Famous Givers and Their Gifts

Sarah Knowles Bolton

Famous Givers and Their Gifts

ISBN: 978-1-64799-202-6

TO

THE MEMORY

OF

William Frederick Poole,

THE ORIGINATOR

OF

"POOLE'S INDEX."

PREFACE

While it is interesting to see how men have built up fortunes, as a rule, through industry, saving, and great energy, it is even more interesting to see how those fortunes have been or may be used for the benefit of mankind.

In a volume of this size, of course, it is impossible to speak of but few out of many who have given generously of their wealth, both in this country and abroad.

The book has been written with the hope that others may be incited to give through reading it, and may see the results of their giving in their lifetime. A sketch of George Peabody may be found in "Poor Boys who became Famous;" a sketch of Johns Hopkins in "How Success is Won."

S. K. B.

CONTENTS

	PAGE
JOHN LOWELL, JR., AND HIS FREE LECTURES	1
STEPHEN GIRARD AND HIS COLLEGE FOR ORPHANS	18
ANDREW CARNEGIE AND HIS LIBRARIES	35
THOMAS HOLLOWAY; HIS SANATORIUM AND COLLEGE	53
CHARLES PRATT AND HIS INSTITUTE	64
THOMAS GUY AND HIS HOSPITAL	76
SOPHIA SMITH AND HER COLLEGE FOR WOMEN	90
JAMES LICK AND HIS TELESCOPE	101
LELAND STANFORD AND HIS UNIVERSITY	117
CAPTAIN THOMAS CORAM AND HIS FOUNDLING ASYLUM	136
HENRY SHAW AND HIS BOTANICAL GARDEN	144
JAMES SMITHSON AND THE SMITHSONIAN INSTITUTION	150
PRATT, LENOX, MARY MACRAE STUART, NEWBERRY, CRERAR, ASTOR, REYNOLDS AND THEIR LIBRARIES	154
FREDERICK H. RINDGE AND HIS GIFTS	165
ANTHONY J. DREXEL AND HIS INSTITUTE	167
PHILIP D. ARMOUR AND HIS INSTITUTE	171
LEONARD CASE AND HIS SCHOOL OF APPLIED SCIENCE	175
ASA PACKER AND LEHIGH UNIVERSITY	178
CORNELIUS VANDERBILT AND VANDERBILT UNIVERSITY	181
BARON MAURICE DE HIRSCH	184
ISAAC RICH AND BOSTON UNIVERSITY	186
DANIEL B. FAYERWEATHER AND OTHERS	188
CATHARINE LORILLARD WOLFE	191
MARY ELIZABETH GARRETT	192

MRS. ANNA OTTENDORFER 194

DANIEL P. STONE AND VALERIA G. STONE 196

SAMUEL WILLISTON 197

JOHN F. SLATER AND DANIEL HAND 199

GEORGE T. ANGELL 206

WILLIAM W. CORCORAN 209

JOHN D. ROCKEFELLER AND CHICAGO UNIVERSITY 212

JOHN LOWELL, Jr.,
AND HIS FREE LECTURES

There is often something pathetic about a great gift. The only son of Leland Stanford dies, and the millions which he would have inherited are used to found a noble institution on the Pacific Coast.

The only son of Henry F. Durant, the noted Boston lawyer, dies, and the sorrowing father and mother use their fortune to build beautiful Wellesley College.

The only son of Amasa Stone is drowned while at Yale College, and his father builds Adelbert College of Western Reserve University, to honor his boy, and bless his city and State.

John Lowell, Jr., early bereft of his wife and two daughters, his only children, builds a lasting monument for himself, in his Free Lectures for the People, for all time,—the Lowell Institute of Boston.

John Lowell, Jr., was born in Boston, Mass., May 11, 1799, of distinguished ancestry. His great-grandfather, the Rev. John Lowell, was the first minister of Newburyport. His grandfather, Judge John Lowell, was one of the framers of the Massachusetts Constitution in 1780. He inserted in the bill of rights the clause declaring that "all men are born free and equal," for the purpose, as he said, of abolishing slavery in Massachusetts; and offered his services to any slave who desired to establish his right to freedom under that clause. His position was declared to be constitutional by the Supreme Court of the State in 1783, since which time slavery has had no legal existence in Massachusetts. In 1781 he was elected a member of the Continental Congress, and appointed by President Washington a judge of the District Court of Massachusetts; in 1801 President Adams appointed him chief justice of the Circuit Court. He was brilliant in conversation, an able scholar, and an honest and patriotic leader. He was for eighteen years a member of the corporation of Harvard College.

Judge Lowell had three sons, John, Francis Cabot, and Charles. John, a lawyer, was prominent in all good work, such as the establishment of the Massachusetts General Hospital, the Provident Institution for Savings in the City of Boston, the Massachusetts Agricultural Society, and other helpful projects. "He considered wealth," said Edward Everett, "to be no otherwise valuable but as a powerful instrument of doing good. His liberality went to the extent of his means; and where they stopped, he exercised an almost unlimited control over the means of others. It was difficult to resist the contagion of his enthusiasm; for it was the enthusiasm of a strong, cultivated, and practical mind."

1

Francis Cabot, the second son, was the father of the noted giver, John Lowell, Jr. Charles, the third son, became an eminent Boston minister, and was the father of the poet, James Russell Lowell. On his mother's side the ancestors of John Lowell, Jr., were also prominent. His maternal grandfather, Jonathan Jackson, was a generous man of means, a member of the Congres of 1782, and at the close of the Revolutionary War largely the creditor of the Commonwealth of Massachusetts. He was the treasurer of the State and of Cambridge University.

John Lowell, Jr., must have inherited from such ancestors a love of country, a desire for knowledge, and good executive ability. He was reared in a home of comfort and intelligence. His father, Francis Cabot, was a successful merchant, a man of great energy, strength of mind, and integrity of character.

In 1810, when young John was about eleven years old, the health of his father having become impaired, the Lowell family went to England for rest and change. The boy was placed at the High School of Edinburgh, where he won many friends by his lovable qualities, and his intense desire to gain information. When he came back to America with his parents, he entered Harvard College in 1813, when he was fourteen years old. He was a great reader, especially along the line of foreign travel, and had a better knowledge of geography than most men. After two years at Cambridge, he was obliged to give up the course from ill health, and seek a more active live. When he was seventeen, and the year following, he made two voyages to India, and acquired a passion for study and travel in the East.

His father, meantime, had become deeply interested in the manufacture of cotton in America. The war of 1812 had interrupted our commerce with Europe, and America had been compelled to manufacture many things for herself. In 1789 Mr. Samuel Slater had brought from England the knowledge of the inventions of Arkwright for spinning cotton. These inventions were so carefully guarded from the public that it was almost impossible for any one to leave England who had worked in a cotton-mill and understood the process of manufacture. Parliament had prohibited the exportation of the new machinery. Without the knowledge of his parents, Samuel Slater sailed to America, carrying the complicated machinery in his mind. At Pawtucket, R.I., he set up some Arkwright machinery from memory, and, after years of effort and obstacles, became successful and wealthy.

Mr. Lowell determined to weave cotton, and if possible use the thread already made in this country. He proposed to his brother-in-law, Mr. Patrick Tracy Jackson, that they put some money into experiments, and try to make a power-loom, as this newly invented machine could not be obtained from abroad. They procured the model

2

of a common loom, and after repeated failures succeeded in reinventing a fairly good power-loom.

The thread obtained from other mills not proving available for their looms, spinning machinery was constructed, and land was purchased on the Merrimac River for their mills; in time a large manufacturing city gathered about them, and was named Lowell, for the energetic and upright manufacturer.

When the war of 1812 was over, Mr. Lowell knew that the overloaded markets of Europe and India would pour their cotton and other goods into the United States. He therefore went to Washington in the winter of 1816, and after overcoming much opposition, obtained a protective tariff for cotton manufacture. "The minimum duty on cotton fabrics," says Edward Everett, "the corner-stone of the system, was proposed by Mr. Lowell, and is believed to have been an original conception on his part. To this provision of law, the fruit of the intelligence and influence of Mr. Lowell, New England owes that branch of industry which has made her amends for the diminution of her foreign trade; which has left her prosperous under the exhausting drain of her population to the West; which has brought a market for his agricultural produce to the farmer's door; and which, while it has conferred these blessings on this part of the country, has been productive of good, and nothing but good, to every other portion of it."

At Mr. Lowell's death he left a large fortune to his four children, three sons and a daughter, of whom John Lowell, Jr., was the eldest. Like his father, John was a successful merchant; but as his business was carried on largely with the East Indies, he had leisure for reading. He had one of the best private libraries in Boston, and knew the contents of his books. He did not forget his duties to his city. He was several times a member of the Common Council and the Legislature of the State, believing that no person has a right to shirk political responsibility.

In the midst of this happy and useful life, surrounded by those who were dear to him, in the years 1830 and 1831, when he was thirty-two years of age, came the crushing blow to his domestic joy. His wife and both children died, and his home was broken up. He sought relief in travel, and in the summer of 1832 made a tour of the Western States. In the autumn of the same year, November, 1832, he sailed for Europe, intending to be absent for some months, or even years. As though he had a premonition that his life would be a brief one, and that he might never return, he made his will before leaving America, giving about two hundred and fifty thousand dollars—half of his property—"to found and sustain free lectures," "for the promotion of the moral and intellectual and physical instruction or education of the citizens of Boston."

The will provides for courses in physics, chemistry, botany, zoölogy, mineralogy, the literature of our own and foreign nations, and historical and internal evidences in favor of Christianity.

The management of the whole fund, with the selection of lecturers, is left to one trustee, who shall choose his successor; that trustee to be, "in preference to all others, some male descendant of my grandfather, John Lowell, provided there be one who is competent to hold the office of trustee, and of the name of Lowell." The trustees of the Boston Athenæum are empowered to look over the accounts each year, but have no voice in the selection of the lecturers. "The trustee," says Mr. Lowell in his will, "may also from time to time establish lectures on any subject that, in his opinion, the wants and taste of the age may demand."

None of the money given by will is ever to be used in buildings; Mr. Lowell probably having seen that money is too often put into brick and stone to perpetuate the name of the donor, while there is no income for the real work in hand. Ten per cent of the income of the Lowell fund is to be added annually to the principal. It is believed that through wise investing the fund is already doubled, and perhaps trebled.

"The idea of a foundation of this kind," says Edward Everett, "on which, unconnected with any place of education, provision is made, in the midst of a large commercial population, for annual courses of instruction by public lectures, to be delivered gratuitously to all who choose to attend them, as far as it is practicable within our largest halls, is, I believe, original with Mr. Lowell. I am not aware that, among all the munificent establishments of Europe, there is anything of this description upon a large scale."

After Mr. Lowell reached Europe in the fall of 1832, he spent the winter in Paris, and the summer in England, Scotland, and Ireland. He was all the time preparing for his Eastern journey,—in the study of languages, and the knowledge of instruments by which to make notes of the course of winds, the temperature, atmospheric phenomena, the height of mountains, and other matters of interest in the far-off lands which he hoped to enter. Lord Glenelg, the Secretary of State for the Colonies, gave him special facilities for his proposed tour into the interior of India.

The winter of 1833 was spent in the southwestern part of France, in visiting the principal cities of Lombardy, in Nice and Genoa, reaching Florence early in February, 1834. In Rome he engaged a Swiss artist, an excellent draftsman and painter, to accompany him, and make sketches of scenery, ruins, and costumes throughout his whole journey.

After some time spent in Naples and vicinity, he devoted a month to the island of Sicily. He writes to Princess Galitzin, the granddaughter of the famous Marshal Suvorof, whom he had met in Florence: "Clear

4

and beautiful are the skies in Sicily, and there is a warmth of tint about the sunsets unrivalled even in Italy. It resembles what one finds under the tropics; and so does the vegetation. It is rich and luxuriant. The palm begins to appear; the palmetto, the aloe, and the cactus adorn every woodside; the superb oleander bathes its roots in almost every brook; the pomegranate and a large species of convolvulus are everywhere seen. In short, the variety of flowers is greater than that of the prairies in the Western States of America, though I think their number is less. Our rudbeckia is, I think, more beautiful than the chrysanthemum coronarium which you see all over Sicily; but there are the orange and the lemon."

Mr. Lowell travelled in Greece, and July 10 reached Athens, "that venerable, ruined, dirty little town," he wrote, "of which the streets are most narrow and nearly impassable; but the poor remains of whose ancient taste in the arts exceed in beauty everything I have yet seen in either Italy, Sicily, or any other portions of Greece."

Late in September Mr. Lowell reached Smyrna, and visited the ruins of Magnesia, Tralles, Nysa, Laodicea, Tripolis, and Hierapolis. He writes to a friend in America; "I then crossed Mount Messogis in the rain, and descended into the basin of the river Hermus, visited Philadelphia, the picturesque site of Sardis, with its inaccessible citadel, and two solitary but beautiful Ionic columns."

Early in December Mr. Lowell sailed from Smyrna in a Greek brig, coasting along the islands of Mitylene, Samos, Patmos, and Rhodes, arrived in Alexandria in the latter part of the month, and proceeded up the river Nile. On Feb. 12, 1835, he writes to his friends from the top of the great pyramid:—

"The prospect is most beautiful. On the one side is the boundless desert, varied only by a few low ridges of limestone hills. Then you have heaps of sand, and a surface of sand reduced to so fine a powder, and so easily agitated by the slightest breeze that it almost deserves the name of fluid. Then comes the rich, verdant valley of the Nile, studded with villages, adorned with green date-trees, traversed by the Father of Rivers, with the magnificent city of Cairo on its banks; but far narrower than one could wish, as it is bounded, at a distance of some fifteen miles, by the Arabian desert, and the abrupt calcareous ridge of Mokattam. Immediately below the spectator lies the city of the dead, the innumerable tombs, the smaller pyramids, the Sphinx, and still farther off and on the same line, to the south, the pyramids of Abou Seer, Sakkârà, and Dashoor."

While journeying in Egypt, Mr. Lowell, from the effects of the climate, was severely attacked by intermittent fever; but partially recovering, proceeded to Thebes, and established his temporary home on the ruins of a palace at Luxor. After examining many of its wonderful structures carved with the names and deeds of the Pharaohs, he was again prostrated by illness, and feared that he should not recover. He had thought out more details about his noble gift to the people of Boston; and, sick and among strangers, he completed in that ancient land his last will for the good of humanity. "The few sentences," says Mr. Everett, "penned with a tired hand, on the top of a palace of the Pharaohs, will do more for human improvement than, for aught that appears, was done by all of that gloomy dynasty that ever reigned."

Mr. Lowell somewhat regained his health, and proceeded to Sioot, the capital of Upper Egypt, to lay in the stores needed for his journey to Nubia. While at Sioot, he saw the great caravan of Darfour in Central Africa, which comes to the Nile once in two years, and is two or three months in crossing the desert. It usually consists of about six hundred merchants, four thousand slaves, and six thousand camels laden with ivory, tamarinds, ostrich-feathers, and provisions for use on the journey.

Mr. Lowell writes in his journal: "The immense number of tall and lank but powerful camels was the first object that attracted our attention in the caravan. The long and painful journey, besides killing perhaps a quarter of the original number, had reduced the remainder to the condition of skeletons, and rendered their natural ugliness still more appalling. Their skins were stretched, like moistened parchment scorched by the fire, over their strong ribs. Their eyes stood out from their shrunken foreheads; and the arched backbone of the animals rose sharp and prominent above their sides, like a butcher's cleaver. The fat that usually accompanies the middle of the backbone, and forms with it the camel's bunch, had entirely disappeared. They had occasion for it, as well as for the reservoir of water with which a bountiful nature has furnished them, to enable them to undergo the laborious journey and the painful fasts of the desert. Their sides were gored with the heavy burdens they had carried.

"The sun was setting. The little slaves of the caravan had just driven in from their dry pasture of thistles, parched grass, and withered herbage these most patient and obedient animals, so essential to travellers in the great deserts, and without which it would be as impossible to cross them as to traverse the ocean without vessels. Their conductors made them kneel down, and gradually poured beans between their lengthened jaws. The camels, not having been used to this food, did not like it; they would have greatly preferred a bit of old, worn-out mat, as we have found to our cost in the desert. The most mournful cries, something between the braying of an ass and the lowing of a cow, assailed our ears in all directions, because these poor creatures were obliged to eat what was not good for them; but they offered no resistance otherwise. When transported to the Nile, it is said that the change of food and water kills most of them in a little time."

In June Mr. Lowell resumed his journey up the Nile, and was

again ill for some weeks. The thermometer frequently stood at 115 degrees. He visited Khartoom, and then travelled for fourteen days across the desert of Nubia to Sowakeen, a small port on the western coast of the Red Sea. Near here, Dec. 22, he was shipwrecked on the island of Dassá, and nearly lost his life. In a rainstorm the little vessel ran upon the rocks. "All my people behaved well," Mr. Lowell writes. "Yanni alone, the youngest of them, showed by a few occasional exclamations that it is hard to look death in the face at seventeen, when all the illusions of life are entire. As for swimming, I have not strength for that, especially in my clothes, and so thorough a ducking and exposure might of itself make an end of me."

Finally they were rescued, and sailed for Mocha, reaching that place on the 1st of January, 1836. Mr. Lowell was much exhausted from exposure and his recent illness. His last letters were written, Jan. 17, at Mocha, while waiting for a British steamer on her way to Bombay, India. From Mr. Lowell's journal it is seen that the steamboat Hugh Lindsay arrived at Mocha from Suez, Jan. 20; that Mr. Lowell sailed on the 23d, and arrived at Bombay, Feb. 10. He had reached the East only to die. After three weeks of illness, he expired, March 4, 1836, a little less than thirty-seven years of age. For years he had studied about India and China, and had made himself ready for valuable research; but his plans were changed by an overruling Power in whom he had always trusted. Mr. Lowell had wisely provided for a greater work than research in the East, the benefits of which are inestimable and unending.

Free public lectures for the people of Boston on the Lowell foundation were begun on the evening of Dec. 31, 1839, by a memorial address on Mr. Lowell by Edward Everett, in the Odeon, then at the corner of Federal and Franklin Streets, before two thousand persons.

The first course of lectures was on geology, given by that able scientist, Professor Benjamin Silliman of Yale College. "So great was his popularity," says Harriette Knight Smith in the New England Magazine for February, 1895, "that on the giving out of tickets for his second course, on chemistry, the following season, the eager crowds filled the adjacent streets, and crushed in the windows of the 'Old Corner Bookstore,' the place of distribution, so that provision for the same had to be made elsewhere. To such a degree did the enthusiasm of the public reach at that time, in its desire to attend these lectures, that it was found necessary to open books in advance to receive the names of subscribers, the number of tickets being distributed by lot. Sometimes the number of applicants for a single course was eight or ten thousand." The same number of the magazine contains a valuable list of all the speakers at the Institute since its beginning. The usual method now is to advertise the lectures in the Boston papers a week or more in advance; and then all persons desiring to attend meet at a designated place, and receive tickets in the order of their coming. At the appointed hour, the doors of the building where the lectures are given are closed, and no one is admitted after the speaker begins. Not long since I met a gentleman who had travelled seven miles to attend a lecture, and failed to obtain entrance. Harriette Knight Smith says, "This rule was at first resisted to such a degree that a reputable gentleman was taken to the lockup and compelled to pay a fine for kicking his way through an entrance door. Finally the rule was submitted to, and in time praised and copied."

For seven years the Lowell Institute lectures were given in the Odeon, and for thirteen years in Marlboro Chapel, between Washington and Tremont, Winter and Bromfield Streets. Since 1879 they have been heard in Huntington Hall, Boylston Street, in the Rogers Building of the Massachusetts Institute of Technology.

Since the establishment of the free lectures, over five thousand have been given to the people by some of the most eminent and learned men of both hemispheres,—Lyell, Tyndall, Wallace, Holmes, Lowell, Bryce, and more than three hundred others. Sir Charles Lyell lectured on Geology, Professor Asa Gray on Botany, Oliver Wendell Holmes on English Poetry of the Nineteenth Century, E. H. Davis on Mounds and Earthworks of the Mississippi Valley, Lieutenant M. F. Maury on Winds and Currents of the Sea, Mark Hopkins (President of Williams College) on Moral Philosophy, Charles Eliot Norton on The Thirteenth Century, Henry Barnard on National Education, Samuel Eliot on Evidences of Christianity, Burt G. Wilder on The Silk Spider of South Carolina, W. D. Howells on Italian Poets of our Century, Professor John Tyndall on Light and Heat, Dr. Isaac I. Hayes on Arctic Discoveries, Richard A. Proctor on Astronomy, General Francis A. Walker on Money, Hon. Carroll D. Wright on The Labor Question, H. H. Boyesen on The Icelandic Saga Literature, the Rev. J. G. Wood on Structure of Animal Life, the Rev. H. R. Haweis on Music and Morals, Alfred Russell Wallace on Darwinism and Some of Its Applications, the Rev. G. Frederick Wright on The Ice Age in North America, Professor James Geikie on Europe During and after the Ice Age, John Fiske on The Discovery and Colonization of America, Professor Henry Drummond on The Evolution of Man, President Eliot of Harvard College on Recent Educational Changes and Tendencies.

Professor Tyndall, after his Lowell lectures, gave the ten thousand dollars which he had received for his labors in America in scholarships to the University of Pennsylvania, Harvard University, and Columbia College.

Mr. John Amory Lowell, a cousin of John Lowell, Jr., and the trustee appointed by him, at the suggestion of Lyell, a mutual friend, invited Louis Agassiz to come to Boston, and give a course of lectures before the Institute in 1846. He came; and the visit resulted in the building, by Mr. Abbott Lawrence, of the Lawrence Scientific School in connection with Harvard College, and the retaining of the brilliant and noble Agassiz in this country as a professor of zoölogy and geology. The influence of such lectures upon the intellectual growth and moral welfare of a city can scarcely be estimated. It is felt through the State, and eventually through the nation.

Mr. Lowell in his will planned also for other lectures, "those more erudite and particular for students;" and for twenty years there have been "Lowell free courses of instruction in the Institute of Technology," given usually in the evening in the classrooms of the professors. These are the same lectures usually given to regular students, and are free alike to men and women over eighteen years of age. These courses of instruction include mathematics, mechanics, physics, drawing, chemistry, geology, natural history, navigation, biology, English, French, German, history, architecture, and engineering. Through the generosity of Mr. Lowell, every person in Boston may become educated, if he or she have the time and desire. Over three thousand such lectures have been given.

For many years the Lowell Institute has furnished instruction in science to the school-teachers of Boston. It now furnishes lectures on practical and scientific subjects to workingmen, under the auspices of the Wells Memorial Workingmen's Institute.

As the University Extension Lectures carry the college to the people, so more and more the Lowell fund is carrying helpful and practical intelligence to every nook and corner of a great city. Young people are stimulated to endeavor, encouraged to save time in which to gain knowledge, and to become useful and honorable citizens. When more "Settlements" are established in all the waste places, we shall have so many the more centres for the diffusion of intellectual and moral aid.

Who shall estimate the power and value of such a gift to the people as that of John Lowell, Jr.? The Hon. Edward Everett said truly, "It will be, from generation to generation, a perennial source of public good,—a dispensation of sound science, of useful knowledge, of truth in its most important associations with the destiny of man. These are blessings which cannot die. They will abide when the sands of the desert shall have covered what they have hitherto spared of the Egyptian temples; and they will render the name of Lowell in all-wise and moral estimation more truly illustrious than that of any Pharaoh engraven on their walls."

The gift of John Lowell, Jr., has resulted in other good work besides the public lectures. In 1850 a free drawing-school was established in Marlboro Chapel, and continued successfully for twenty-nine years, till the building was taken for business purposes. The pupils were required to draw from real objects only, through the whole course.

In 1872 the Lowell School of Practical Design, for the purpose of promoting Industrial Art in the United States, was established, and the Massachusetts Institute of Technology assumed the responsibility of conducting it. The Lowell Institute bears the expenses of the school, and tuition is free to all pupils.

There is a drawing-room and a weaving-room, though applicants must be able to draw from nature before they enter. In the weaving-room are two fancy chain-looms for dress-goods, three fancy chain-looms for woollen cassimeres, one gingham loom, and one Jacquard loom. Samples of brocaded silk, ribbons, alpacas, and fancy woollen goods are constantly provided for the school from Paris and elsewhere.

The course of study requires three years; and students are taught the art of designing, and making patterns from prints, ginghams, delaines, silks, laces, paper-hangings, carpets, oilcloths, etc. They can also weave their designs into actual fabrics of commercial sizes of every variety of material. The school has proved a most helpful and beneficent institution. It is an inspiration to visit it, and see the happy and earnest faces of the young workers, fitting themselves for useful positions in life.

The Lowell Institute has been fortunate in its management. Mr. John Amory Lowell was the able trustee for more than forty years; and the present trustee, Mr. Augustus Lowell, like his father, has the great work much at heart. Dr. Benjamin E. Cotting, the curator from the formation of the Institute, a period of more than half a century, has won universal esteem for his ability, as also for his extreme courtesy and kindness.

John Lowell, Jr., humanly speaking, died before his lifework was scarcely begun. The studious, modest boy, the thorough, conscientious man, planning a journey to Africa and India, not for pleasure merely, but for helpfulness to science and humanity, died just as he entered the long sought-for land. A man of warm affections, he went out from a broken home to die among strangers.

He was so careful of his moments that, says Mr. Everett, "he spared no time for the frivolous pleasures of youth; less, perhaps, than his health required for its innocent relaxations, and for exercise." Whether or not he realized that the time was short, he accomplished more in his brief thirty-seven years than many men in fourscore and ten. It would have been easy to spend two hundred and fifty thousand dollars in houses and lands, in fine equipage and social festivities; but Mr. Lowell had a higher purpose in life.

After five weeks of illness, thousands of miles from all who were dear to him, on the ruins of Thebes, in an Arab village built on the remains of an ancient palace, Mr. Lowell penned these words: "As the most certain and the most important part of true philosophy appears to me to be that which shows the connection between God's revelations and the knowledge of good and evil implanted by him in our nature, I wish a course of lectures to be given on natural religion, showing its conformity to that of our Saviour.

"For the more perfect demonstration of the truth of those moral and religious precepts, by which alone, as I believe, men can be secure of happiness in this world and that to come, I wish a course of lectures to be delivered on the historical and internal evidences in favor of Christianity. I wish all disputed points of faith and ceremony to be avoided, and the attention of the lecturers to be directed to the moral doctrines of the Gospel, stating their opinion, if they will, but not engaging in controversy, even on the subject of the penalty for disobedience. As the prosperity of my native land, New England, which is sterile and unproductive, must depend hereafter, as it has heretofore depended, first on the moral qualities, and second on the intelligence and information of its inhabitants, I am desirous of trying to contribute towards this second object also."

The friend of the people, Mr. Lowell desired that they should learn from the greatest minds of the age without expense to themselves. It should be an absolutely free gift.

The words from the Theban ruins have had their ever broadening influence through half a century. What shall be the result for good many centuries from now? Tens of thousands of fortunes have been and will be spent for self, and the names of the owners will be forgotten. John Lowell, Jr., did not live for himself, and his name will be remembered.

Others in this country have adopted somewhat Mr. Lowell's plan of giving. The Hon. Oakes Ames, the great shovel manufacturer, member of Congress for ten years, and builder of the Union Pacific Railroad, left at his death, May 8, 1873, a fund of fifty thousand dollars "for the benefit of the school children of North Easton, Mass." The income is thirty-five hundred dollars a year, part of which is used in furnishing magazines to children—each family having children in the schools is supplied with some magazine; part for an industrial school where they are taught the use of tools; and part for free lectures yearly to the school children, adults also having the benefit of them. Thirty or more lectures are given each winter upon interesting and profitable subjects by able lecturers.

Some of the subjects already discussed are as follows: The Great Yellowstone Park, A Journey among the Planets, The Chemistry of a Match, Paris, its Gardens and Palaces, A Basket of Charcoal, Tobacco and Liquors, Battle of Gettysburg, The Story of the Jeannette, Palestine, Electricity, Picturesque Mexico, The Sponge and Starfish, Sweden, Physiology, History of a Steam-Engine, Heroes and Historic

Places of the Revolution, The Four Napoleons, The World's Fair, The Civil War, and others.

What better way to spend an evening than in listening to such lectures? What better way to use one's money than in laying the foundation of intelligent and good citizenship in childhood and youth?

The press of North Easton says, "The influence and educational power of such a series of lectures and course of instruction in a community cannot be measured or properly gauged. From these lectures a stream of knowledge has gone out which, we believe, will bear fruit in the future for the good of the community. Of the many good things which have come from the liberality of Mr. Ames, this, we believe, has been the most potent for good of any."

Judge White of Lawrence, Mass., left at his death a tract of land in the hands of three trustees, which they were to sell, and use the income to provide a course of not less than six lectures yearly, especially to the industrial classes. The subjects were to be along the line of good morals, industry, economy, the fruits of sin and of virtue. The White fund amounts to about one hundred thousand dollars.

Mrs. Mary Hemenway of Boston, who died March 6, 1894, will always be remembered for her good works, not the least of which are the yearly courses of free lectures for young people at the Old South Church. When the meeting-house where Benjamin Franklin was baptized, where the town meeting was held after the Boston Massacre in 1770, and just before the tea was thrown overboard in 1773, and which the British troops used for a riding-school in 1775,—when this historic place was in danger of being torn down because business interests seemed to demand the location, Mrs. Hemenway, with other Boston women, came forward in 1876 to save it. She once said to Mr. Larkin Dunton, head master of the Boston Normal School, "I have just given a hundred thousand dollars to save the Old South; yet I care nothing for the church on the corner lot. But, if I live, such teaching shall be done in that old building, and such an influence shall go out from it, as shall make the children of future generations love their country so tenderly that there can never be another civil war in this country."

Mrs. Hemenway was patriotic. When asked why she gave one hundred thousand dollars to Tileston Normal School in Wilmington, N.C.,—her maiden name was Tileston,—and thus provide for schools in the South, she replied, "When my country called for her sons to defend the flag, I had none to give. Mine was but a lad of twelve. I gave my money as a thank-offering that I was not called to suffer as other mothers who gave their sons and lost them. I gave it that the children of this generation might be taught to love the flag their fathers tore down."

In December, 1878, Miss C. Alice Baker began at the Old South

12

Church a series of talks to children on New England history, between eleven and twelve o'clock on Saturdays, which she called, "The Children's Hour." From the relics on the floor and in the gallery, telling of Colonial times, she riveted their attention, thus showing to the historical societies of this country how easily they might interest and profit the children of our public schools, if these were allowed to visit museums in small companies with suitable leaders.

From this year, 1878, the excellent work has been carried on. Every year George Washington's birthday is appropriately celebrated at the Old South Meeting-house, with speeches and singing of national patriotic airs by the children of the public schools. In 1879 Mr. John Fiske, the noted historical writer, gave a course of lectures on Saturday mornings upon The Discovery and Colonization of America. These were followed in succeeding years by his lectures on The American Revolution, and others that are now published in book form. These were more especially for the young, but adults seemed just as eager to hear them as young persons.

Regular courses of free lectures for young people were established in the summer of 1883, more especially for those who did not leave the city during the long summer vacations. The lectures are usually given on Wednesday afternoons in July and August. A central topic is chosen for the season, such as Early Massachusetts History, The War for the Union, The War for Independence, The Birth of the Nation, The American Indians, etc.; and different persons take part in the course.

With each lecture a leaflet of four or eight pages is given to those who attend, and these leaflets can be bound at the end of the season for a small sum. "These are made up, for the most part, from original papers treated in the lectures," says Mr. Edwin D. Mead who prepares them, "in the hope to make the men and the public life of the periods more clear and real." These leaflets are very valuable, the subjects being, "The Voyages to Vinland, from the Saga of Eric the Red," "Marco Polo's Account of Japan and Java," "The Death of De Soto from the Narrative of a Gentleman of Elvas," etc. They are furnished to the schools at the bare cost of paper and printing. Mr. Mead, the scholarly author, and editor of the *New England Magazine*, has been untiring in the Old South work, and has been the means of several other cities adopting like methods for the study of early history, especially by young people.

Every year since 1881 four prizes, two of forty dollars, and two of twenty-five dollars each, have been offered to high school pupils soon to graduate, and also to those recently graduated, for the best essays on assigned topics of American history. Those who compete and do not win a prize receive a present of valuable books in recognition of their effort. From the first, Mrs. Hemenway was

13

the enthusiastic friend and promoter of the Old South work. She spent five thousand a year, for many years, in carrying it forward, and left provision for its continuation at her death. It is not too much to say that these free lectures have stimulated the study of our early history all over the country, and made us more earnest lovers of our flag and of our nation. The world has little respect for a "man without a country."

> "Breathes there the man with soul so dead
> Who never to himself hath said,
>   'This is my own, my native land!'
> Whose heart hath ne'er within him burned
> As home his footsteps he hath turned
>   From wandering on a foreign strand?"

Mrs. Hemenway did not cease her good work with her free lectures for young people. It is scarcely easier to stop in an upward career than in a downward. When the heart and hand are once opened to the world's needs, they can nevermore be closed.

Mrs. Hemenway, practical with all her wealth, believed that everybody should know how to work, and thus not only be placed above want, but dignify labor. She said, "In my youth, girls in the best families were accustomed to participate in many of the household affairs. Some occasionally assisted in other homes. As for myself, I read not many books. They were not so numerous as now. I was reared principally on household duties, the Bible, and Shakespeare."

Mrs. Hemenway began by establishing kitchen gardens in Boston, opened on Saturdays. I remember going to one of them at the North End, in 1881, through the invitation of Mrs. Hemenway's able assistant, Miss Amy Morris Homans. In a large, plain room of the "Mission" I found twenty-four bright little girls seated at two long tables. They were eager, interesting children, but most had on torn and soiled dresses and poor shoes.

In front of each stood a tiny box, used as a table, on which were four plates, each a little over an inch wide; four knives, each three inches long, and forks to correspond; goblets, and cups and saucers of the same diminutive sizes.

At a signal from the piano, the girls began to set the little tables properly. First the knives and forks were put in their places, then the very small napkins, and then the goblets. In front of the "lady of the house" were set the cups and saucers, spoon-holder, water-pitcher, and coffee-pot.

Then they listened to a useful and pleasant talk from the leader; and when the order was given to clear the tables, twenty-four pairs of little hands put the pewter dishes, made to imitate silver, into a pitcher, and the other things into dishpans, about four or five inches wide, singing a song to the music of the piano as they washed the dishes. These children also learned to sweep and dust, make beds, and perform other household duties. Each pupil was given a complete set of new clothes by Mrs. Hemenway.

Many persons had petitioned to have sewing taught in the public schools of Boston, as in London; but there was opposition, and but little was accomplished. Mrs. Hemenway started sewing-schools, obtained capable teachers, and in time sewing became a regular part of the public-school work, with a department of sewing in the Boston Normal School; so that hereafter the teacher will be as able in her department as another in mathematics. Drafting, cutting, and fitting have been added in many schools, so that thousands of women will be able to save expense in their homes through the skill of their own hands.

Mrs. Hemenway knew that in many homes food is poorly cooked, and health is thereby impaired. Mr. Henry C. Hardon of Boston tells of this conversation between two teachers: "Name some one thing that would enable your boys to achieve more, and build up the school."—"A plate of good soup and a thick slice of bread after recess," was the reply. "I could get twice the work before twelve. They want new blood."

Mrs. Hemenway started cooking-schools in Boston, which she called school kitchens; and when it was found to be difficult to secure suitable teachers, she established and supported a normal school of cooking. Boston, seeing the need of proper teachers in its future work in the schools, has provided a department of cooking in the city Normal School.

Mrs. Hemenway believed in strong bodies, aided to become such by physical training. She offered to the School Committee of Boston to provide for the instruction of a hundred teachers in the Swedish system, on condition that they be allowed to use the exercises in their classes in case they chose to do so. The result proved successful, and now over sixty thousand in the public schools take the Swedish exercises daily.

Mrs. Hemenway established the Boston Normal School of Gymnastics, from which teachers have gone to Radcliffe College, Cambridge; Bryn Mawr, Pennsylvania; Denver, Colorado; Drexel Institute, Philadelphia; their average salary being slightly less than one thousand dollars, the highest salary reaching eighteen hundred dollars. Boston has now made the teaching of gymnastics a part of its normal-school work, so that every graduate goes out prepared to direct the work in the school. Mrs. Hemenway gave generously to aid the Boston Teachers' Mutual Benefit Association; for she said, "Nothing is too good for the Boston teachers." She was a busy woman, with no time for fashionable life, though she welcomed to her elegant home all who had any helpful work to do in the world. She used her wealth and her social position to help humanity. She died leaving her impress on a great city and State, and through that upon the nation.

New York State and City are now carrying out an admirable plan of free lectures for the people. The State appropriates twenty-five thousand dollars annually that free lectures may be given "in natural history, geography, and kindred subjects by means of pictorial representation and lectures, to the free common schools of each city and village of the State that has, or may have, a superintendent of free common schools." These illustrated lectures may also be given "to artisans, mechanics, and other citizens."

This has grown largely out of the excellent work done by Professor Albert S. Bickmore of the American Museum of Natural History, Eighth Avenue and Seventy-seventh Street, Central Park, New York. In 1869, when the Museum was founded, the teachers of the public schools were required to give object-lessons on animals, plants, human anatomy, and physiology, and came to the Museum to the curator of the department of ethnology, Professor Bickmore, for assistance. His lectures, given on Saturday forenoons, illustrated by the stereopticon, were upon the body,—the muscular system, nervous system, etc.; the mineral kingdom,—granite, marble, coal, petroleum, iron, etc.; the vegetable kingdom,—evergreens, oaks, elms, etc.; the animal kingdom,—the sea, corals, oysters, butterflies, bees, ants, etc.; physical geography,—the Mississippi Valley, Yellowstone National Park, Mexico, Egypt, Greece, Italy, West Indies, etc.; zoölogy,—fishes, reptiles, and birds, the whale, dogs, seals, lions, monkeys, etc.

These lectures became so popular and helpful that the trustees of the Museum hired Chickering Hall for some of the courses, which were attended by over thirteen hundred teachers each week. Professor Bickmore also gives free illustrated lectures to the people on the afternoons of legal holidays at the Museum, under the auspices of the State Department of Public Instruction.

New York State has done a thing which might well be copied in other States. Each normal school of the State, and each city and village superintendent of schools, may be provided with a stereopticon, all needed lantern slides, and the printed lectures of Professor Bickmore, for use before the schools. In this way children have object-lessons which they never forget.

The Museum, in co-operation with the Board of Education of the city of New York, is providing free lectures for the people at the Museum on Saturday evenings, by various lecturers. The Board, under the direction of Dr. Henry M. Leipziger, is doing good work in its free illustrated lectures for the people in many portions of the city. These are given in the evenings, and often at the grammar-school buildings, a good use to which to put them. Such subjects are chosen as The Navy in the Civil War, The Progress of the Telegraph, Life in the Arctic Regions, Emergencies and How to Meet Them (by some physician), Iron and Steel Ship-building, The Care of the Eyes and Teeth, Burns and Scotland, Andrew Jackson, etc. Rich and poor are alike welcome to the lectures, and all classes are present.

A city or State that does such work for the people will reap a hundred-fold in coming generations.

STEPHEN GIRARD
AND HIS COLLEGE FOR ORPHANS

Near the city of Bordeaux, France, on May 20, 1750, the eldest son of Pierre Girard and his wife, Anne Marie Lafargue, was born. The family were well-to-do; and Pierre was knighted by Louis XV. for bravery on board the squadron at Brest, in 1744, when France and England were at war. The king gave Pierre Girard his own sword, which Pierre at his death ordered to be placed in his coffin, and it was buried with him. Although the Girard family were devoted to the sea, Pierre wished to have his boys become professional men; and this might have been the case with the eldest son, Stephen, had not an accident changed his life.

When the boy was eight years old, his right eye was destroyed. Some wet oyster-shells were thrown upon a bonfire, and the heat breaking the shells, a ragged piece flew into the eye. To make the calamity worse, his playmates ridiculed his appearance with one eye closed; and he became sensitive, and disinclined to play with any one save his brother Jean.

He was a grave and dignified lad, inclined to be domineering, and of a quick temper. His mother tried to teach him self-control, and had she lived, would doubtless have softened his nature; but a second mother coming into the home, who had several children of her own, the effect upon Stephen was disastrous. She seems not to have understood his nature; and when he rebelled, the father sided with the new love, and bade his son submit, or find a home as best he could.

"I will leave your house," replied the passionate boy, hurt in feelings as well as angered. "Give me a venture on any ship that sails from Bordeaux, and I will go at once, where you shall never see me again."

A business acquaintance, Captain Jean Courteau, was about to sail to San Domingo in the West Indies. Pierre Girard gave his son sixteen thousand livres, about three thousand dollars; and the lad of fourteen, small for his age, went out into the world as a cabin-boy, to try his fortune.

If his mother had been alive he would have been homesick, but as matters were at present the Girard house could not be a home to him. His first voyage lasted ten months; the three thousand dollars had gained him some money, and the trip had made him in love with the sea. He returned for a brief time to his brothers and sisters, and then made five other voyages, having attained the rank of lieutenant of the vessel.

When he was twenty-three, he was given authority to act as "captain of a merchant vessel," and sailed away from Bordeaux forever. After stopping at St. Marc's in the island of San Domingo, young Girard sailed for New York, which he reached in July, 1774. With shrewd business ability he disposed of the articles brought in his ship, and in so doing attracted the interest of a prosperous merchant, Mr. Thomas Randall, who was engaged in trade with New Orleans and the West Indies.

Mr. Randall asked the energetic young Frenchman to take the position of first officer in his ship L'Aimable Louise. This resulted so satisfactorily that Girard was taken into partnership, and became master of the vessel in her trade with New Orleans and the West Indies.

After nearly two years, in May, 1776, Girard was returning from the West Indies, and in a fog and storm at sea found himself in Delaware Bay, and learned that a British fleet was outside. The pilot, who had come in answer to the small cannon fired from Girard's ship, advised against his going to New York, as he would surely be captured, the Revolutionary War having begun. As he had no American money with him, a Philadelphia gentleman who came with the pilot loaned him five dollars. This five-dollar loan proved a blessing to the Quaker City, when in after years she received millions from the merchant who came by accident into her borders.

Captain Girard sold his interest in L'Aimable Louise, and opened a small store on Water Street, putting into it his cargo from the West Indies. He hoped to go to sea again as soon as the war should be over, and conferred with Mr. Lum, a plain shipbuilder near him on Water Street, about building a ship for him. Mr. Lum had an unusually beautiful daughter, Mary, a girl of sixteen, with black hair and eyes, and very fair complexion. Though eleven years older than Mary, Stephen Girard fell in love with her, and was married to her, June 6, 1777, before his family could object, as they soon did strenuously, when they learned that she was poor and below him in social rank.

About three years after the marriage, Jean visited his brother Stephen in America, and seems to have appreciated the beautiful and modest girl to whom the family were so opposed. Henry Atlee Ingram, LL.B., in his life of Girard, quotes several letters from Jean after he had returned to France, or when at Cape François, San Domingo: "Be so kind as to assure my dear sister-in-law of my true affection.... Say a thousand kind things to her for me, and assure her of my unalterable friendship.... Thousands and thousands of friendly wishes to your dear wife. Say to her that if anything from here would give her pleasure, to ask me for it. I will do everything in the world to prove to her my attachment.... I send by Derussy the jar which your lovely wife filled for me with gherkins, full of an excellent guava jelly for you people, besides two orange-trees. He has promised me to take care of them. I hope he will, and embrace, as well as you, my ever dear Mary."

Three or four months after his marriage, Lord Howe having threatened the city, Mr. Girard took his young wife to Mount Holly, N.J., to a little farm of five or six acres which he had purchased the previous year for five hundred dollars. Here they lived in a one-story-and-a-half frame house for over a year, when they returned to Philadelphia and he resumed his business. He had decided already to become a citizen of the Republic, and took the oath of allegiance, Oct. 27, 1778.

Mr. Lum at once began to build the sloop which Mr. Girard was planning when he first met Mary, and she was named the Water-Witch. Until she was shipwrecked, five or six years later, Mr. Girard believed she could never cause him loss. Already he was worth over one hundred and fifty thousand dollars, made by his own energy, prudence, and ability; but he lived with great simplicity, and was accumulating wealth rapidly. In 1784 he built his second vessel, named, in compliment to Jean, the Two Brothers.

The next year, 1785, when he was thirty-five years old, the great sorrow of his life came upon him. The beautiful wife, only a little beyond her teens, became melancholy, and then hopelessly insane. Mr. Ingram believes the eight years of Mary Girard's married life were happy years, though the contrary has been stated. Without doubt Mr. Girard was very fond of her, though his unbending will and temper, and the ignoring of her relatives, were not calculated to make any woman continuously happy. Evidently Jean, who had lived in the family, thought no blame attached to his brother; for he wrote from Cape François: "It is impossible to express to you what I felt at such news. I do truly pity the frightful state I imagine you to be in, above all, knowing the regard and love you bear your wife.... Conquer your grief, and show yourself by that worthy of being a man; for, dear friend, when one has nothing with which to reproach one's self, no blow, whatsoever it may be, should crush him."

After a period of rest, Mrs. Girard seemed to recover. Stephen and Jean formed a partnership, and the former sailed to the Mediterranean on business for the firm. After three years the partnership was dissolved by mutual consent, Stephen preferring to transact business alone. As soon as these matters were settled, he and his wife were to take a journey to France, which country she had long been anxious to visit. Probably the family would then see for themselves that the unassuming girl made an amiable, sensible wife for their eldest son.

In the midst of preparations, the despondency again returned; and by the advice of physicians, Mrs. Girard was taken to the Pennsylvania Hospital, at Eighth and Spruce Streets, Aug. 31, 1790, where she remained till her death in 1815, insane for over twenty-five years. She retained much of the beauty of her girlhood, lived on the first floor of the hospital in large rooms, had the freedom of the grounds, and was "always sitting in the sunlight." Her mind became almost a blank; and when the housekeeper came bringing the little daughters of Jean, Mrs. Girard scarcely recognized her.

To add still more to Mr. Girard's sorrow, after his wife had been at the hospital several months, on March 3, 1791, a daughter was born to her, who was named for the mother, Mary Girard. The infant was taken into the country to be cared for, and lived but a few months. It was buried in the graveyard of the parish church.

Bereft of his only child, his home desolate, Mr. Girard plunged more than ever into the whirl of business. He built six large ships, naming some of them after his favorite authors,—Voltaire, Helvetius, Montesquieu, Rousseau, Good Friends, and North America,—to trade with China and India, and other Eastern countries. He would send grain and cotton to Bordeaux, where, after unloading, his ships would reload with fruit and wine for St. Petersburg. There they would dispose of their cargo, and take on hemp and iron for Amsterdam. From there they would go to Calcutta and Canton, and return, laden with tea and silks, to Philadelphia.

Little was known about the quiet, taciturn Frenchman; but every one supposed he was becoming very rich, which was the truth. He was not always successful. He says in one of his letters, "We are all the subjects of what you call 'reverses of fortune.' The great secret is to make good use of fortune, and when reverses come, receive them with *sang froid*, and by redoubled activity and economy endeavor to repair them." His ship Montesquieu, from Canton, China, arrived within the capes of Delaware, March 26, 1813, not having heard of the war between America and England, and was captured with her valuable cargo, the fruits of the two years' voyage. The ship was valued at $20,000, and the cargo over $164,000. He immediately tried to ransom her, and did so with $180,000 in coin. When her cargo was sold, the sales amounted to nearly $500,000, so that Girard's quickness and good sense, in spite of the ransom, brought him large gains. The teas were sold for over two dollars a pound, on account of their scarcity from the war.

Mr. Girard rose early and worked late. He spent little on clothes or for daily needs. He evidently did not care simply to make money; for he wrote his friend Duplessis at New Orleans: "I do not value fortune. The love of labor is my highest ambition.... I observe with pleasure that you have a numerous family, that you are happy in the possession of an honest fortune. This is all that a wise man has a right to wish for. As to myself, I live like a galley-slave, constantly occupied, and often passing the night without sleeping. I am wrapped up in a labyrinth of affairs, and worn out with care."

To another he wrote: "When I rise in the morning my only effort is to labor so hard during the day that when the night comes I may be enabled to sleep soundly." He had the same strong will as in his boyhood, but he usually controlled his temper. He kept his business to himself, and would not permit his clerks to gossip about his affairs. They had to be men of correct habits while in his employ. Having some suspicion of one of the officers of his ship Voltaire, he wrote to Captain Bowen: "I desire you not to permit a drunken or immoral man to remain on board of your ship. Whenever such a man makes disturbance, or is disagreeable to the rest of the crew, discharge him whenever you have the opportunity. And if any of my apprentices should not conduct themselves properly, I authorize you to correct them as I would myself. My intention being that they shall learn their business, so after they are free they may be useful to themselves and their country."

Mr. Girard gave minute instructions to all his employees, with the direction that they were to "break owners, not orders." Miss Louise Stockton, in "A Sylvan City, or Quaint Corners in Philadelphia," tells the following incident, illustrative of Mr. Girard's inflexible rule: "He once sent a young supercargo with two ships on a two years' voyage. He was to go first to London, then to Amsterdam, and so from port to port, selling and buying, until at last he was to go to Mocha, buy coffee, and turn back. At London, however, the young fellow was charged by the Barings not to go to Mocha, or he would fall into the hands of pirates; at Amsterdam they told him the same thing. Everywhere the caution was repeated; but he sailed on until he came to the last port before Mocha. Here he was consigned to a merchant who had been an apprentice to Girard in Philadelphia; and he, too, told him he must not dare venture near the Red Sea.

"The supercargo was now in a dilemma. On one side was his master's order; on the other, two vessels, a valuable cargo, and a large sum of money. The merchant knew Girard's peculiarities as well as the supercargo did; but he thought the rule to "break owners, not orders" might this time be governed by discretion. 'You'll not only lose all you have made,' he said, 'but you'll never go home to justify yourself.'

"The young man reflected. After all, the object of his voyages was to get coffee; and there was no danger in going to Java, so he turned his prow, and away he sailed to the Chinese seas. He bought coffee at four dollars a sack, and sold it in Amsterdam at a most enormous advance, and then went back to Philadelphia in good order, with large profits, sure of approval. Soon after he entered the counting-room Girard came in. He looked at the young fellow from under his bushy brows, and his one eye gleamed with resentment. He did not greet him, nor welcome

22

him, nor congratulate him, but, shaking his angry hand, cried, 'What for you not go to Mocha, sir?' And for the moment the supercargo wished he had. But this was all Girard ever said on the subject. He rarely scolded his employees. He might express his opinion by cutting down a salary, and when a man did not suit him he dismissed him."

When one of Girard's bookkeepers, Stephen Simpson, apparently with little or no provocation, assaulted a fellow bookkeeper, injuring him so severely about the head that the man was unable to leave his home for more than a week, Girard simply laid a letter on Simpson's desk the next morning, reducing his salary from fifteen hundred dollars to one thousand per annum. The clerk was very angry, but did not give up his situation. When an errand-boy was caught in the act of stealing small sums of money from the counting-house, Mr. Girard put a more intricate lock on the money-drawer, and made no comment. The boy was sorry for his conduct, and gave no further occasion for complaint.

Girard believed in labor as a necessity for every human being. He used to say, "No man shall be a gentleman on *my* money." If he had a son he should labor. He said, "If I should leave him twenty thousand dollars, he would be lazy or turn gambler." Mr. Ingram tells an amusing incident of an Irishman who applied to Mr. Girard for work. "Engaging the man for a whole day, he directed the removal from one side of his yard to the other of a pile of bricks, which had been stored there awaiting some building operations; and this task, which consumed several hours, being completed, he was accosted by the Irishman to know what should be done next. 'Why, have you finished that already?' said Girard; 'I thought it would take all day to do that. Well, just move them all back again where you took them from; that will use up the rest of the day;' and upon the astonished Irishman's flat refusal to perform such fruitless labor, he was promptly paid and discharged, Girard saying at the same time, in a rather aggrieved manner, 'I certainly understood you to say that you wanted *any* kind of work.'"

Absorbed as Mr. Girard was in his business, cold and unapproachable as he seemed to the people of Philadelphia, he had noble qualities, which showed themselves in the hour of need. In the latter part of July, 1793, yellow fever in its most fatal form broke out in Water Street, within a square of Mr. Girard's residence. The city was soon in a panic. Most of the public offices were closed, the churches were shut up, and people fled from the city whenever it was possible to do so. Corpses were taken to the grave on the shafts of a chaise driven by a negro, unattended, and without ceremony.

"Many never walked in the footpath, but went in the middle of the streets, to avoid being infected in passing houses wherein people had died. Acquaintances and friends avoided each other in the streets, and only signified their regard by a cold nod. The old custom of shaking hands fell into such disuse that many shrank back with affright at even the offer of a hand. The death-calls echoed through the silent, grass-grown streets; and at night the watcher would hear at his neighbor's door the cry, 'Bring out your dead!' and the dead were brought. Unwept over, unprayed for, they were wrapped in the sheet in which they died, and were hurried into a box, and thrown into a great pit, the rich and the poor together."

"Authentic cases are recorded," says Henry W. Arey in his "Girard College and its Founder," "where parent and child and husband and wife died deserted and alone, for want of a little care from the hands of absent kindred."

In the midst of this dreadful plague an anonymous call for volunteer aid appeared in the *Federal Gazette*, the only paper which continued to be published. All but three of the "Visitors of the Poor" had died, or had fled from the city. The hospital at Bush Hill needed some one to bring order out of chaos, and cleanliness out of filth. Two men volunteered to do this work, which meant probable death. To the amazement of all, one of these was the rich and reticent foreigner, Stephen Girard. The other man was Peter Helm. The former took the interior of the hospital under his charge. For two months Mr. Girard spent from six to eight hours daily in the hospital, and the rest of the time helped to remove the sick and the dead from the infected districts round about. He wrote to a friend in Baltimore: "The deplorable situations to which fright and sickness have reduced the inhabitants of our city demand succor from those who do not fear death, or who at least do not see any risk in the epidemic which now prevails here. This will occupy me for some time; and if I have the misfortune to succumb, I will have at least the satisfaction to have performed a duty which we all owe to each other."

Mr. Ingram quotes from the *United States Gazette* of Jan. 13, 1832, the account of Girard at this time, witnessed by a merchant who was hurrying by with a camphor-saturated handkerchief pressed to his mouth: "A carriage, rapidly driven by a black servant, broke the silence of the deserted and grass-grown street. It stopped before a frame house in Farmer's Row, the very hotbed of the pestilence; and the driver, first having bound a handkerchief over his mouth, opened the door of the carriage, and quickly remounted to the box. A short, thick-set man stepped from the coach, and entered the house.

"In a minute or two the observer, who stood at a safe distance watching the proceedings, heard a shuffling noise in the entry, and soon saw the visitor emerge, supporting, with extreme difficulty, a tall, gaunt, yellow-visaged victim of the pestilence. His arm was around the waist of the sick man, whose yellow face rested against his own, his long, damp, tangled hair mingling with his benefactor's, his feet dragging helpless upon the pavement. Thus, partly dragging, partly lifted, he was drawn to the carriage door, the driver averting his face

24

from the spectacle, far from offering to assist. After a long and severe exertion, the well man succeeded in getting the fever-stricken patient into the vehicle, and then entering it himself, the door was closed, and the carriage drove away to the hospital, the merchant having recognized in the man who thus risked his life for another, the foreigner, Stephen Girard."

Twice after this, in 1797 and 1798, when the yellow fever again appeared in Philadelphia, Mr. Girard gave his time and money to the sick and the poor.

In January, 1799, he wrote to a friend in France: "During all this frightful time I have constantly remained in the city, and without neglecting my public duties, I have played a part which will make you smile. Would you believe it, my friend, that I have visited as many as fifteen sick people in one day, and what will surprise you still more, I have lost only one patient, an Irishman, who would drink a little."

Busy, as a mariner, merchant, and helper of the sick and the poor, Mr. Girard found time to aid the Republic, to which he had become ardently attached. Besides serving for several terms in the City Council, and as Warden of the Port for twenty-two years, during the war of 1812 he rendered valuable financial aid. In 1810 Mr. Girard, having about one million dollars in the hands of Baring Bros. & Co., London, ordered the whole of it to be used in buying stock and shares of the Bank of the United States. When the charter of the bank expired in 1811, Mr. Girard purchased the whole outfit, and opened "The Bank of Stephen Girard," with a capital of one million two hundred thousand dollars. About this time, 1811, an attempt was made by two men to kidnap Mr. Girard by enticing him into a house to buy goods, then seize him, and carry him to a small ship in the Delaware, where he would be confined till he had paid the money which they demanded. The plot was discovered. After the men were arrested, and in prison for several months, one was declared insane, and the other was acquitted on the ground of comparative ignorance of the plot.

Everybody believed in Mr. Girard's honesty, and in the safety of his bank. He made temporary loans to the Government, never refusing his aid. When near the close of the war the Government endeavored to float a loan of five million dollars, the bonds to bear interest at seven per cent per annum, and a bonus offered to capitalists, there was so much indifference or fear of future payment, or opposition to the war with Great Britain, that only $20,000 were subscribed for. Mr. Girard determined to stake his whole fortune to save the credit of his adopted country. He put his name opposite the whole of the loan still unsubscribed for.

The effect was magical. People at once had faith in the Government, professed themselves true patriots, and persisted in taking shares from Mr. Girard, which he gave them on the original terms. "The sinews of war were thus furnished," says Mr. Arey, "public confidence was restored, and a series of brilliant victories resulted in a peace, to which he thus referred in a letter written in 1815 to his friend Morton of Bordeaux: 'The peace which has taken place between this country and England will consolidate forever our independence, and insure our tranquillity.'"

Soon after the close of the war, on Sept. 13, 1815, word was sent to Mr. Girard that his wife, still insane, was dying. Years before, when he found that she was incurable, he had sought a divorce, which those who admire him most must wish that he had never attempted; and the bill failed. He was now sixty-five, and growing old. His life had been too long in the shadow ever to be very full of light.

He asked to be sent for when all was over. Toward sunset, when Mary Girard was in her plain coffin, word was sent to him. He came with his household, and followed her to her resting-place, in the lawn at the north front of the hospital. "I shall never forget the last and closing scene," writes Professor William Wagner. "We all stood about the coffin, when Mr. Girard, filled with emotion, stepped forward, kissed his wife's corpse, and his tears moistened her cheek."

She was buried in silence, after the manner of the Friends, who manage the hospital. After the coffin was lowered, Mr. Girard looked in, and saying to Mr. Samuel Coates, "It is very well," returned to his home.

Mary Girard's grave, and that of another who died in 1807, giving the hospital five thousand dollars on condition that he be buried there, are now covered by the Clinic Building, erected in 1868. The bodies were not disturbed, as there is no cellar under the structure. As a reward for the care of his wife, soon after the burial Mr. Girard gave the hospital about three thousand dollars, and small sums of money to the attendants and nurses. It was his intention to be buried beside his wife, but this plan was changed later.

The next year, 1816, President Madison having chartered the second Bank of the United States, there were so few subscribers that it was evident that the scheme would fail. At the last moment Mr. Girard placed his name against the stock not subscribed for,—three million one hundred thousand dollars. Again confidence was restored to a hesitating and timid public. Some years later, in 1829, when the State of Pennsylvania was in pressing need for money to carry on its daily functions, the governor asked Mr. Girard to loan the State one hundred thousand dollars, which was cheerfully done.

As it was known that Mr. Girard had amassed great wealth, and had no children, he was constantly besought to give, from all parts of the country. Letters came from France, begging that his native land be remembered through some grand institution of benevolence.

Ambitious though Mr. Girard was, and conscious of the power of

26

money, he had without doubt been saving and accumulating for other reasons than love of gain. His will, made Feb. 16, 1830, by his legal adviser, Mr. William J. Duane, after months of conference, showed that Mr. Girard had been thinking for years about the disposition of his millions. When persons seemed inquisitive during his life, he would say, "My deeds must be my life. When I am dead, my actions must speak for me."

To the last Mr. Girard was devoted to business. "When death comes for me," he said, "he will find me busy, unless I am asleep in bed. If I thought I was going to die to-morrow, I should plant a tree, nevertheless, to-day."

His only recreation from business was going daily to his farm of nearly six hundred acres, in Passyunk Township, where he set out choice plants and fruit-trees, and raised the best produce for the Philadelphia market. His yellow-bodied gig and stout horse were familiar objects to the townspeople, though he always preferred walking to riding.

His home in later years, a four-story brick house, was somewhat handsomely furnished, with ebony chairs and seats of crimson plush from France, a present from his brother Étienne; a tall writing-cabinet, containing an organ given him by Joseph Bonaparte, the brother of Napoleon, and the ex-king of Spain and Naples, who usually dined with Mr. Girard on Sunday; a Turkey carpet, and marble statuary purchased in Leghorn by his brother Jean. The home was made cheerful by his young relatives. He had in his family the three daughters of Jean, and two sons of Étienne, whom he educated.

He loved animals, always keeping a large watch-dog at his home and on each of his ships, saying that his property was thus much more efficiently protected than through the services of those to whom he paid wages. He was very fond of children, horses, dogs, and canary-birds. In his private office several canaries swung in brass cages; and these he taught to sing with a bird organ, which he imported from France for that purpose.

When Mr. Girard was seventy-six years of age a violent attack of erysipelas in the head and legs led him to confine himself thereafter to a vegetable diet as long as he lived. The sight of his one eye finally grew so dim that he was scarcely able to find his way about the streets, and he was often seen to grope about the vestibule of his bank to find the door. On Feb. 12, 1820, as he was crossing the road at Second and Market Streets, he was struck and badly injured by a wagon, the wheel of which passed over his head and cut his face. He managed to regain his feet and reach his home. While the doctors were dressing the wound and cleansing it of the sand, he said, "Go on, Doctor, I am an old sailor; I can bear a good deal."

After some months he was able to return to his bank; but in

December, 1831, nearly two years after the accident, an attack of influenza, then prevailing, followed by pneumonia, caused his death. He lay in a stupor for some days, but finally rallied, and walked across the room. The effort was too great, and putting his hand against his forehead, he exclaimed, "How violent is this disorder! How very extraordinary it is!" and soon died, without speaking again, at five o'clock in the afternoon of Dec. 26, 1831, nearly eighty-two years old.

He was given a public funeral by the city which he had so many times befriended. A great concourse of people gathered to watch the procession or to join it, all houses being closed along the route, the city officials walking beside the coffin carried in an open hearse. So large a funeral had never been known in Philadelphia, said the press. The body was taken to the Holy Trinity Roman Catholic Church, and placed in the vault of Baron Henry Dominick Lallemand, General of Artillery under Napoleon I., who had married the youngest daughter of Girard's brother Jean. Mr. Girard was born in the Romish Church, and never severed his connection, although he attended a church but rarely. He liked the Friends, and modelled his life after their virtues; but he said it was better for a man to die in the faith in which he was born. He gave generously to all religious denominations and to the poor.

When Mr. Girard's will was read, it was apparent for what purpose he had saved his money. He gave away about $7,500,000, a remarkable record for a youth who left home at fourteen, and rose from a cabin-boy to be one of the wealthiest men of his time.

The first gift in the will, and the largest to any existing corporation, was $30,000 to the Pennsylvania hospital where Mary Girard died and was buried, the income to be used in providing nurses. To the Institution for the Deaf and Dumb, Mr. Girard left $20,000; to the Philadelphia Orphan Asylum, $10,000; public schools, $10,000; to purchase fuel forever, in March and August, for distribution in January among poor white housekeepers of good character, the income from $10,000; to the Society for poor masters of ships and their families, $10,000; to the poor among the Masonic fraternity of Pennsylvania, $20,000; to build a schoolhouse at Passyunk, where he had his farm, $6,000; to his brother Étienne, and to each of the six children of this brother, $5,000; to each of his nieces from $10,000 to $60,000; to each captain of his vessels $1,500, and to each of his housekeepers an annuity or yearly sum of $500, besides various amounts to servants; to the city of Philadelphia, to improve her Delaware River front, to pull down and remove wooden buildings within the city limits, and to widen and pave Water Street, the income of $500,000; to the Commonwealth of Pennsylvania, for internal improvements by canal navigation, $300,000; to the cities of New Orleans and Philadelphia, "to promote the health and general prosperity of the inhabitants," 280,000 acres of land in the State of Louisiana.

The city of Philadelphia has been fortunate in her gifts. The Elias Boudinot Fund, for supplying the poor of the city with fuel, furnished over three hundred tons of coal last year; "and this amount will increase annually, by reason of the larger income derived from the 12,000 acres of land situated in Centre County, the property of this trust." The investments and cash balance on Dec. 31, 1893, amounted to $40,600.

Benjamin Franklin, at his death, April 17, 1790, gave to each of the two cities, Philadelphia and Boston, in trust, £1,000 ($5,000), to be loaned to young married mechanics under twenty-five years of age, to help them start in business, in sums not to exceed £60, nor to be less than £15, at five per cent interest, the money to be paid back by them in ten annual payments of ten per cent each. Two respectable citizens were to become surety for the payment of the money. This Franklin did because two men helped him when young to begin business in Philadelphia by a loan, and thus, he said, laid the foundation of his fortune. A bequest somewhat similar was founded in London more than twenty years previously, in 1766,—the Wilson's Loan Fund, "to lend sums of £100 to £300 to young tradesmen of the city of London, etc., at two per cent per annum."

Dr. Franklin estimated that his $5,000 at interest for one hundred years would increase to over $600,000 (£131,000); and then the managers of the fund were to lay out $500,000 (£100,000) says the will, "in public works, which may be judged of most general utility to the inhabitants, such as fortifications, bridges, aqueducts, public buildings, baths, pavements, or whatever may make living in the town more convenient to its people, and render it more agreeable to strangers resorting hither for health or a temporary residence." In Philadelphia Dr. Franklin hoped the £100,000 would be used in bringing by pipes the water of the Wissahickon Creek to take the place of well water, and in making the Schuylkill completely navigable. If these things had been done by the end of the hundred years, the money could be used for other public works.

The remaining £31,000 was to be put at interest for another hundred years, when it would amount to £4,600,000 or $23,000,000. Of this amount £1,610,000 was to be given to Philadelphia, and the same to Boston, and the balance, £3,000,000 or $15,000,000, paid to each State. The figures are of especial interest, as showing how fast money will accumulate if kept at interest.

The descendants of Franklin have tried to break the will, but have not succeeded. The Board of Directors of City Trusts of Philadelphia report for the year ending Dec. 31, 1893, that the fund of $5,000 for the first hundred years, though not equalling the sum which Franklin hoped, has yet reached the large amount of $102,968.48. The Boston fund, says Mr. Samuel F. McCleary, the treasurer, amounted, at the end of a hundred years, to $431,395.70. Of this sum, $328,940 was paid to the city of Boston, and $102,455.70 was put at interest for another hundred years. This has already increased to $110,806.83. What an amount of good some other man or woman might do with $5,000!

It remains to be seen to what use the two cities will put their gifts. Perhaps they will provide work for the unemployed in making good roads or in some other useful labor, or instead of loaning money to mechanics, as Franklin intended, perhaps they will erect tenement houses for mechanics or other working people, as is done by some cities in England and Scotland, following the example so nobly set by George Peabody, when he gave his $3,000,000, which has now doubled, to build houses for the London poor. He said, "If judiciously managed for two hundred years, its accumulation will amount to a sum sufficient to buy the city of London."

If Stephen Girard's $300,000 to the State of Pennsylvania had been given for the making of good roads, thousands of the unemployed might have been provided with labor, tens of thousands of poor horses saved from useless over-work in hauling loads over muddy roads where the wheels sink to the hubs, and the farmers saved thousands of dollars in carrying their produce to cities.

Stephen Girard had a larger gift in mind than those to his adopted city and State. He said in his will, "I have been for a long time impressed with the importance of educating the poor, and of placing them, by the early cultivation of their minds, and the development of their moral principles, above the many temptations to which, through poverty and ignorance, they are exposed; and I am particularly desirous to provide for such a number of poor male white orphan children, as can be trained in one institution, a better education, as well as a more comfortable maintenance, than they usually receive from the application of the public funds."

With this object in view, a college for orphan boys, Mr. Girard gave to "the Mayor, Aldermen, and citizens of Philadelphia, all the residue and remainder of my real and personal estate" in trust; first, to erect and maintain a college for poor white male orphans; second, to establish "a competent police;" and third, "to improve the general appearance of the city itself, and, in effect, to diminish the burden of taxation, now most oppressive, especially on those who are the least able to bear it," "after providing for the college as my primary object."

He left $2,000,000, allowing "as much of that sum as may be necessary in erecting the college," which was "to be constructed with the most durable materials, and in the most permanent manner, avoiding needless ornament." He gave the most minute directions in his will for its size, material, "marble or granite," and the training and education of the inmates.

This residue "and remainder of my real and personal estate" had grown in 1891 to more than $15,000,000, with an income yearly of about $1,500,000. Truly Stephen Girard had saved and labored for a magnificent and enduring monument! The Girard estate is one of the largest owners of real estate in the city of Philadelphia. Outside of the city some of the Girard land is valuable in coal production. In the year 1893, 1,542,652 tons of anthracite coal were mined from the Girard land. More than $4,500,000 received from its coal has been invested, that the college may be doubly sure of its support when the coal-mines are exhausted.

Girard College, of white marble, in the form of a Greek temple, was begun in May, 1833, two years after Mr. Girard's death, and was fourteen years and six months in building. A broad platform, reached by eleven marble steps, supports the main building. Thirty-four Corinthian columns form a colonnade about the structure, each column six feet in diameter and fifty-five feet high, and each weighing one hundred and three tons, and costing about $13,000 apiece. They are beautiful and substantial, and yet $13,000 would support several orphans for a year or more.

The floors and roof are of marble; and the three-story building weighs over 76,000 tons, the average weight on each superficial foot of foundation being, according to Mr. Arey, about six tons. Four auxiliary white marble buildings were required by the will of Mr. Girard for dormitories, schoolrooms, etc. The whole forty-five acres in which stand the college buildings are surrounded, according to the given instructions, by a wall ten feet high and sixteen inches thick, covered with a heavy marble capping.

The five buildings were completed Nov. 13, 1847, at a cost of nearly $2,000,000 ($1,933,821.78); and on Jan. 1, 1848, Girard College was opened with one hundred orphans. In the autumn one hundred more were admitted, and on April 1, 1849, one hundred more. Those born in the city of Philadelphia have the first preference, after them those born in the State, those born in New York City where Mr. Girard first landed in America, and then those born in New Orleans where he first traded. They must enter between the ages of six and ten, be fatherless, although the mother may be living, and must remain in the college till they are between fourteen and eighteen, when they are bound out by the mayor till they are twenty-one, to learn some suitable trade in the arts, manufacture, or agriculture, their tastes being consulted as far as possible. Each orphan has three suits of clothing, one for every day, one better, and one usually reserved for Sundays.

The first president of Girard College was Alexander Dallas Bache, a great-grandson of Benjamin Franklin, and head of the Coast Survey of the United States. He visited similar institutions in Europe, and purchased the necessary books and apparatus for the school.

While the college was building, the heirs, with the not unusual disregard of the testator's desires, endeavored to break the will. Mr. Girard had given the following specific direction in his will: "I enjoin and require that no ecclesiastic, missionary, or minister of any sect whatsoever shall ever hold or exercise any station or duty whatever in the said college, nor shall any such person ever be admitted for any purpose, or as a visitor, within the premises appropriated to the purposes of the said college:—In making this restriction I do not mean to cast any reflection upon any sect or person whatsoever; but as there is such a multitude of sects, and such a diversity of opinion amongst them, I desire to keep the tender minds of the orphans, who are to derive advantage from this bequest, free from the excitement which clashing doctrines and sectarian controversy are so apt to produce. My desire is that all the instructors and teachers in the college shall take pains to instil into the minds of the scholars the purest principles of morality, so that on their entrance into active life they may from inclination and habit evince benevolence toward their fellow-creatures, and a love of truth, sobriety, and industry, adopting at the same time such religious tenets as their matured reason may enable them to prefer." The heirs of Mr. Girard claimed that by reason of the above the college was "illegal and immoral, derogatory and hostile to the Christian religion;" but it was the unanimous decision of the Supreme Court that there was in the will "nothing inconsistent with the Christian religion, or opposed to any known policy of the State."

On Sept. 30, 1851, the body of Stephen Girard was removed from the Roman Catholic Church, but not without a lawsuit by the heirs on account of its removal, to the college, and placed in a sarcophagus in the vestibule. The ceremony was entirely Masonic, the three hundred orphans witnessing it from the steps of the college. Over fifteen hundred Masons were in the procession, and each deposited his palm-branch upon the coffin. In front of the sarcophagus is a statue of Mr. Girard, by Gevelot of Paris, costing thirty thousand dollars.

Girard College now has ten white marble auxiliary buildings for its nearly or quite two thousand orphans. There are more applicants than there is room to accommodate. Its handsome Gothic chapel is also of white marble, erected in 1867. Here each day the pupils gather for worship morning and evening, the exercises, non-sectarian in character, consisting of a hymn, reading from the Bible, and prayer. On Sundays the pupils assemble in their section rooms at nine in the morning and two in the afternoon for religious reading and instruction; and at 10.30 and 3 they attend worship in the chapel, addresses being given by the president, A. H. Fetterolf, Ph.D. LL.D., or some invited layman.

In 1883 the Technical Building was erected in the western part of the grounds. Here instruction is given in metal and woodwork, mechanical drawing, shoemaking, blacksmithing, carpentry, foundry, plumbing, steam fitting, and electrical mechanics. Here the pupils learn about the dynamo, motor, lighting by electricity, telegraphy, and the like. About six hundred boys in this department spend five hours a week in this practical work.

At the World's Columbian Exposition at Chicago, in the exhibit made by Girard College, one could see the admirable work of the students in a single-span bridge, a four horse-power yacht steam-engine, a vertical engine, etc. The whole exhibit was given at the close of the Exposition to Armour Institute, to which the founder, Mr. Philip D. Armour, has given $1,500,000.

To the west of the main college building is the monument erected by the Board of Directors to the memory of Girard College boys killed in the Civil War. A life-size figure of a soldier stands beneath a canopy supported by four columns of Ohio sandstone. The granite base is overgrown with ivy. On one side are the names of the fallen; on the other, these words, from Mr. Girard's will, "And especially do I desire that, by every proper means, a pure attachment to our Republican institutions, and to the sacred rights of conscience, as guaranteed by our happy constitutions, shall be formed and fostered in the minds of the scholars."

On May 20, each year, the anniversary of Mr. Girard's birth, the graduates of Girard College gather from all parts of the country to do honor to the generous giver. Games are played, the cadets parade, and a dinner is provided for scholars and guests. The pupils seem happy and contented. Their playgrounds are large; and they have a bathing-pool for swimming in summer, and skating in winter. They receive a good education in mathematics, astronomy, geology, history, chemistry, physics, French, Spanish, with some Latin and Greek, with a course in business, shorthand, etc. Through all the years they have "character lessons," which every school should have throughout our country,—familiar conversations on honesty, the dignity of labor, perseverance, courage, self-control, bad language, value and use of time, truthfulness, temperance, good temper, the good citizen and his duties, kindness to animals, patriotism, the study of the lives and deeds of noble men and women, the Golden Rule of play,—"No fun unless it is fun on both sides," and similar topics. Oral and written exercises form a part of this work. There is also a department of military science, a two years' course being given, with one recitation a week. A United States army officer is one of the college faculty, and commandant of the battalion.

The annual cost of clothing and educating each of the two thousand orphans, including current repairs on the buildings, is a little more than three hundred dollars. On leaving college, each boy receives a trunk with clothing and books, amounting to about seventy-five dollars.

Probably Mr. Girard, with all his far-sightedness, could not have foreseen the great good to the nation, as well as to the individual, in thus fitting, year after year, thousands of poor orphans for useful positions in life. Mr. Arey well says: "When in the fulness of time many homes have been made happy, many orphans have been fed, clothed, and educated, and many men rendered useful to their country and themselves, each happy home, or rescued child, or useful citizen, will be a living monument to perpetuate the name and embalm the memory of the dead 'Mariner and Merchant.'"

ANDREW CARNEGIE
AND HIS LIBRARIES

"This, then, is held to be the duty of the man of wealth: First, to set an example of modest, unostentatious living, shunning display or extravagance; to provide moderately for the legitimate wants of those dependent upon him; and after doing so, to consider all surplus revenues which come to him simply as trust funds, which he is called upon to administer, and strictly bound as a matter of duty to administer in the manner which, in his judgment, is best calculated to produce the most beneficial results for the community,—the man of wealth thus becoming the mere trustee and agent for his poorer brethren."

Thus wrote Andrew Carnegie in his "Gospel of Wealth," published in the *North American Review* for June, 1889. This article so interested Mr. Gladstone that he asked the editor of the *Review* to permit its republication in England, which was done. When the world follows this "Gospel," and those who have means consider themselves "trustees for their poorer brethren," and their money as "trust funds," we shall see little of the heartbreak and the poverty of the present age.

> "Ring in the valiant man and free,
> The larger heart, the kindlier hand;
> Ring out the darkness of the land,
> Ring in the Christ that is to be."

Andrew Carnegie was born at Dunfermline, Scotland, Nov. 25, 1835, into a poor but honest home. His father, William Carnegie, was a weaver, a man of good sense, strongly republican, though living under a monarchy, and well-read upon the questions of the day. The mother was a woman of superior mind and character, to whom Andrew was unusually devoted, till her death in 1886, when he had reached middle life.

When Andrew was twelve years of age and his brother Thomas five, the parents decided to make their home in the New World, coming to New York in a sailing-vessel in 1847. They travelled to Pittsburg, Penn., and lived for some time in Allegheny City.

Andrew had been sent to school in Dunfermline, and, having a fondness for books, was a bright, ambitious boy at twelve, ready to begin the struggle for a living so as to make the family burdens lighter. Work was not easily found; but finally he obtained employment as a bobbin-boy in a cotton factory, at $1.20 a week.

Mr. Carnegie, when grown to manhood, wrote in the *Youth's Companion*, April 23, 1896:—

"I cannot tell you how proud I was when I received my first week's own earnings. One dollar and twenty cents made by myself, and given to me because I had been of some use in the world! No longer entirely dependent upon my parents, but at last admitted to the family partnership as a contributing member, and able to help them! I think this makes a man out of a boy sooner than almost anything else, and a real man too, if there be any germ of true manhood in him. It is everything to feel that you are useful.

"I have had to deal with great sums. Many millions of dollars have since passed through my hands. But the genuine satisfaction I had from that one dollar and twenty cents outweighs any subsequent pleasure in money-getting. It was the direct reward of honest manual labor; it represented a week of very hard work, so hard that but for the aim and end which sanctified it, slavery might not be much too strong a term to describe it.

"For a lad of twelve to rise and breakfast every morning, except the blessed Sunday morning, and go into the streets and find his way to the factory, and begin work while it was still dark outside, and not be released until after darkness came again in the evening, forty minutes' interval only being allowed at noon, was a terrible task.

"But I was young, and had my dreams; and something within always told me that this would not, could not, should not last—I should some day get into a better position. Besides this, I felt myself no longer a mere boy, but quite 'a little man;' and this made me happy."

Another place soon opened for the lad, where he was set to fire a boiler in a cellar, and to manage the small steam-engine which drove the machinery in a bobbin factory. "The firing of this boiler was all right," says Mr. Carnegie; "for fortunately we did not use coal, but the refuse wooden chips, and I always liked to work in wood. But the responsibility of keeping the water right and of running the engine, and the danger of my making a mistake and blowing the whole factory to pieces, caused too great a strain, and I often awoke and found myself sitting up in bed through the night trying the steam-gauges. But I never told them at home that I was having a 'hard tussle.' No! no! everything must be bright to them.

"This was a point of honor; for every member of the family was working hard except, of course, my little brother, who was then a child, and we were telling each other only all the bright things. Besides this, no man would whine and give up—he would die first.

"There was no servant in our family, and several dollars per week were earned by 'the mother' by binding shoes after her daily work was done! Father was also hard at work in the factory. And could I complain?"

36

Wages were small, and in every leisure moment Andrew looked for something better to do. He went one day to the office of the Atlantic and Ohio Telegraph Company, and asked for work as a messenger. James Douglas Reid, the manager, was a Scotchman, and liked the lad's manner. "I liked the boy's looks," said Mr. Reid afterwards; "and it was easy to see that though he was little he was full of spirit. His pay was $2.50 a week. He had not been with me a full month when he began to ask whether I would teach him to telegraph. I began to instruct him, and found him an apt pupil. He spent all his spare time in practice, sending and receiving by sound, and not by tape as was largely the custom in those days. Pretty soon he could do as well as I could at the key, and then his ambition carried him away beyond doing the drudgery of messenger work."

The boy liked his new occupation. He once wrote: "My entrance into the telegraph office was the transition from darkness to light; from firing a small engine in a dirty cellar to a clean office where there were books and papers. That was a paradise to me, and I bless my stars that sent me to be a messenger-boy in a Pittsburg telegraph office."

When Andrew was fourteen his father died, leaving him the only support of his mother and brother, seven years old. He believed in work, and never shirked any duty, however hard.

He soon found employment as telegraph operator with the Pennsylvania Railroad Company. At fifteen he was train-despatcher, a place of unusual responsibility for a boy; but his energy, carefulness, and industry were equal to the demands on him.

When he was sixteen Andrew had thought out a plan by which trains could be run on single tracks, and the telegraph be used to govern their running. "His scheme was the one now in universal use on the single-tracked roads in the country; namely, to run trains in opposite directions until they approached within comparatively a few miles, and then hold one at a station until the other had passed." This thought about the telegraph brought Andrew into notice among those above him; and he was transferred to Altoona, the headquarters of the general manager.

Young Carnegie had done what he recommends others to do in his "How to win Fortune," in the New York *Tribune*, April 13, 1890. He says, "George Eliot put the matter very pithily: 'I'll tell you how I got on. I kept my ears and my eyes open, and I made my master's interest my own.'

"The condition precedent for promotion is that the man must first attract notice. He must do something unusual, and especially must this be beyond the strict boundary of his duties. He must suggest, or save, or perform some service for his employer which he could not be censured for not having done. When he has thus attracted the notice of his immediate superior, whether that be only the foreman of a gang, it matters not; the first great step has been taken, for upon his immediate superior promotion depends. How high he climbs is his own affair."

Carnegie "kept his eyes and ears open." In his "Triumphant Democracy" he relates the following incident: "Well do I remember that, when a clerk in the service of the Pennsylvania Railroad Company, a tall, spare, farmer-looking kind of man came to me once when I was sitting on the end seat of the rear car looking over the line. He said he had been told by the conductor that I was connected with the railway company, and he wished me to look at an invention he had made. With that he drew from a green bag (as if it were for lawyers' briefs) a small model of a sleeping-berth for railway cars. He had not spoken a minute before, like a flash, the whole range of the discovery burst upon me. 'Yes,' I said, 'that is something which this continent must have.' I promised to address him upon the subject as soon as I had talked over the matter with my superior, Thomas A. Scott.

"I could not get that blessed sleeping-car out of my head. Upon my return I laid it before Mr. Scott, declaring that it was one of the inventions of the age. He remarked, 'You are enthusiastic, young man; but you may ask the inventor to come and let me see it.' I did so; and arrangements were made to build two trial cars, and run them on the Pennsylvania Railroad. I was offered an interest in the venture, which, of course, I gladly accepted. Payments were to be made ten per cent per month after the cars were delivered, the Pennsylvania Railroad Company guaranteeing to the builders that the cars should be kept upon its line and under its control.

"This was all very satisfactory until the notice came that my share of the first payment was $217.50. How well I remember the exact sum; but two hundred and seventeen dollars and a half were as far beyond my means as if it had been millions. I was earning fifty dollars per month, however, and had prospects, or at least I always felt that I had. What was to be done? I decided to call on the local banker, Mr. Lloyd, state the case, and boldly ask him to advance the sum upon my interest in the affair. He put his hand on my shoulder, and said, 'Why, of course, Andie, you are all right. Go ahead. Here is the money.'

"It is a proud day for a man when he pays his last note, but not to be named in comparison with the day in which he makes his first one, and *gets a banker to take it*. I have tried both, and I know. The cars paid the subsequent payments from their earnings. I paid my first note from my savings, so much per month; and thus did I get my foot on fortune's ladder. It is easy to climb after that. A triumphant success was scored. And thus came sleeping-cars into the world. 'Blessed be the man who invented sleep,' says Sancho Panza. Thousands upon thousands will echo the sentiment, 'Blessed be the man who invented sleeping-cars.' Let me record his name, and testify my gratitude to him, my dear, quiet, modest, truthful, farmer-looking friend, T. T. Woodruff, one of the benefactors of the age."

Mr. Pullman later engaged in sleeping-car building, and Carnegie advised his firm "to capture Mr. Pullman." "There was a capture," says Mr. Carnegie, "but it did not quite take that form. They found themselves swallowed by this ogre, and Pullman monopolized everything."

While a very young man, Carnegie was appointed superintendent of the Western Division of the Pennsylvania Railroad. As superintendent he became the friend of Colonel Scott; and, together with some others, they bought several farms along the line of the road, which proved very valuable oil-lands. Mr. Carnegie says of the Storey Farm, Oil Creek, "We purchased the farm for $40,000; and so small was our faith in the ability of the earth to yield for any considerable time the hundred barrels per day which the property was then producing, that we decided to make a pond capable of holding one hundred thousand barrels of oil, which we estimated would be worth, when the supply ceased, $1,000,000. Unfortunately for us the pond leaked fearfully, evaporation also caused much loss; but we continued to run oil in to make the losses good day after day, until several hundred thousand barrels had gone in this fashion.

"Our experience with the farm may be worth reciting. Its value rose to $5,000,000; that is, the shares of the company sold in the market upon this basis; and one year it paid in cash dividends $1,000,000—rather a good return upon an investment of $40,000. So great was the yield in the district that in two years oil became almost valueless, often selling as low as thirty cents per barrel, and not infrequently it was suffered to run to waste as utterly worthless.

"But as new uses were found for the oil, prices rose again; and to remove the difficulty of high freights, pipes were laid, first for short distances, and then to the seaboard, a distance of about three hundred miles. Through these pipes, of which six thousand two hundred miles have been laid, the oil is now pumped from two thousand one hundred wells. It costs only ten cents to pump a barrel of oil to the Atlantic. The value of petroleum and its products *exported* up to January, 1884, exceeds in value $625,000,000."

Within ten years from the time when Mr. Carnegie and his friends bought the oil-farms, their investment had returned them four hundred and one per cent, and the young Scotchman could count himself a rich man. Before this, however, he had entered the iron and steel industry, in which his great wealth has been made. With a little money which he had saved, he borrowed $1,250 from a bank, and, with five other persons, established the Keystone Bridge Works of Pittsburg, with the small capital of $6,000. This was a success from the first, and in latter years has had a capital of $1,000,000. It has built bridges all over the country, and structural frames for many public buildings in New York, Chicago, and other cities. From this time forward Mr. Carnegie's career has been a most successful one. He has become chief owner in the Union Iron Works, the Edgar Thomson Steel Works, the Homestead Steel Works, formerly a rival company, the Duquesne Works of the Allegheny Bessemer Steel Company, and several other iron and coke companies. The capital of these companies is about $30,000,000, and about twenty-five thousand men are employed.

"In 1890 Carnegie Bros. & Co., Limited," says the *Engineering and Mining Journal* for July 4, 1891, "had a capacity to produce 600,000 tons of steel rails per annum, or over twenty-five per cent of the total capacity of all the rolling-mills of the United States, while its products of steel girders, plates, nails, and other forms of manufactured iron and steel are greater than at any other works in this country, and exceed the amount turned out at the famous Krupp Works in Germany." The company has supplied the United States Government with a large amount of armor plates for our new ships, and also filled a large order for the Russian Government.

The Edgar Thomson Steel Works have an annual capacity of 1,000,000 gross tons of ingots, 600,000 gross tons of rails and billets, and 50,000 gross tons of castings. The Duquesne Furnaces have a yearly capacity of 700,000 gross tons of pig-iron; the Lucy Furnaces, 200,000 gross tons yearly; the Duquesne Steel Works, an annual capacity of 450,000 gross tons of ingots. The Homestead Steel Works have an annual capacity of 375,000 gross tons of Bessemer steel and ingots, and 400,000 gross tons of open-hearth steel ingots. The Upper Union Mills have an annual output of 140,000 gross tons of steel bars and steel universal mill-plates, etc.; the Lower Union Mills, an annual capacity of 65,000 gross tons of mill-plates, bridge-work, car-forgings, etc.

The industrious, ambitious boy was not satisfied merely to amass wealth. He had always been a great reader and thinker. In 1883 Charles Scribner's Sons published a book by this successful telegraph operator and iron manufacturer, "An American Four-in-Hand in Britain." The trip was suggested by Mr. Black's novel, "The Strange Adventures of a Phaeton," and extended from Brighton to Inverness, a distance of eight hundred and thirty-one miles.

Mr. Carnegie and his party of chosen friends made the journey by coach in seven weeks, from July 17 to Aug. 3, 1881, and had a most enjoyable as well as instructive trip. *The Critic* gives Mr. Carnegie well-merited praise, saying that "he has produced a book of travel as fresh as though he had been exploring Thibet or navigating the River of Golden Sand." The book is dedicated to "My favorite heroine, my mother," who was the queen dowager of the volume, and whose happiness during the journey seemed to be the chief concern of her devoted son.

This book had so cordial a reception that the following year, 1884, another volume was published, "Round the World," covering a trip made in 1878-1879; Mr. Carnegie having sailed from San Francisco to Japan, and thence through the lands of the East. As he starts, his mother puts in his hand Shakespeare in thirteen small volumes; and these are his company and delight in the long ocean voyage. Through China, India, and other countries, he observes closely, learns much, and tells it in a way that is always interesting. "Life at the East," he says, "lacks two of its most important elements,—the want of intelligent and refined women as the companion of man, and a Sunday. It has been a strange experience to me to be for several months without the society of some of this class of women,—sometimes many weeks without even speaking to one, and often a whole week without even seeing the face of an educated woman. And, bachelor as I am, let me confess what a miserable, dark, dreary, and insipid life this would be without their constant companionship."

Ten years later, in 1886, Mr. Carnegie published a book that had a very wide reading, and at once placed the author prominently before the New World and the Old World as well, "Triumphant Democracy, or Fifty Years' March of the Republic."

The book showed extensive research, a deep love for his adopted country, America, a warm heart, and an able mind. He wrote: "To the beloved Republic, under whose equal laws I am made the peer of any man, although denied political equality by my native land, I dedicate this book, with an intensity of gratitude and admiration which the native-born citizen can neither feel nor understand."

No one can read this book without being amazed at the power and possibilities of the Republic, and without a deeper love for, and pride in the greatness and true worth of, his country. The style is bright and attractive, and the facts stated remarkable. Americans must always be debtors to the Scotchman who has shown them how to prize their native land.

Mr. Carnegie wrote the book "as a labor of love," to show the people of the Old World the advantages of a republic over a monarchical form of government, and to Americans, "a juster estimate than prevails in some quarters of the political and social advantages which they so abundantly possess over the people of the older and less advanced lands, that they may be still prouder and even more devoted, if possible, to their institutions than they are."

Mr. Carnegie shows by undisputed facts that America, so recently a colony of Great Britain, has now become "the wealthiest nation in the world," "the greatest agricultural nation," "the greatest manufacturing nation," "the greatest mining nation in the world." "In the ten years from 1870 to 1880," says Mr. Carnegie, "eleven and a half millions were added to the population of America. Yet these only added three persons

41

to each square mile of territory; and should America continue to double her population every thirty years, instead of every twenty-five years as hitherto, seventy years must elapse before she will attain the density of Europe. The population will then reach two hundred and ninety millions."

Mr. Carnegie has said in his "Imperial Federation," published in the *Nineteenth Century*, September, 1891, "Even if the United States increase is to be much less rapid than it has been hitherto, yet the child is born who will see more than 400,000,000 under her sway. No possible increase of the race can be looked for in all the world combined comparable to this. Green truly says that its 'future home is to be found along the banks of the Hudson and the Mississippi.'"

It will surprise many to know that "the whole United Kingdom (England, Scotland, and Ireland) could be planted in Texas, and leave plenty of room around it."

"The farms of America equal the entire territory of the United Kingdom, France, Belgium, Germany, Austria, Hungary, and Portugal. The corn-fields equal the extent of England, Scotland, and Belgium; while the grain-fields generally would overlap Spain. The cotton-fields cover an area larger than Holland, and twice as large as Belgium."

The growth of manufactures in America is amazing. In thirty years, from 1850 to 1880, Mr. Carnegie says there was an increase of nearly six hundred per cent, while the increase in British manufactures was little more than a hundred per cent. The total in America in 1880 was $5,560,000,000; in the United Kingdom, $4,055,000,000.

"Probably the most rapid development of an industry that the world has ever seen," says Mr. Carnegie, "is that of Bessemer steel in America." In 1870 America made 40,000 tons of Bessemer; in 1885, fifteen years later, she made 1,373,513 tons, which was 74,000 tons more than Great Britain made. "This is advancing not by leaps and bounds, it is one grand rush—a rush without pause, which has made America the greatest manufacturer of Bessemer steel in the world.... One is startled to find that more yards of carpet are manufactured in and around the city of Philadelphia alone than in the whole of Great Britain. It is not twenty years since the American imported his carpets, and now he makes more at one point than the greatest European manufacturing nation does in all its territory."

Of the manufacture of boots and shoes by machinery, Mr. Carnegie says, "A man can make three hundred pairs of boots in a day, and a single factory in Massachusetts turns out as many pairs yearly as thirty-two thousand bootmakers in Paris.... Twenty-five years ago the American conceived the idea of making watches by machinery upon a gigantic scale. The principal establishment made only five watches per day as late as 1854. Now thirteen hundred per day is the daily task, and six thousand watches per month are sent to the London agency."

42

The progress in mining has been equally remarkable. "To the world's stock of gold," says Mr. Carnegie, "America has contributed, according to Mulhall, more than fifty per cent. In 1880 he estimated the amount of gold in the world at 10,355 tons, worth $7,240,000,000. Of this the New World contributed 5,302 tons, or more than half. One of the most remarkable veins of metal known is the Comstock Lode in Nevada.... In fourteen years this single vein yielded $180,000,000. In one year, 1876, the product of the lode was $18,000,000 in gold, and $20,500,000 in silver,—a total of $38,500,000. Here, again, is something which the world never saw before.

"America also leads the world in copper, the United States and Chili contributing nearly one-half the world's supply.... On the south shore of Lake Superior this metal is found almost pure, in masses of all sizes, up to many tons in weight. It was used by the native Indians, and traces of their rude mining operations are still visible."

Mr. Carnegie says the anthracite coal-fields of Pennsylvania will produce 30,000,000 tons per year for four hundred and thirty-nine years; and he thinks by that time "men will probably be burning the hydrogen of water, or be fully utilizing the solar rays or the tidal energy." The coal area of the United States comprises 300,000 square miles; and Mr. Carnegie "is almost ashamed to confess it, she has three-quarters of all the coal area of the earth."

While Mr. Carnegie admires and loves the Republic, he is devoted to the mother country, and is a most earnest advocate of peace between us. He writes: "Of all the desirable political changes which it seems to me possible for this generation to effect, I consider it by far the most important for the welfare of the race, that every civilized nation should be pledged, as the Republic is, to offer peaceful arbitration to its opponent before the senseless, inhuman work of human slaughter begins."

In his "Imperial Federation" he writes: "War between members of our race may be said to be already banished; for English-speaking men will never again be called upon to destroy each other.... Both parties in America, and each successive government, are pledged to offer peaceful arbitration for the adjustment of all international difficulties,—a position which it is to be hoped will soon be reached by Britain, at least in regard to all the differences with members of the same race.

"Is it too much to hope that, after this stage has been reached, and occupied successfully for a period, another step forward will be taken, and that, having jointly banished war between themselves, a general council should be evolved by the English-speaking nations, to which may at first only be referred all questions of dispute between them?...

"The Supreme Court of the United States is extolled by the

statesmen of all parties in Britain, and has just received the compliment of being copied in the plan for the Australian Commonwealth. Building upon it, may we not expect that a still higher Supreme Court is one day to come, which shall judge between the nations of the entire English-speaking race, as the Supreme Court at Washington already judges between States which contain the majority of the race?"

Mr. Carnegie believes that the powers of the council would increase till the commanding position of the English-speaking race would make other races listen to its demands for peace, and so war be forever done away with. Mr. Carnegie rightly calls war "international murder," and, like Tennyson, looks forward to that blessed time when—

> "All men's good
> Be each man's rule, and universal Peace
> Lie like a shaft of light across the land,
> And like a lane of beams athwart the sea."

Mr. Carnegie has also written, in the *North American Review* for June, 1891, "The A. B. C. of Money," urging the Republic to keep "its standard in the future, as in the past, not fluctuating silver, but unchanging gold."

In his articles in the newspapers, and in his public addresses, he has given good advice to young men, in whom he takes the deepest interest. He believes there never were so many opportunities to succeed as now for the sober, frugal, energetic young man. "Real ability, the capacity for doing things, never was so eagerly searched for as now, and never commanded such rewards.... The great dry-goods houses that interest their most capable men in the profits of each department succeed, when those fail that endeavor to work with salaried men only. Even in the management of our great hotels it is found wise to take into partnership the principal men. In every branch of business this law is at work; and concerns are prosperous, generally speaking, just in proportion as they succeed in interesting in the profits a larger and larger proportion of their ablest workers. Co-operation in this form is fast coming in all great establishments." To young men he says, "Never enter a barroom.... It is low and common to enter a barroom, unworthy of any self-respecting man, and sure to fasten upon you a taint which will operate to your disadvantage in life, whether you ever become a drunkard or not."

"Don't smoke.... The use of tobacco requires young men to withdraw themselves from the society of women to indulge the habit. I think the absence of women from any assembly tends to lower the tone of that assembly. The habit of smoking tends to carry young men into the society of men whom it is not desirable that they should choose as their intimate associates. The practice of chewing tobacco was once common. Now it is considered offensive. I believe the race is soon to take another step forward, and that the coming man is to consider smoking as offensive as chewing was formerly considered."

"Never speculate. Never buy or sell grain or stocks upon a margin.... The man who gambles upon the exchanges is in the condition of the man who gambles at the gaming-table. He rarely, if ever, makes a permanent success."

"Don't indorse.... There are emergencies, no doubt, in which men should help their friends; but there is a rule that will keep one safe. No man should place his name upon the obligation of another if he has not sufficient to pay it without detriment to his own business. It is dishonest to do so."

Mr. Carnegie has not only written books and made money, he has distinguished himself as a giver of millions, and that while he is alive. He has seen too many wills broken, and fortunes misapplied, when the money was not given away till death. He says of Mr. Tilden's bequest of over $5,000,000 for a free library in the city of New York: "How much better if Mr. Tilden had devoted the last years of his own life to the proper administration of this immense sum; in which case neither legal contest nor any other cause of delay could have interfered with his aims."

Of course money is sometimes so tied up in business that it cannot be given during a man's life; "yet," says Mr. Carnegie, "the day is not far distant when the man who dies leaving behind him millions of available wealth, which was free for him to administer during life, will pass away 'unwept, unhonored, and unsung,' no matter to what uses he leaves the dross which he cannot take with him. Of such as these the public verdict will then be, 'The man who dies thus rich dies disgraced.'"

He believes large estates left at death should be taxed by the State, as is the case in Pennsylvania and some other States. Mr. Carnegie does not favor large gifts left to families. "Why should men leave great fortunes to their children?" he asks. "If this is done from affection, is it not misguided affection? Observation teaches that, generally speaking, it is not well for the children that they should be so burdened. Neither is it well for the State. Beyond providing for the wife and daughters moderate sources of income, and very moderate allowances indeed, if any, for the sons, men may well hesitate; for it is no longer questionable that great sums bequeathed often work more for the injury than for the good of the recipients. There are instances of millionnaires' sons unspoiled by wealth, who, being rich, still perform great services to the community. Such are the very salt of the earth, as valuable as unfortunately they are rare." Again Mr. Carnegie says of wealth left to the young, "It deadens their energies, destroys their ambition, tempts them to destruction, and renders it almost impossible that they should lead lives creditable to themselves or valuable to the State. Such as are not deadened by wealth deserve double credit, for they have double temptation."

In the *North American Review* for December, 1889, Mr. Carnegie suggests what he considers seven of the best uses for surplus wealth: The founding of great universities; free libraries; hospitals or any means to alleviate human suffering; public parks and flower-gardens for the people, conservatories such as Mr. Phipps has given to the park at Allegheny City, which are visited by thousands; suitable halls for lectures, elevating music, and other gatherings, free, or rented for a small sum; free swimming-baths for the people; attractive places of worship, especially in poor localities. Mr. Carnegie's own great gifts have been largely along the line which he believes the "best gift to a community,"—a free public library. He thinks with John Bright that "it is impossible for any man to bestow a greater benefit upon a young man than to give him access to books in a free library."

"It is, no doubt," he says, "possible that my own personal experience may have led me to value a free library beyond all other forms of beneficence. When I was a working-boy in Pittsburg, Colonel Anderson of Allegheny—a name I can never speak without feelings of devotional gratitude—opened his little library of four hundred books to boys. Every Saturday afternoon he was in attendance at his house to exchange books. No one but he who has felt it can ever know the intense longing with which the arrival of Saturday was awaited that a new book might be had. My brother and Mr. Phipps, who have been my principal business partners through life, shared with me Colonel Anderson's precious generosity; and it was when revelling in the treasures which he opened to us that I resolved, if ever wealth came to me, that it should be used to establish free libraries, that other poor boys might receive opportunities similar to those for which we were indebted to that noble man."

"How far that little candle throws his beams!
So shines a good deed in a naughty world."

Again Mr. Carnegie says, "I also come by heredity to my preference for free libraries. The newspaper of my native town recently published a history of the free library in Dunfermline, and it is there recorded that the first books gathered together and opened to the public were the small collections of three weavers. Imagine the feelings with which I read that one of these three men was my honored father. He founded the first library in Dunfermline, his native town; and his son was privileged to found the last.... I have never heard of a lineage for which I would exchange that of the library-founding weaver."

Mr. Carnegie has given for the Edinburgh Free Library, Scotland, $250,000; for one in his native town of Dunfermline, $90,000; and several thousand dollars each to libraries in Aberdeen, Peterhead, Inverness, Ayr, Elgin, Wick and Kirkwall, besides contributions towards public halls and reading-rooms at Newburgh, Aberdour, and many other places abroad. Mr. Carnegie's mother laid the corner-stone for the free library in Dunfermline. He writes in his "American Four-in-Hand in Britain," "There was something of the fairy-tale in the fact that she had left her native town, poor, thirty odd years before, with her loved ones, to found a new home in the great Republic, and was to-day returning in her coach, to be allowed the privilege of linking her name with the annals of her beloved native town in one of the most enduring forms possible."

When the corner-stone of the Peterhead Free Library in Scotland was laid, Aug. 8, 1891, the wife of Mr. Carnegie was asked to lay the stone with square and trowel, and endeared herself to the people by her hearty interest and attractive womanhood. She was presented with the silver trowel with ivory handle which she had used, and with a vase of Peterhead granite from the employees of the Great North of Scotland Granite Works.

Mr. Carnegie did not marry till he was fifty-two years of age, in 1887, the year following the death of his mother and only brother Thomas. The latter died Oct. 19, 1886. Mr. Carnegie's wife, who is thoroughly in sympathy with her husband's constant giving, was Miss Louise Whitfield, the daughter of the late Mr. John Whitfield of New York, of the large importing firm of Whitfield, Powers, & Co. Mr. Carnegie had been an intimate friend of the family for many years, and knew well the admirable qualities and cultivation of the lady he married. He once wrote: "There is no improving companionship for man in an ignorant or frivolous woman." Miss Whitfield acted upon the advice which Mr. Carnegie has given in some of his addresses: "To the young ladies I say, 'Marry the man who loves most his mother.'" Mr. Carnegie now has two homes, one in New York City, the other at Cluny Castle, Kingussie, Scotland. He gives little personal attention to business, having delegated those matters to others. "I throw the responsibility upon others," he once said, "and allow them full swing." Mr. Carnegie is a man of great energy, with cheerful temperament, sound judgment, earnestness, and force of character. He has a large, well-shaped head, high forehead, brown hair and beard, and expressive face.

Mr. Carnegie's gifts in his adopted country have been many and large. To the Johnstown Free Library, Pennsylvania, he has given $40,000. To the Jefferson County Library at Fairfield, Iowa, he has given $40,000, which provides an attractive building for books, museum, and lecture-hall. The late Senator James F. Wilson gave the ground for the fire-proof building. The library owes much of its success to its librarian, Mr. A. T. Wells, who has given his life to the work, having held the position for thirty-two years. For many years he labored without salary, giving both time and money.

To the Braddock Free Library, Mr. Carnegie has given $200,000. Braddock, ten miles east of Pittsburg, has a population of 16,000, mainly the employees of the Edgar Thomson Steel Works; and the village of Homestead lies just opposite. The handsome library building has a very attractive reading-room, which is filled in the evening and much used during the day by the families of the employees. There is also a large reading-room exclusively for boys and girls, where are found juvenile books and periodicals. The librarian, Miss Helen Sperry, writes: "There is a great deal of local pride in the library, and it grows constantly in the affection of the people."

The building was much enlarged in 1894 to accommodate the Carnegie Club of six hundred men and boys. The new portion contains a hall capable of seating eleven hundred persons, a large gymnasium, bathrooms, swimming-pool, bowling-alleys, etc.

"In order to encourage public spirit in Braddock," says the *Review of Reviews* for October, 1895, "a selection of books on municipal improvement, streets and roads, public health, and other subjects in which the community should be interested, was placed on the library shelves; and it is said that these books have been consulted by the municipal officers, and results are already apparent." This is a good example for other librarians. Much work is being done in local history and in co-operation with the public schools.

To the Carnegie Free Library of Allegheny City, Mr. Carnegie has given $300,000, the city making an annual appropriation of $15,000 to carry on its work. The building is of gray granite, Romanesque in style, with a shelving capacity of about 75,000 volumes. The library has a delivery-room, a general reading-room, women's reading-room, reference-room, besides trustees' and librarians' rooms. The building also contains, on the first floor, a music-hall, with a seating-capacity of eleven hundred, where free concerts are given every Saturday afternoon on a ten-thousand-dollar organ; there is an art-gallery on the second floor, and a lecture-room. The latter seats about three hundred persons, and is used for University Extension lectures, meetings of the Historical Society, etc. A room adjoining is for the accommodation of scientific societies. The city appropriates about $8,000 yearly for the music-hall, fuel, repairs, etc.

The Allegheny Free Library was formally opened by President Harrison on Feb. 13, 1890. Mr. Carnegie said, in presenting the gift of the library, "My wife,—for her spirit and influence are here to-night,—

48

my wife and I realize to-night how infinitely more blessed it is to give than to receive.... I wish that the masses of working men and women, the wage-earners of all Allegheny, will remember and act upon the fact that this is their library, their gallery, and their hall. The poorest citizen, the poorest man, the poorest woman, that toils from morn till night for a livelihood, as, thank Heaven, I had that toil to do in my early days, as he walks this hall, as he reads the books from these alcoves, as he listens to the organ, and admires the works of art in this gallery, equally with the millionnaire and the foremost citizen, I want him to exclaim in his own heart, 'Behold, all this is mine. I support it, and I am proud to support it. I am joint proprietor here.'" "Since the library opened four years ago," says Mr. William M. Stevenson, the librarian, "over 1,000,000 books and periodicals have been put into the hands of readers.... The concerts have been exceedingly popular, and incidentally have helped the library by drawing people to the library who might otherwise have remained in ignorance of the popularity and usefulness of the institution."

Mr. Carnegie's greatest gift has been the Pittsburg Library. It is a magnificent building of gray Ohio sandstone, in the Italian Renaissance style of architecture, with roof of red tile. The architects were Longfellow, Alden, and Harlow, their plan being chosen from the one hundred and two sets of plans offered. The library building is 393 feet long and 150 feet wide, with two graceful towers, each 162 feet high, and has capacity for 300,000 volumes. The entire "stack" or set of shelves for books is made of iron in six stories, and is as nearly fireproof as possible. The lower stories are for the circulating-books; the upper stories for reference-books.

The library proper is in the centre of the building, reached by a broad flight of stone steps. Above, cut in stone, are the words, "Carnegie Library; Free to the People." The vestibule, finished in marble with mosaic floors, is handsomely decorated. On the first floor are the circulating-library, "its blue-ceiling panels bordered with an interlace in orange and white," a periodical room on either side, one for scientific and technical, the other for popular and literary magazines, with rooms for cataloguing and for the library officials.

"The reference reading-room on the second floor, large, beautiful, and well-lighted," says the efficient librarian, Mr. Edwin H. Anderson, "is for quiet study. Here reference-books, such as encyclopædias, dictionaries, atlases, etc., are at hand, on the shelves along the walls, to be freely consulted." This room is of a greenish tone, with ivory-colored pilasters and arches, and a *fleur-de-lis* pattern painted in the wall-panels, from the "mark" of a famous Florentine printer and engraver four centuries ago.

Across the corridor from the reference reading-room are five smaller rooms for special collections of books. One is occupied by a

49

musical library of two thousand volumes, of the late Karl Merz, which was bought and presented to the library by several citizens of Pittsburg. Another will contain the collection to be purchased from the fund left by Mr. J. D. Bernd, and will bear his name. Another will be used for art-books, and another for science.

The children are to have a reading-room, made attractive by juvenile books, magazines, and copies of good pictures. A large and well-lighted room in the basement is used for the leading newspapers of the country.

The library has a wing on either side, one containing the art-gallery, and the other the science museum. The former has three large picture-rooms on the second floor, painted in dull red, with a wall-space of 8,300 feet for the exhibition of paintings and prints. A corridor 148 feet long, in which statuary will be placed, is decorated with copies of the frieze of the Parthenon. The basement of this wing will be devoted to the various departments of the art-schools of Pittsburg.

In the science museum three large, well-lighted rooms on the second floor will be used for collections in zoölogy, botany, and mineralogy. "The closely allied branches of geology, the study of the earth's crust; paleontology, the study of life in former ages; anthropology, the natural history of the human species; archæology, the science of antiquity; and ethnology and ethnography, treating of the origin, relation, characteristic costumes and habits of the human races, will, no doubt, receive as much attention as space and funds will permit."

It is also expected that works of skill and invention will be gathered into an industrial museum for the benefit especially of the many artisans of Pittsburg. Courses of free lectures will be given to teachers, to pupils, and to the public, as in the American Museum of Natural History of New York. Below the three rooms in the museum are three lecture-rooms, which can be used separately or as one room.

In one end of the large library building, and separated from it by a thick wall so as to deaden sound, is the music-hall, semi-circular in plan, with seats for two thousand one hundred persons, and a stage for sixty musicians and a chorus of two hundred. Much Sienna marble is used, the floor is mosaic, the walls are painted a deep rose-color, and the architecture proper in a soft ivory tone, with gilded ornamentation. Two free concerts, or organ recitals, are given each week through the year, on the large modern concert organ, built expressly for this hall. Musical lectures are also given, free from technicalities, illustrated by choir, organ, and piano. This is certainly taking music, art, and science to the people as a free gift. To this noble work Mr. Carnegie has given $2,100,000. Of this amount, $800,000 was for the main building, $300,000 for the seven branch libraries or distributing stations, and $1,000,000 as an endowment fund for the art-gallery.

From the annual income of this art-fund, which will be about $50,000, at least three of the pictures purchased are to be the work of American artists exhibited that year, preferably in the Pittsburg gallery.

The city of Pittsburg agrees to appropriate $40,000 annually for the maintenance of the library system. Mr. Carnegie has always felt that the people should bear a part of the burden. He said at the opening of the library, Nov. 5, 1895, "Every citizen of Pittsburg, even the very humblest, now walks into this, his own library; for the poorest laborer contributes his mite indirectly to its support. The man who enters a library is in the best society this world affords; the good and the great welcome him, surround him, and humbly ask to be allowed to become his servants; and if he himself, from his own earnings, contributes to its support, he is more of a man than before.... If library, hall, gallery, or museum be not popular, and attract the manual toilers and benefit them, it will have failed in its mission; for it was chiefly for the wage-earners that it was built, by one who was himself a wage-earner, and who has the good of that class at heart."

Mr. Carnegie has said elsewhere, "Every free library in these days should contain upon its shelves all contributions bearing upon the relations of labor and capital from every point of view,—socialistic, communistic, co-operative, and individualist; and librarians should encourage visitors to read them all."

The library stands near the entrance of the valuable park of about 439 acres given to the city by Mrs. Schenley in 1889. "This lady," says Mr. Carnegie, "although born in Pittsburg, married an English gentleman while yet in her teens. It is forty years and more since she took up her residence in London among the titled and wealthy of the world's metropolis; but still she turns to the home of her childhood, and by means of Schenley Park links her name with it forever. A noble use this of great wealth by one who thus becomes her own administrator."

Near the library are the $125,000 conservatories given to the people by Mr. Phipps, and a source of most elevating pleasure. Mr. Carnegie's gifts in and about Pittsburg amount already to $5,000,000; yet he is soon to build a library for Homestead, and one each for Duquesne and the town of Carnegie. "Such other districts as may need branch libraries," says Mr. Carnegie, "we ardently hope we may be able to supply; for to provide free libraries for all the people of Pittsburg is a field which we would fain make our own, as chief part of our life-work. I have dropped into the plural, for there is one always with me to prompt, encourage, suggest, discuss, and advise, and fortunately, sometimes, when necessary, gently to criticise; whose heart is as keenly in this work as my own, preferring it to any other as the best possible use of surplus wealth, and without whose wise and zealous co-operation I often feel little useful work could be done."

Mr. Carnegie has given $50,000 to Bellevue Hospital Medical College, New York, for a histological laboratory. He is also the founder of the magnificent Music Hall on the corner of Fifty-second Street and Seventh Avenue, New York City. The press says his investment in the Music Hall Company Limited equals nine-tenths of the full cost of the hall. "It was the dearest wish of the elder Damrosch that a grand concert-hall suitable for oratorio, choral, and symphony performances might be built in New York. The questions of cost, endowment, etc., have been discussed many times by his associates and successors, without definite result. It was the liberality and public spirit of Andrew Carnegie which finally made possible the establishment of a completely equipped home for music."

The main hall, exquisite in its decorations of ivory white, gold, and old rose, will seat about three thousand persons, with standing-room for a thousand more. In the decorations 1,217 lamps are placed. Of these, 189 are in the ceiling and the walls of the stage, 339 around the boxes and balconies, and 689 in the main ceiling. When the electric current is turned on at night the effect is magical. The electric-light plant consists of four dynamos, each weighing 20,000 pounds. Besides the main hall, there are several smaller rooms for recitals, lectures, readings, receptions, and studios.

Mr. Carnegie will need no other monument than his great libraries, the influence of which will increase in the coming centuries.

52

THOMAS HOLLOWAY:
HIS SANATORIUM AND COLLEGE

Thomas Holloway, one of England's most munificent givers, was born in Devonport, England, Sept. 22, 1800. His father, who had been a warrant officer in a militia regiment, had become a baker in Devonport.

Finding that he could support his several children better by managing an inn, he removed to Penzance, and took charge of Turk's Head Inn on Chapel Street. His son Thomas went to school at Camborne and Penzance until he was sixteen.

He was a saving lad, for the family were obliged to be economical. He must also have been energetic, for this quality he displayed remarkably through life. After his father died, he and his mother and his brother Henry opened a grocery and bakery shop in the marketplace at Penzance. Mrs. Holloway, the mother, was the daughter of a farmer at Trelyon, Lelant Parish, Cornwall, and knew how to help her sons make a living in the Penzance shop.

When Thomas was twenty-eight he seems to have tired of this kind of work or of the town, for he went to London to struggle with its millions in making a fortune. It seemed extremely improbable that he would make money; but if he did not make, he was too poor to lose much.

For twelve years he worked in various situations, some of the time being "secretary to a gentleman," showing that he had improved his time while in school to be able to hold such a position. In 1836 he had established himself as "a merchant and foreign commercial agent" at 13 Broad Street Buildings.

One of the men for whom Mr. Holloway, then thirty-six years old, did business, was Felix Albinolo, an Italian from Turin, who sold leeches and the "St. Come et St. Damien Ointment." Mr. Holloway introduced the Italian to the doctors at St. Thomas's Hospital, who liked the ointment, and gave testimonials in its favor.

Mr. Holloway, hoping that he could make some money out of it, prepared an ointment somewhat similar, and announced it for sale, Oct. 15, 1837. He stated in his advertisement in the paper that "Holloway's Family Ointment" had received the commendation of Herbert Mayo, senior surgeon at Middlesex Hospital, Aug. 19, 1837.

Albinolo warned the people in the same paper that the surgeon's letter was given in connection with his ointment, the composition of which was a secret. Whether this was true or not, the surgeon made no denial of Mr. Holloway's statement. A year later, as Albinolo could not sell his wares, and was in debt, he was committed to the debtors' prison, and nothing more is known of him or his ointment.

There were various reports about the Holloway ointment, and the pills which he soon after added to his stock. It was said that for the making of one or both of these preparations an old German woman had confided her knowledge to Mr. Holloway's mother, and she in turn had told her son. Mr. Holloway as long as he lived had great faith in his medicines, and believed they would sell if they could be brought to the notice of the people.

Every day he took his pills and his ointment to the docks to try to interest the captains and passengers sailing to all parts of the world. People, as usual, were indifferent to an unknown man and unknown medicines, and Mr. Holloway went back to his rooms day after day with little money or success. He advertised in the press as much as he was able, indeed, more than he was able; for he got into debt, and, like Albinolo, was thrust into a debtors' prison on White Cross Street. He effected a release by arranging with his creditors, whom he afterwards paid in full, with ten per cent interest, it is said, to such as willingly granted his release.

Mr. Holloway had married an unassuming girl, Miss Jane Driver, soon after he came to London; and she was assisting in his daily work. Mr. Holloway used to labor from four o'clock in the morning till ten at night, living, with his wife, over his patent-medicine warehouse at 244 Strand. He told a friend years afterwards that the only recreation he and his wife had during the week was to take a walk in that crowded thoroughfare. Speaking of the great labor and anxiety in building up a business, he said, "If I had then offered the business to any one as a gift they would not have accepted it."

The constant advertising created a demand for the medicines. In 1842, five years after he began to make his pills and ointment, Mr. Holloway spent £5,000 in advertising; in 1845 he spent £10,000; in 1851, £20,000; in 1855, £30,000; in 1864, £40,000; in 1882, £45,000, and later £50,000, or $250,000, each year.

Mr. Holloway published directions for the use of his medicines in nearly every known language,—Chinese, Turkish, Armenian, Arabic, and most of the vernaculars of India. He said he "believed he had advertised in every respectable newspaper in existence." The business had begun to pay well evidently in 1850, about twelve years after he started it; for in that year Mr. Holloway obtained an injunction against his brother, who had commenced selling "Holloway's Pills and Ointment at 210 Strand." Probably the brother thought a partnership in the bakery in their boyish days had fitted him for a partnership in the sale of the patent medicines.

In 1860 Mr. Holloway sent a physician to France to introduce his preparations; but the laws not being favorable to secret remedies, not much was accomplished. When the new Law Courts were built in London, Mr. Holloway moved his business to 533 New Oxford Street, since renumbered 78, where he employed one hundred persons, besides the scores in his branch offices.

"Of late years," says the Manchester *Guardian*, "his business became a vast banking-concern, to which the selling of patent medicines was allied; and he was understood to say some few years ago that his profits as a dealer in money approached the enormous sum of £100,000 a year.... The ground-floor of his large establishment in Oxford Street was occupied with clerks engaged in bookkeeping. On the first and second floors one might gain a notion of the profits of pill-making by seeing young women filling boxes from small hillocks of pills containing a sufficient dose for a whole city. On the topmost floor were Mr. Holloway's private apartments."

Later in life Mr. Holloway moved to a country home, Tittenhurst, Sunninghill, which is about six miles from Windsor, and on the borders of the great park of eighteen hundred acres, where he lived without any display, and where his wife died, Sept. 25, 1871, at the age of seventy-one.

He never had any desire for title or public prominence, and when, after his gifts had made him known and honored, a baronetcy was suggested to him, he would not consent to it. Mr. Holloway had worked untiringly; he had not spent his money in extravagant living; and now, how should he use it for the best good of his country?

The noble Earl of Shaftesbury had been giving much of his early life to the amelioration of the insane. He had visited asylums in England, and seen lunatics chained to their beds, living on bread and water, or shut up in dark, filthy cells, neglected, and often abused. He ascertained that over seventy-five per cent may be cured if treatment is given in the first twelve months; only five per cent if given later. He was astonished to find that no one seemed to care about these unfortunates.

He longed to see an asylum built for the insane of the middle classes. He addressed public meetings in their behalf; and Mr. Holloway was in one of these meetings, and listened to Lord Shaftesbury's fervent appeal. His heart was greatly moved; and he visited Shaftesbury, and together they conferred about the great gift which was consummated later. It is said also that at Mr. Gladstone's breakfast-table, Mrs. Gladstone advised with Mr. Holloway about the need of convalescent homes.

In the year 1873 Mr. Holloway put aside nearly £300,000 ($1,500,000) for an institution for the insane of the middle classes, such as professional men, clerks, teachers, and governesses, as the lower classes were quite well provided for in public asylums.

A picturesque spot was chosen for the Holloway Sanatorium,—

forty acres of ground near Virginia Water, which is six miles from Windsor, though within the royal domains. Virginia Water is a beautiful artificial lake, about seven miles in circumference, a mile and a half long, and one-third of a mile wide. The lake was formed in 1746, in order to drain the moorland, by William, Duke of Cumberland, uncle of George III. Near by is an obelisk with this inscription: "This obelisk was raised by the command of George II., after the battle of Culloden, in commemoration of the services of his son William, Duke of Cumberland, the success of his arms, and the gratitude of his father." This lake, with its adjacent gardens, pavilions, and cascades, was the favorite summer retreat of George IV., who built there a fishing-temple richly decorated. A royal barge, thirty-two feet long, for the use of royalty, is stationed on the lake.

In the midst of this attractive scenery Mr. Holloway caused his forty acres to be laid out with tasteful flower-beds, walks, and thousands of trees and shrubs. Occupied with his immense business, he yet had time to watch the growth of his great benevolent project.

Mr. W. H. Crossland, who had built the fine Town Hall at Rochdale, was chosen as the architect, and began at Virginia Water the stately and handsome Sanatorium in the English Renaissance style of architecture, of red brick with stone trimmings. There is a massive and lofty tower in the centre. The interior is finished in gray marble, which is enriched with cheerful colors and plentiful gilding. The great lecture or concert hall, adorned with portraits of distinguished persons by Mr. Girardot and other artists, has a very richly gilded roof. The refectory is decorated by a series of beautiful fancy groups after Watteau, forming a frieze.

The six hundred rooms of the building, great and small, on the four floors, are exquisitely finished and furnished, all made as attractive as possible, that those of both sexes who are weary and broken in mind may have much to interest them in their long days of absence from home and friends. Students of the National Art Training School, under Mr. Poynter, did much of the art work. There are no blank walls.

The Holloway Sanatorium, which is five hundred feet by two hundred feet in extent, has a model laundry in a separate building, pretty red brick houses for the staff and those who are not obliged to sleep in the building, a pleasure-house for rest and recreation for the inmates, and a handsome chapel.

Four hundred or more patients can be accommodated. A moderate charge is made for those who can afford to pay, and only those persons thought to be curable are received. As much freedom is allowed as possible, that the inmates may not unnecessarily feel the surveillance under which they are obliged to live.

The Sanatorium was opened June 15, 1885, by the Prince of

Wales, accompanied by the Princess, their three daughters, and the Duke of Cambridge. Mr. Martin Holloway, the brother-in-law of Mr. Thomas Holloway, spoke of the uses of the Sanatorium, and the Prince of Wales replied in a happy manner.

Many inmates were received at once, and the institution has proved a great blessing.

To what other uses should Mr. Holloway put his large fortune? He and Mrs. Holloway had long thought of a college for women, and after her death he determined to build one as a memorial to her who had helped him through all those days of poverty and self-sacrifice.

In 1875 Mr. Holloway held a conference with the blind Professor Henry Fawcett, Member of Parliament, and his able wife, Mrs. Millicent Garrett Fawcett, Mr. Samuel Morley, M.P., Sir James Kay-Shuttleworth, Bart., Mr. David Chadwick, M.P., Dr. Hague of New York, and others interested in the higher education of women. Mr. Holloway foresaw, with these educators, that in the future women would seek a university education like their brothers. "For many years," says Mr. Martin Holloway, "his mind was dominated by the idea that if a higher form of education would ennoble women, the sons of such mothers would be nobler men."

On May 8, 1876, Mr. Holloway purchased, and conveyed in trust to Mr. Henry Driver Holloway and Mr. George Martin Holloway, his brother-in-law, and Mr. David Chadwick, M.P., ninety-five acres on the southern slope of Egham Hill, Surrey, for his college for women. It is in the midst of most picturesque and beautiful scenery, rich in historical associations. Egham is five miles from Windsor, near the Thames, and on the borders of Runnymede, so called from the Saxon Runemede, or Council Meadow, where the barons, June 15, 1215, compelled King John to sign the Magna Charta. A building was erected to commemorate this important event, and the table on which the charter was signed is still preserved.

Near by is Windsor Great Park, with seven thousand fallow deer in its eighteen hundred acres, and its noted long walk, an avenue of elms three miles in length, extending from the gateway of George IV., the principal entrance to Windsor Castle, to Snow Hill, crowned by a statue of George III., by Westmacott. Not far away from Egham are lovely Virginia Water and Staines, from Stana, the Saxon for stone, where one sees the city boundary stone, on which is inscribed, "God preserve the city of London, A.D. 1280." This marks the limit of jurisdiction of the Lord Mayor of London over the Thames.

After Mr. Holloway had decided to build his college, he visited the chief cities of Europe with Mr. Martin Holloway to ascertain what was possible about the best institutions of learning, and the latter made a personal inspection of colleges in the United States. Mr. Holloway was seventy-six, and too old for a long journey to America.

Plans were prepared by Mr. W. H. Crossland of London, who spent much time in France studying the old French châteaux before he began his work on the college. The first brick was laid Sept. 12, 1879. Mr. Holloway wished this structure to be the best of its kind in England, if not in the world. The *Annual Register* says in regard to Mr. Holloway's two great gifts, "When their efficiency or adornment was concerned, his customary principle of economy failed to restrain him."

The college is a magnificent building in the style of the French Renaissance, reminding one of the Louvre in Paris, of red brick with Portland stone dressings, with much artistic sculpture.

"It covers," says a report prepared by the college authorities, "more ground than any other college in the world, and forms a double quadrangle, measuring 550 feet by 376 feet. The general design is that of two long, lofty blocks running parallel to each other, and connected in the middle and at either end by lower cross buildings.... The quadrangles each measure about 256 feet by 182 feet. Cloisters run from east to west on two sides of each quadrangle, with roofs whose upper sides are constructed as terraces, the capitals being arranged as triplets."

No pains or expense have been spared to finish and furnish this college with every comfort, even luxury. There are over 1,000 rooms, and accommodations for about 300 students. Each person has two rooms, one for sleeping and one for study; and there is a sitting-room for every six persons. The dining-hall is 100 feet long, 30 wide, and 30 high. The semi-circular ceiling is richly ornamented. The recreation-hall, which is in reality a picture-gallery, is 100 feet long, 30 wide, and 50 high, with beautiful ceiling and floor of polished marquetry. The pictures here were collected by Mr. Martin Holloway, and cost about £100,000, or half a million dollars. Sir Edwin Landseer's famous picture, "Man proposes, God disposes," was purchased for £6,000. It was painted in 1864 by Landseer, who received £2,500 for it. It represents an arctic incident suggested by the finding of the relics of Sir John Franklin.

Here are "The Princes in the Tower" and "Princess Elizabeth in Prison at St. James," by Sir John Millais; "The Babylonian Marriage Market" and "The Suppliants," by Edwin Long; "The Railway Station," by W. P. Frith; and other noted works. The gallery is open to the public every Thursday afternoon, and in the summer months on Saturdays also. There are several thousand visitors each year.

The college has twelve rooms with deadened walls for practising music, a gymnasium, six tennis-courts (three of asphalt and three of grass), a large swimming-bath, a lecture theatre, museum, a library with carved oak bookcases reaching nearly to the ceiling, and an immense kitchen which serves for a school for cookery. Electric lights and steam heat are used throughout the buildings, and there are open fireplaces for the students' rooms.

The chapel, 130 feet long by 30 feet wide, says the London *Graphic* for July 10, 1886, "is a singularly elaborate building in the Renaissance style.... In its decoration a strong tendency to the Italian school of the latter part of the sixteenth century is apparent. This is especially the case with the roof, which bears a kind of resemblance to that of the Sistine Chapel at Rome, though it cannot in any way be said to be a copy of that magnificent work.... The choir, or nave, is seated with oak benches arranged stall-ways, as is usual in the college chapels of Oxford and Cambridge.... The roof is formed of an elliptic barrel-vault, the lower portions of which are adorned with statues and candelabra in high relief, and the upper portion by painted enrichments. The former are a very remarkable series of works by the Italian sculpture Fucigna, who had learned his art in the studios of Tenerani and Rauch at Rome. These were his last works, and he did not live to complete them. The figures represent the prophets and other personages from the Old Testament on the left side, and apostles, evangelists, and saints from the New Testament on the right. The baldachino is constructed of walnut and oak, richly carved; and the organ front, at the opposite end of the chapel, is a beautiful example of wood-carving."

The building and furnishing of the college cost £600,000, the endowment £300,000, the pictures £100,000, making in all about one million sterling, or five million dollars. The deed of foundation states that "the college is founded by the advice and counsel of the founder's dear wife." When Mrs. Holloway was toiling with her husband over the shop in the Strand, with no recreation during the week except a walk, as he said, in that crowded thoroughfare, how little she could have realized that this beautiful monument would be built to her memory!

Mr. Holloway did not live to see his college completed; as he died, after a brief illness of bronchitis, at Tittenhurst, Wednesday, Dec. 26, 1883, aged eighty-three, and was buried in St. Michael's Churchyard, Sunninghill, Jan. 4, 1884.

Mr. Martin Holloway faithfully carried out his relative's wishes; and when the college was ready for occupancy, it was opened by Queen Victoria in person, on Wednesday, June 30, 1886. The day was fine; and Egham was gayly decorated for the event with flowers, banners, and arches. The Queen, with Princess Beatrice and her husband, the late Prince Henry of Battenberg, the Duke of Connaught, and other members of the royal family, drove over from Windsor through Frogmore, where Prince Albert is buried, and Runnymede to Egham, in open carriages, each carriage drawn by four gray horses ridden by postilions. Outriders in scarlet preceded the procession, which was accompanied by an escort of Life Guards.

Reaching the college at 5.30 P.M., the Queen and Princess Beatrice were each presented with a bouquet by Miss Driver Holloway, and were conducted to the chapel, where a throne had been prepared for her Majesty. Princess Beatrice, Prince Henry of Battenberg, and the Duke of Cambridge stood on her left, with the Duke of Connaught, the Archbishop of Canterbury, and others on her right. The choir sang an ode composed by Mr. Martin Holloway, and the Archbishop of Canterbury offered prayer.

The Queen then admired the decorations of the chapel, and proceeded to the picture gallery, where the architect presented to her an album with illustrations of the college, and the contractor, Mr. J. Thompson, offered her a beautiful key of gold. The top of the stem is encircled by two rows of diamonds; and the bow at the top is an elegant piece of gold, enamel, and diamonds. A laurel wreath of diamonds surrounds the words, "Opened by H. M. the Queen, June 30, 1886."

The Queen was then conducted to the upper quadrangle, where she seated herself in a chair of state on a dais, under a canopy of crimson velvet. A great concourse of people were gathered to witness the formal opening of the college. The lawn was also crowded, six hundred children being among the people. After the band of the Royal Artillery played to the singing of the national anthem, "God save the Queen," Mr. Martin Holloway presented an address to her Majesty in a beautiful casket of gold. "The casket rests on four pediments, on each of which is seated a female figure," says the London *Times*, "which are emblematical of education, science, music, and painting. On the front panel is a view of Royal Holloway College, on either side of which is a medallion containing the royal and imperial monogram, V.R.I., executed in colored enamel. Underneath the view is the monogram of the founder, Mr. Thomas Holloway, in enamel."

At one end of the casket are the royal arms, and at the opposite end the Holloway arms and motto, "Nil Desperandum," richly emblazoned in enamel. The casket is surmounted by a portrait model of Mr. Holloway, seated in a classic chair, being a reduction from the model from life taken by Signor Fucigna.

After the address in the casket was presented to Queen Victoria, the Earl of Kimberley, the minister in attendance, stepped forward, and said, "I am commanded by her Majesty to declare the college open." Trumpets were blown by the Royal Scots' Greys, cheers were given, the archbishop pronounced the benediction, and the choir sang "Rule Britannia." The Queen before her departure expressed her pleasure and satisfaction in the arrangement of the institution, and commanded that it be styled, "The Royal Holloway College."

More than a year later, on Friday, Dec. 16, 1887, a statue of the Queen was unveiled in the upper quadrangle of the college by Prince Christian. A group of the founder and his wife in the lower quadrangle was also unveiled. Both statues are of Tyrolese marble, and are the work of Prince Victor of Hohenlohe-Langenburg. The Rt. Hon. Earl Granville, K.G., made a very interesting address.

The college has done admirable work during the ten years since its opening. The founder desired that ultimately the college should confer degrees, but at present the students qualify for degrees at existing universities. In the report for 1895 of Miss Bishop, the principal, she says, "We have now among our students, past and present, fifty-one graduates of the University of London (twenty-one in honors), and twenty-one students who have obtained Oxford University honors.... This is the second year that a Holloway student has won the Gilchrist medal, which is awarded to the first woman on the London B.A. list, provided she obtains two-thirds of the possible marks." In 1891 a Holloway student was graduated from the Royal University of Ireland with honors.

Students are received who do not wish to work for a university examination, "provided they are *bona fide* students, with a definite course of work in view," says the college report for 1895. They must be over seventeen, pass an entrance examination, and remain not less than one year. There are twelve entrance scholarships of the value of £50 to £75 a year, and twelve founder's scholarships of £30 a year, besides bursaries of the same value. The charge for board, lodging, and instruction is £90 or $450 a year.

Courses of practical instruction are given in cookery, ambulance-work, sick-nursing, wood-carving, and dressmaking. Mr. Holloway states in his deed: "The curriculum of the college shall not be such as to discourage students who desire a liberal education apart from the Greek and Latin languages; and proficiency in classics shall not entitle students to rewards of merit over others equally proficient in other branches of knowledge." While the governors, some of whom rightly must always be women, may provide instruction in subjects which seem most suitable, Mr. Holloway expresses his sensible belief that "the education of women should not be exclusively regulated by the traditions and methods of former ages."

The students at Holloway, according to an article in Harper's *Bazar*, March 10, 1894, by Miss Elizabeth C. Barney, have a happy as well as busy life. She says, "The girls have a running-club, which requires an entrance examination of each candidate for election, the test being a rousing sprint around the college—one-third of a mile—within three minutes, or fail. After this has been successfully passed, the condition of continued membership is a repetition of this performance eight times every two weeks, on pain of a penny fine for every run neglected. On stormy days the interior corridors are not a bad course, inasmuch as each one measures one-tenth of a mile in length."

"Nor are in-door amusements less in vogue than out-door sports. There are the 'Shakespeare Evenings' and the 'French Evenings,' the 'Fire Brigade' and the 'Debating Society,' and a host of other more or less social events.... The Debating Society is an august body, which holds its sittings in the lecture theatre, and deals with all the questions of the United Kingdom in the most irreproachable Parliamentary style. They divide into Government and Opposition, and pass and reject bills in a way which would do credit to the nation in Parliament assembled."

The girls also, she says, "have a string orchestra of violins and 'celli, numbering about fifteen performers. The girls meet one evening a week in the library for practice, and enter into it more as recreation before study than as serious work. They play very well indeed together, and sometimes give concerts for the rest of the college."

A writer in the Atlanta *Constitution* for April 3, 1892, thus describes the drill of the fair fire brigade: "'The Holloway Volunteer Brigade' formed in three sections of ten students each, representing the occupants of different floors. They were drawn up in line at 'Right turn! Quick march! Position!' Then each section went quite through with two full drills.

"A fire in sitting-room No. 10 was supposed. At command 'Get to work!' the engine was run down to the doorway, a 'chain' of recruits was formed to the nearest source of water-supply, and the buckets were handed in line that the engine might be kept in full play. The pump was vigorously applied by two girls, while another worked the small hose quickly and ingeniously, so that the engine was at full speed in less than a minute. When the drill was concluded with the orders 'Knock off!' and 'Make up!' everything had been put in its own place.

"Then came the 'Hydrant Drill,' which was conducted at the hydrant nearest the point of a supposed outbreak of fire. In this six students from each section took part. Directly the alarm was given one hundred feet of canvas hose was run out, and an additional length (regulated, of course, by the distance) was joined to it. At the words 'Turn on!' by the officer known as 'branch hoseman,' the hose was directed so that, had there been water in it, it must have streamed onto the supposed fire. This drill was also accomplished in only a minute; and at the commands 'Knock off!' and 'Make up!' the hose-pipes were promptly disconnected, the pipe that is always kept attached to the hydrant was 'flaked down,' and an extra one hundred feet 'coiled up' on the bight with astonishing rapidity. The drills are genuine realities, and the students thoroughly enjoy them."

There is also a way of escape for the students in case of fire. The "Merryweather Chute," a large tube of specially woven fire-proof canvas, is attached to a wrought-iron frame that fits the window opening. There is also a drill with this chute. When the word is given, "Make ready to go down chute," the young woman draws her dress around her, steps feet foremost into the tube, and regulates her speed by means of a rope made fast to the frame, and running through the chute to the ground. Fifty students can descend from a window in five minutes with no fear after they have practised.

Mr. Holloway and his wife worked hard to accumulate their fortune, but they placed it where it will do great good for centuries to come. In so doing they made for themselves an honored name and lasting remembrance.

CHARLES PRATT
AND HIS INSTITUTE

"It is a good thing to be famous, provided that the fame has been honestly won. It is a good thing to be rich when the image and superscription of God is recognized on every coin. But the sweetest thing in the world is to be *loved*. The tears that were shed over the coffin of Charles Pratt welled up out of loving hearts.... I count his death to have been the sorest bereavement Brooklyn has ever suffered; for he was yet in his vigorous prime, with large plans and possibilities yet to be accomplished.

"Charles Pratt belonged to the only true nobility in America,—the men who do not inherit a great name, but make one for themselves." Thus wrote the Rev. Dr. Theodore L. Cuyler of Brooklyn, after Mr. Pratt's death in 1891.

Charles Pratt, the founder of Pratt Institute, was born at Watertown, Mass., Oct. 2, 1830. His father, Asa Pratt, a cabinet-maker, had ten children to support, so that it became necessary for each child to earn for himself whenever that was possible.

When Charles was ten years old, he left home, and found a place to labor on a neighboring farm. For three years the lad, slight in physique, but ambitious to earn, worked faithfully, and was allowed to attend school three months in each winter. At thirteen he was eager for a broader field, and, going to Boston, was employed for a year in a grocery store. Soon after he went to Newton, and there learned the machinist's trade, saving every cent carefully, because he had a plan in his mind; and that plan was to get an education, even if a meagre one, that he might do something in the world.

Finally he had saved enough for a year's schooling, and going to Wilbraham Academy, at Wilbraham, Mass., "managed," as he afterwards said, "to live on one dollar a week while I studied." Fifty dollars helped to lay the foundation for a remarkably useful and noble life.

When the year was over and the money spent, having learned already the value of depending upon himself rather than upon outside help, the youth became a clerk in a paint-and-oil store in Boston. Here the thirst for knowledge, stimulated but only partially satisfied by the short year at the academy, led him to the poor man's blessing,—the library. Here he could read and think, and be far removed from evil associations.

When he was twenty-one, in 1851, Charles Pratt went to New York as a clerk for Messrs. Schanck & Downing, 108 Fulton Street, in the oil, paint, and glass business. The work was constant; but he was happy in it, because he believed that work should be the duty and pleasure of all. He never changed in this love for labor. He said years afterwards, when he was worth millions, "I am convinced that the great problem which we are trying to solve is very much wrapped up in the thought of educating the people to find happiness in a busy, active life, and that the occupation of the hour is of more importance than the wages received." He found "happiness in a busy, active life," when he was earning fifty dollars a year as well as when he was a man of great wealth.

Years later Mr. Pratt's son Charles relates the following incident, which occurred when his father came to visit him at Amherst College: "He was present at a lecture to the Senior class in mental science. The subject incidentally discussed was 'Work,' its necessary drain upon the vital forces, and its natural and universal distastefulness. On being asked to address the class, my father assumed to present the matter from a point of view entirely different from that of the text-book, and maintained that there was no inherent reason why man should consider his daily labor, of whatever nature, as necessarily disagreeable and burdensome, but that the right view was the one which made of work a delight, a source of real satisfaction, and even pleasure. Such, indeed, it was to him; he believed it might prove to be such to all others."

After Mr. Pratt had worked three years for his New York firm, in connection with two other gentlemen he bought the paint-and-oil business of his employers, and the new firm became Raynolds, Devoe, & Pratt. For thirteen years he worked untiringly at his business; and in 1867 the firm was divided, the oil portion of the business being carried on by Charles Pratt & Co. In the midst of this busy life the influence of the Mercantile Library of Boston was not lost. He had become associated with the Mercantile Library of New York, and both this and the one in Boston had a marked influence on his life and his great gifts.

When the immense oil-fields of Pennsylvania began to be developed, about 1860, Mr. Pratt was one of the first to see the possibilities of the petroleum trade. He began to refine the crude oil, and succeeded in producing probably the best upon the market, called "Pratt's Astral Oil." Mr. Pratt took a just pride in its wide use, and was pleased, says a friend, "when the Rev. Dr. Buckley told him that he had found that the Russian convent on Mount Tabor was lighted with Pratt's Astral Oil. He meant that the stamp 'Pratt' should be like the stamp of the mint,—an assurance of quality and quantity."

For years he was one of the officers of the Standard Oil Company, and of course a sharer in its enormous wealth. Nothing seemed more improbable when he was spending a year at Wilbraham Academy, living on a dollar a week, than this ownership of millions. Now, as then, he was saving of time as well as money.

Says Mr. James McGee of New York, "He brought to business a hatred of waste. He disliked waste of every kind. He was not willing that the smallest material should be lost. He did not believe in letting time go to waste. He was punctual at his engagements, or gave good excuse for his tardiness. Speaking of an evening spent in congratulations, he said that it was time lost; it would have been better spent in reviewing mistakes, that they might be corrected. It is said that a youth who had hurried into business applied to Mr. Pratt for advice as to whether he should go West. He questioned the young man as to how he occupied his time; what he did before business hours, and what after; what he was reading or doing to improve his mind. Finding that the young man was taking no pains to educate himself, he said emphatically, 'No; don't go West. They don't want you.'"

Active as Mr. Pratt was in the details of a great business, he found time for other work. Desiring an education, which he in his early days could not obtain, he provided the best for his children. He became deeply interested in Adelphi Academy, Brooklyn, was a trustee, and later president of the Board. In 1881 he erected the wing of the main building; and six years later, in 1887, he gave $160,000 for the erection of a new building.

He gave generously to the Baptist Church in Brooklyn in which he worshipped, and from the pews of which he was seldom absent on the Sabbath. He bestowed thousands upon struggling churches. He generously aided Rochester Theological Seminary. He gave to Amherst College, through his son Charles M. Pratt, about $40,000 for a gymnasium, and through his son Frederick B. Pratt thirteen acres for athletic grounds. He helped foreign missions and missions at home with an open hand.

"There were," says Dr. Cuyler, "innumerable little rills of benevolence that trickled into the homes of the needy and the hearts of the straitened and suffering. I never loved Charles Pratt more than when he was dealing with the needs of a bright orphan girl, whose case appealed strongly to his sympathies. After inquiring into it carefully, he said to me, 'We must be careful when trying to aid this young lady, not to cripple her energies, or lower her sense of independence.'

"The last time his hand ever touched paper was to sign a generous check for the benefit of our Brooklyn Bureau of Charities. Almost the last words that he ever wrote was this characteristic sentence: 'I feel that life is so short that I am not satisfied unless I do each day the best I can.'"

Mr. Pratt was not willing to spend his life in accumulating millions except for a purpose. He once told Dr. Cuyler, "The greatest humbug in this world is the idea that the mere possession of money can make any man happy. I never got any satisfaction out of mine until I began to do good with it."

He did not wish his wealth to build fine mansions for himself, for he preferred to live simply. He had no pleasure in display. "He needed," says his minister, Dr. Humpstone, "neither club nor playhouse to afford him rest; his home sufficed. For those who use such diversions he had no criticism. In these matters he was neither narrow nor ascetic. He was the brother of his own children. His home was to him the fairest spot on earth. He filled it with sunshine. Outside of his business, his church, and his philanthropy, it was his only sphere."

He was a man of few words and much self-control. Dr. Humpstone relates this incident, told him by a friend: "Some one made upon Mr. Pratt, openly, a bitter personal attack. The future revealed that this charge was entirely unmerited, and the man who made it lived to regret his act; but the moment revealed the greatness of our dead friend's love. He said no word; only a face pale with pain revealed how determined was his effort at self-control, and how keen was his suffering. When his accuser turned to go, he bade him good-morning, as though he had left a blessing and not a bane behind him. As I recall the past at this moment, I think of no word he ever spoke in my hearing that was proof of an unloving spirit in him."

For years Mr. Pratt had been thinking about industrial education; "such education as enables men and women to earn their own living by applied knowledge and the skilful use of their hands in the various productive industries." He knew that the majority of young men and women are born poor, and must struggle for a livelihood, and, whether poor or rich, ought to know how to be self-supporting, and not helpless members of the community. The study of algebra and English literature might be a delight, but not all can be teachers or clerks in stores; some must be machinists, carpenters, and skilled workmen in various trades.

Mr. Pratt never forgot that he had been a poor boy. He never grew cold in manner and selfish in life. "He presented," says Mr. James MacAlister, President of the Drexel Institute, Philadelphia, "the rare spectacle of a rich man in strong sympathy with the industrial revolution that was progressing around him. His ardent desire was to recognize labor, to improve it, to elevate it; and his own experience taught him that the best way to do this was to put education into the handiwork of the laborer."

Mr. Pratt gained information from all possible sources about the kind of an institution which should be built to provide the knowledge of books and the knowledge of earning a living. He travelled widely in his own country, corresponded with the heads of various schools, such as The Rose Polytechnic Institute at Terre Haute, Ind., the Institute of Technology in Boston, and with Dr. John Eaton, then Commissioner of

67

Education, Dr. Felix Adler of New York, and others. Then Mr. Pratt took his son, Mr. F. B. Pratt, and his private secretary, Mr. Heffley, to twenty of the leading cities in England, France, Austria, Switzerland, and Germany, to see what the Old World was doing to educate her people in self-help.

He found great industrial schools on the Continent supported by the city or state, where every boy or girl could learn the theory or practice, or both, of the trade to be followed for a livelihood. On leaving the schools the pupils could earn a dollar or more a day. Our own country was sadly backward in such matters. The public schools had introduced manual training only to a very limited extent. Mr. Pratt determined to build an institute where any who wished to engage in "mechanical, commercial, and artistic pursuits" should have a thorough "theoretic and practical knowledge." It should dignify labor, because he believed there should be no idlers among rich or poor. It should teach "that personal character is of greater consequence than material productions."

Mr. Pratt, on Sept. 11, 1885, bought a large piece of land on Ryerson Street, Brooklyn, a total of 32,000 square feet, and began to carry out in brick and stone his noble thought for the people. He not only gave his millions, but he gave his time and thought in the midst of his busy life. He said, "*The giving which counts, is the giving of one's self.* The faithful teacher who gives his strength and life without stint or hope of reward, other than the sense of fidelity to duty, gives most; and so the record will stand when our books are closed at the day of final accounting."

Mr. Pratt at first erected the main building six stories high, 100 feet by 86, brick with terra-cotta and stone trimmings, and the machine-shop buildings, consisting of metal-working and wood-working shops, forge and foundry rooms, and a building 103 feet by 95 for bricklaying, stone-carving, plumbing, and the like. Later the high-school building was added; and a library building has recently been erected, the library having outgrown its rooms. In the main building, occupying the whole fourth floor as well as parts of several other floors, is the art department of the Institute. Here, in morning, afternoon, and evening classes, under the best instructors, a three years' course in art may be taken, in drawing, painting, and clay-modelling; also courses in architectural and mechanical drawing, where in the adjacent shops the properties of materials and their power to bear strain can be learned. Many students take a course in design, and are thus enabled to win good positions as designers of book-covers, tiles, wall-papers, carpets, etc. The normal art course of two years fits for teaching. Of those who left the Institute between 1890 and 1893, having finished the course, seventy-six became supervisors of drawing in public schools, or teach art elsewhere, with salaries aggregating $47,620. Courses are also given in wood-carving and art needlework. Though there were but twelve in the class in the art department at the opening of the Institute in 1887, in three years the number of pupils had increased to about seven hundred.

Mr. Pratt instituted another department in the main building,—that of domestic science. There are morning, afternoon, and evening classes in sewing, cooking, and other household matters. A year's course, two lessons a week, is given in dressmaking, cutting, fitting, and draping, or the course may be taken in six months if time is limited; a course in millinery with five lessons a week, and the full course in three months if the person has little time to give; lectures in hygiene and home nursing, that women in their homes may know what to do in cases of sickness; classes in laundry work, in plain and fancy cooking, and preparing food for invalids. There are Normal courses to fit teachers for schools and colleges to give instruction in house sanitation, ventilation, heating, cooking, etc.

This department of domestic science has been most useful and popular. As many as 2,800 pupils have been enrolled in a single year. A club of men came to take lessons in cooking preparatory to camp-life. Nurses come from the training-schools in hospitals to learn how to cook for invalids. Many teachers have gone out from this department. The Institute has not been able to supply the demand for sewing-women and dressmakers during the busy season.

Mr. Pratt rightly thought "that a knowledge of household employments is thoroughly consistent with the grace and dignity and true womanliness of every American girl.... The housewife who knows how to manage the details of her home has more courage than one who is dependent upon servants, no matter how faithful they may be. She is a better mistress; for she can sympathize with them, and appreciate their work when well done."

Mr. Pratt had another object in view, as he said, "To help those families who must live on small incomes,—say, not over $400 or $500 per year,—teaching the best disposition of this money in wise purchase, economical use of material, and little waste. One aim of this department is to make the home of the workingman more attractive."

Mr. Pratt said in the last address which he ever made to his Institute: "Home is the centre from which the life of the nation emanates; and the highest product of modern civilization is a contented, happy home. How can we help to secure such homes? By teaching the people that happiness, to some extent at least, consists in having something to occupy the head and hand, and in doing some useful work."

In the department of commerce, there are day and evening classes in phonography, typewriting, bookkeeping, commercial law,

German, and Spanish, as the latter language, it is believed, will be used more in our commercial relations in the future.

There is a department of music to encourage singing among the people, with courses in vocal music, and in the art of teaching music; this has over four hundred students. In the department of kindergartens in the Institute Mr. Pratt took a deep interest. A model kindergarten is conducted with training-classes, and classes for mothers, who may thus be able to introduce it into their homes. The high-school department, a four years' course, combining the academic and the manual training, has proved very valuable. It was originally intended to make the Institute purely manual, but later it was felt to be wise to give an opportunity for a completer education by combining head-work and hand-work. The school day is from nine o'clock till three. Of the seven periods into which this time is divided, three are devoted to recitations, one to study,—the lessons are prepared at home,—one to drawing, and two to the workshop, in wood, forging, tinsmithing, machine-tool work, etc. When the high school was opened, Mr. Pratt said, "We believe in the value of co-education, and are pleased to note the addition of more than twenty young women to this entering class."

The high school has some excellent methods. "For making the machinery of National and State elections clear," says Mr. F. B. Pratt, the secretary of the Institute and son of the founder, "the school has conducted a campaign and election in close imitation of the actual process.... Every morning the important news of the preceding day has been announced and explained by selected pupils." The Institute annually awards ten scholarships to ten graduates of the Brooklyn grammar schools, five boys and five girls, who pass the best entrance examinations for the high school of Pratt Institute. The pupils after leaving the high school are fitted to enter any scientific institution of college grade.

Mr. Pratt was "so much impressed with the far-reaching influence of good books as distributed through a free library," that he established a library in the Institute for the use of the pupils, and for the public as well. It now has fifty thousand volumes, with a circulation of over two hundred thousand volumes. In connection with it, there are library training-classes, graduates of which have found good positions in various libraries.

A museum was begun by Mr. Pratt in 1887, as an aid to the students in their work. The finest specimens of glass, earthenware, bronzes, iron-work, and minerals were obtained from the Old World, specimens of iron and steel from our own country to illustrate their manufacture in the various articles of use; much attention will be given to artistic work in iron after the manner of Quentin Matsys; lace, ancient and modern; all common cloth, with kind of weave and price; various wools and woollen goods from many countries.

In the basement of the main building Mr. Pratt opened a lunch-room, a most sensible department, especially for those who live at some distance from the Institute. Dinners at a reasonable price are served from twelve to two o'clock, and suppers three nights a week from six to seven P.M. Over forty thousand meals are served yearly. Soups, cold meats, salads, sandwiches, tea, coffee, milk, and fruit are usually offered.

Another thought of Mr. Pratt, who seemed not to overlook anything, was the establishing of an association known as "The Thrift." Mr. Pratt said, "Pupils are taught some useful work by which they can earn money. It seems a natural thing that the next step should be to endeavor to teach them how to save this money; or, in other words, how to make a wise use of it. It is not enough that one be trained so that he can join the bands of the world's workers and become a producer; he needs quite as much to learn habits of economy and thrift in order to make his life a success."

"The Thrift" was divided into the investment branch and the loan branch. The investment shares were $150, payable at the rate of one dollar a month for ten years. The investor would then have $160. Any person could loan money to purchase a home, and make small monthly payments instead of rent. As many persons were unable to save a dollar a month, stamps were sold as in Europe; and a person could buy them at any time, and these could be redeemed for cash. In less than four years, the Thrift had 650 depositors, with a total investment of over $90,000. Twenty-four loans had been made, aggregating over $100,000. The total deposits up to 1895 were $260,000.

Most interesting to me of all the departments of Pratt Institute are the machine-shops and the Trade School Building, where boys can learn a trade. "The aim of these trade classes," says Mr. F. B. Pratt, in the *Independent* for April 30, 1891, "is to afford a thorough grounding in the principles of a mechanical trade, and sufficient practice in its different operations to produce a fair amount of hand skill." The old apprenticeship system has been abandoned, and our boys must learn to earn a living in some other way. The trades taught at Pratt Institute are carpentry, forging, machine-work, plastering, plumbing, blacksmithing, bricklaying, house and fresco painting, etc. There is an evening class of sheet-metal workers, who study patterns for cornices, elbows, and other designs in sheet-metal. Much attention is given to electrical construction and to electricity in general. The day and evening classes are always full. Some of the master-mechanics' associations are cordial in their co-operation and examination of students through their committees. After leaving the Institute, work seems to be readily obtained at good wages.

71

Mr. Pratt wished the instruction here to be of the best. He said, "The demand is for a better and better quality of work, and our American artisans must learn that to claim first place in any trade they must be intelligent.... They must learn to have pride in their work, and to love it, and believe in our motto, 'Be true to your work, and your work will be true to you.'"

The sons of the founder are alive to the necessities of the young in this direction. If it is true that out of the 52,894 white male prisoners in the prisons and reformatory institutions of the United States in 1890 nearly three-fourths were native born, and 31,426 had learned no trade whatever, it is evident that one of the most pressing needs of our time is the teaching of trades to boys and young men.

Mr. Charles M. Pratt, the president of the Institute, says in his Founder's Day Address in 1893 concerning technical instruction: "Our possible service here seems almost limitless. The President of the Board of Education of Boston in a recent address congratulated his fellow-citizens upon the fact that Boston has her system of public schools and kindergartens, and now, and but lately, her public school of manual training; but what is needed, he said, 'is a school of *technical training in the trades*, such as Pratt Institute and other similar institutions furnish. I sincerely trust that the next five years of life and growth here will develop much in this direction.... We are willing to enlarge our present special facilities, or provide new ones for new trade-class requirements, as long as the demand for such opportunities truly exists.'"

One rejoices in such institutions as the New York Trade Schools on First Avenue, between Sixty-seventh and Sixty-eighth Streets, with their day and evening classes in plumbing, gasfitting, bricklaying, plastering, stone-cutting, fresco-painting, wood-carving, carpentry, and the like. A printing department has also been added. This work owes its inception and success to the brain and devotion of the late lamented Richard Tylden Auchmuty, who died in New York, July 18, 1893. Mrs. Auchmuty, the wife of the founder, has given the land and buildings to the school, valued at $220,000, and a building-fund of $100,000. Mr. J. Pierpont Morgan has endowed the school with a gift of $500,000.

Mr. Pratt did not cease working when his great Institute was fairly started. He built in Greenpoint, Long Island, a large apartment building called the "Astral," five stories high, of brick and stone, with 116 suites of rooms, each suite capable of accommodating from three to six persons. The building cost $300,000, and is rented to workingmen and their families, the income to be used in helping to maintain the Institute. A public library was opened in the Astral, with the thought at first of using it only for the people in the building; but it was soon opened to all the inhabitants of Greenpoint, and has been most heartily appreciated and used. Cut in stone over the fireplace in the reading-room of the Astral are the words, "Waste neither time nor money."

When Mr. Pratt made his first address to the students of Pratt Institute on Founder's Day, Oct. 2, 1888, his birthday, taking the Bible from the desk, he said, before reading it and offering prayer, "Whatever I have done, whatever I hope to do, I have done trusting in the Power from above."

Before he built the Institute many persons asked him to use his wealth in other ways; some urged a Theological School, others a Medical School, but his interest in the workingman and the home led him to found the Institute. He rejoiced in the work and its outlook for the future. He said, "I am so grateful, so grateful that the Almighty has inclined my heart to do this thing."

On the second and third Founder's Days, Mr. Pratt spoke with hope and the deepest interest in the work of the Institute. He had been asked often what he had spent for the work, and had prepared a statement at considerable cost of time, but with characteristic modesty he could never bring himself to make it public. "I have asked myself over and over again what good could result from any statement we could make of the amount of money we have spent. The quality and amount of service rendered by the Institute is the only fair estimate of its real value."

In closing his address Mr. Pratt said, "To my sons and co-trustees, who will have this work to carry on when I am gone, I wish to say, 'The world will overestimate your ability, and will underestimate the value of your work; will be exacting of every promise made or implied; will be critical of your failings; will often misjudge your motives, and hold you to strict account for all your doings. Many pupils will make demands, and be forgetful of your service to them. Ingratitude will often be your reward. When the day is dark, and full of discouragement and difficulty, you will need to look on the other side of the picture, which you will find full of hope and gladness.'"

When the next Founder's Day came, Mr. Pratt was gone, and the Institute was in the hands of others. At the close of a day of work and thought in his New York office, Mr. Pratt fell at his post, May 4, 1891, and was carried to his home in Clinton Avenue, Brooklyn. After the funeral, May 7, memorial services were held in the Emmanuel Baptist Church on Sunday afternoon, May 17, with addresses by distinguished men who loved and honored him.

A beautiful memorial chapel was erected by his family on his estate at Dosoris, Glen Cove, Long Island; and there the body of Mr. Pratt was buried, July 31, 1894. The chapel is of granite, in the Romanesque style, with exquisite stained glass windows. The main room is wainscoted with polished red granite, the arching ceiling lined with glass mosaic in blue, gold, and green. At the farther end, in a semi-circular apse reached by two steps through an imposing arch, stands the sarcophagus of Siena marble, with the name, Charles Pratt, and dates of birth and death. The campanile contains the chime of bells so admired by everybody who visited the Columbian Exposition at Chicago, and heard it ring out from the central clock tower in the Building of Manufactures and Liberal Arts. Few, comparatively, will ever see this monument erected by a devoted family to a husband and father; but thousands upon thousands will see the monument which Mr. Pratt built for himself in his noble Institute. Every year thousands come to learn its methods and to copy some of its features, even from Africa and South America. The Earl of Meath, who has done so much for the improvement of his race, said to Dr. Cuyler, "Of all the good things I have seen in America, there is none that I would so like to carry back to London as this splendid establishment."

One may read in Baedeker's "Guide Book of the United States" instructions how to find "the extensive buildings of Pratt Institute, one of the best-equipped technical institutions in the world. None interested in technical education should fail to visit this institution."

During his life, Mr. Pratt gave to the Institute about $3,700,000, and thus had the pleasure of seeing it bear fruit. Of this, $2,000,000 is the endowment fund. Small charges are made to the pupils, but not nearly enough to pay the running expenses. Mr. Pratt's sons are nobly carrying forward the work left to their care by their father, who died in the midst of his labors. Playgrounds have been laid out, a gymnasium provided, new buildings erected, and other measures adopted which they feel that their father would approve were he alive.

Courses of free lectures are given at Pratt Institute to the public as well as the students; a summer school is provided at Glen Cove, Long Island, for such as wish to learn about agriculture, with instruction given in botany, chemistry, physiology, raising and harvesting crops, and the care of animals; nurses are trained in the care and development of children; a bright monthly magazine is published by the Institute; a Neighborship Association has been formed of alumni, teachers, and pupils, which meets for the discussion of such topics as "The relation of the rich to the poor," "The ethics of giving," "Citizenship," etc., and to carry out the work and spirit of the Institute wherever opportunity offers.

Already the influence of Pratt Institute has been very great. Public schools all over the country are adopting some form of manual training whereby the pupils shall be better fitted to earn their living. Mr. Chas. M. Pratt, in one of his Founder's Day addresses, quotes the words of a successful teacher and merchant: "There is nothing under God's heaven so important to the individual as to acquire the power to earn his own living; to be able to stand alone if necessary; to be dependent upon no one; to be indispensable to some one."

About four thousand students receive instruction each year at the Institute. Many go out as teachers to other schools all over the country. As the founder said in his last address, "The world goes on, and Pratt Institute, if it fulfils the hopes and expectations of its founder, must go on, and as the years pass, the field of its influence should grow wider and wider."

On the day that he died, Mr. Herbert S. Adams, the sculptor, had finished a bust of Mr. Pratt in clay. It was put into bronze by the teachers and pupils, and now stands in the Institute, with these words of the founder cut in the bronze: *The giving which counts is the giving of one's self.*"

THOMAS GUY
AND HIS HOSPITAL

One day the rich Matthew Vassar stood before the great London hospital founded by Thomas Guy, and read these words on the pedestal of the bronze statue:—

THOMAS GUY,
SOLE FOUNDER OF THIS HOSPITAL IN HIS LIFETIME
A.D. MDCCXXI.

The last three words made a deep impression. Matthew Vassar had no children. He wished to leave his fortune where it would be of permanent value; and lest something might happen to thwart his plan, he had to do it *in his lifetime.*

Sir Isaac Newton said, "They who give nothing till they die, never give at all." Several years before his death, Matthew Vassar built Vassar College near Poughkeepsie, N.Y.; for he said, "There is not in our country, there is not in the world so far as known, a single fully endowed institution for the education of women. It is my hope to be the instrument, in the hands of Providence, of founding and perpetuating an institution *which shall accomplish for young women what our colleges are accomplishing for young men.*"

To this end he gave a million dollars, and was happy in the results. His birthday is celebrated each year as "Founder's Day." On one of these occasions he said, "This is almost more happiness than I can bear. This one day more than repays me for all I have done."

And what of Thomas Guy, whose example led to Matthew Vassar's noble gift while the latter was alive? He was an economical, self-made bookbinder and bookseller, who became the "greatest philanthropist of his day."

Thomas Guy was born in Horselydown, Southwark, in the outskirts of London, in 1644 or 1645. His father, Thomas Guy, was a lighterman and coalmonger, one who transferred coal from the colliers to the wharves, and also sold it to customers. He was a member of the Carpenters' Company of the city of London, and probably owned some barges.

His wife, Anne Vaughton, belonged to a family of better social position than her husband, as several of her relatives had been mayors in Tamworth, or held other offices of influence.

When the boy Thomas was eight years old, his father died, leaving Mrs. Guy to bring up three small children, Thomas, John, and Anne. The eldest probably went to the free grammar school of

Tamworth, and when fifteen or sixteen years of age was apprenticed for eight years to John Clarke the younger, bookseller and bookbinder in Cheapside, London.

John Clarke was ruined in the great fire of Sept. 2, 1666, which, says H. R. Fox Bourne in his "London Merchants," "destroyed eighty-nine churches, and more than thirteen thousand houses in four hundred streets. Of the whole district within the city walls, four hundred and thirty-six acres were in ruins, and only seventy-five acres were left covered. Property worth £10,000,000 was wasted, and thousands of starving Londoners had to run for their lives, and crouch for days and weeks on the bare fields of Islington and Hampstead, Southwark and Lambeth."

What Thomas Guy was in his later life he probably was as a boy,—hard-working, economical, of good habits, and determined to succeed. When the eight years of apprenticeship were over he was admitted a freeman of the Stationers' Company; and having a little means, he began a business at the junction of Cornhill and Lombard Streets, where he resided through his whole life. His stock of books at the beginning was worth about two hundred pounds.

At this time many English Bibles were printed in Holland on account of the better paper and types found there, and vast numbers were imported to England with large profits. Young Guy, with business shrewdness, soon became an importer of Bibles, and very probably Prayer-books and Psalms.

The King's printers were opposed to such importations, and caused the arrest of booksellers and publishers, so that this Holland trade was largely broken up. It is said that the King's printers so raised the price of Bibles that the poor were unable to buy them. The privilege of printing was limited to London, York, and the Universities of Oxford and Cambridge. Then London and Oxford quarrelled over Bible printing, and each tried to undersell the other.

Thomas Guy and Peter Parker printed Bibles for Oxford, had four presses in use within four months of their undertaking the Oxford work, and showed the greatest activity, skill, and energy in the enterprise. Their work was excellent, and some of their Bibles and other volumes are still found in the English libraries.

These University printers, Parker & Guy, had many lawsuits with other firms, who claimed that the former had made £10,000, or even £15,000, by their connection with Oxford. Doubtless they had made money; but they had done their work well, and deserved their success.

Concerning Oxford Bibles, a writer in *McClure's Magazine* says, "In these days the privilege of printing a Bible is hardly less jealously guarded in the United Kingdom than the privilege of printing a banknote. It is accorded by license to the Queen's printers, and by charter to the Universities of Oxford and Cambridge; and it is, as a matter of fact, at the University of Oxford that the greatest bulk of the work is done. From this famous press there issue annually about one million copies of the sacred book; copies ranging in price from tenpence to ten pounds, and in form from the brilliant Bible, which weighs in its most handsome binding less than four ounces, and measures 3½ by 2-1/8 by ¾ inches, to the superb folio Bible for church use, the page of which measures 19 by 12 inches, which is the only folio Bible in existence—seventy-eight editions in all; copies in all manner of languages, even the most barbarous."

The choicest paper is used, and the utmost care taken with setting the type. It is computed that to set up and "read" a reference Bible costs £1,000.

"The first step is to make a careful calculation, showing what, in the particular type employed, will be the exact contents of each page, from the first page to the last. It must be known before a single type is set just what will be the first and last word on each page. It is not enough that this calculation shall be approximate, it must be exact to the syllable.

"The proofs are then read again by a fresh reader, from a fresh model; and this process is repeated until, before being electrotyped, they have been read five times in all. Any compositor who detects an error in the model gets a reward; but only two such rewards have ever been earned. Any member of the public who is first to detect an error in the authorized text is entitled to one guinea, but the average annual outlay of the press under this head is almost nil."

As soon as Thomas Guy prospered, he gave to various causes. He gave five pounds to help rebuild the schoolhouse at Tamworth, where he had been a student a few years before; and when a little over thirty years of age, in 1678, he bought some land in Tamworth, and erected an almshouse for seven poor women. A good-sized room was used for their library. The whole cost was £200, a worthy beginning for a young man.

A little later Mr. Guy gave ten pounds yearly to a "Spinning School," where the children of the poor were taught how to work, probably some kind of industrial training. Also ten pounds yearly to a Dissenting minister, and the same amount to one of the Established Church.

When Mr. Guy was a little over forty, he gave another £200 for almshouses for poor men at Tamworth; and the town called him, "Our incomparable benefactor."

When Mr. Guy was forty-five years of age, in 1690, he attempted to enter Parliament from Tamworth, but was defeated. This was the second Parliament under William and Mary. In 1694 he was elected sheriff of London, but refused to serve, perhaps on account of the expense, as he disliked display, and paid the penalty of refusing, £400.

In the third Parliament, 1695, Mr. Guy tried again, and succeeded. He was re-elected after an exciting contest in 1698, and again in 1701 and 1702, and in two Parliaments under Queen Anne.

While in Parliament he built a town hall for the people of Tamworth. In 1708, after thirteen years of service, Mr. Guy was rejected. It is said that he promised the people of Tamworth, so much did he enjoy Parliamentary life, that if they would elect him again he would leave his whole fortune to the town, so they should never have a pauper; but for once they forgot their "incomparable benefactor," and Thomas Guy in turn forgot them.

"The cause of Guy's rejection," says the history of Tamworth, "is said to have been his neglect of the gastronomic propensities of his worthy, patriotic, and enlightened constituents, by whom the virtues of fasting appear to have been entirely forgotten. In the anger of the moment he threatened to pull down the town hall which he had built, and to abolish the almshouses. The burgesses, repenting of their rash act, sent a deputation to wait upon him with the offer of re-election in the ensuing Parliament, 1810; but he rejected all conciliation. He always considered that he had been treated with great ingratitude, and he deprived the inhabitants of Tamworth of the advantage of his almshouses." His will provided that persons from certain towns might find a home in his almshouses, his own relatives to be preferred, should any offer themselves; but Tamworth was left out of the list of towns.

Mr. Guy already had become very wealthy. During the wars of William and Anne with Louis XIV., the soldiers and seamen were sometimes unpaid for years, from lack of funds. Tickets were given them, and they were willing to sell these at whatever price they would bring. Mr. Guy bought largely from the seamen, and has been blamed for so doing; but his latest biographers, Messrs. Wilks and Bettany, in their interesting and valuable "Biographical History of Guy's Hospital," think he did it with a spirit of kindness rather than of avarice. "It is at least consistent with his general philanthropy to suppose that, compassionating the poor seamen who could not get their money, he offered them more than they could get elsewhere, and that this accounts for his being so large a purchaser of seamen's tickets. Instead of being to his discredit, we think rather that it is to his credit, and that he managed to benefit a large number of necessitous men, while at the same time, in the future, benefiting himself."

Mr. Guy also made a great amount of money in the South Sea Company. With regard to the South Sea stock, says the *Saturday Magazine*, "Mr. Guy had no hand in framing or conducting that scandalous fraud; he obtained the stock when low, and had the good sense to sell it at the time it was at its height."

Chambers's "Book of Days" gives a very interesting account of this "South Sea Bubble." Harley, Earl of Oxford, who had helped Queen

Anne to get rid of her advisers, the Duke of Marlborough and the proud Duchess, Sarah, with a desire to "restore public credit, and discharge ten millions of the floating debt, agreed with a company of merchants that they should take the debt upon themselves for a certain time, at the interest of six per cent, to provide for which, amounting to £600,000 per annum, the duties for certain articles were rendered permanent. At the same time was granted the monopoly of trade to the South Seas, and the merchants were incorporated as the South Sea Company; and so proud was the minister of his scheme that it was called by his flatterers, 'The Earl of Oxford's Masterpiece.'"

The South Sea Company, after a time, agreed to take upon themselves the whole of the national debt, £30,981,712, about $150,000,000. Sir John Blount, a speculator, first propounded the scheme. It was rumored that Spain, by treaty with England, would grant free trade to all her colonies, and that silver would thus be brought from Potosi, and become as plentiful as iron; and that Mexico would part with gold in abundance for English cotton and woollen goods. It was also said that Spain, in exchange for Gibraltar and Port Mahon, would give up places on the coast of Peru. It was promised that each person who took £100 of stock would make fifty per cent, and probably much more. Mr. Guy took £45,500 of stock, probably the amount which the government owed him for seamen's tickets. Others who had claims "were empowered to subscribe the several sums due to them ... for which he and the rest of the subscribers were to receive an annual interest of six per cent upon their respective subscriptions, until the same were discharged by Parliament."

The speculating mania spread widely. Great ladies pawned their jewels in order to invest. Lords were eager to double and treble their money. A journalist of the time writes: "The South Sea equipages increase daily; the city ladies buy South Sea jewels, hire South Sea maids, take new country South Sea houses; the gentlemen set up South Sea coaches, and buy South Sea estates."

The people seemed wild with speculation. All sorts of companies were established; one with ten million dollars capital to import walnut-trees from Virginia; one with five million dollars capital for a "wheel for perpetual motion." An unknown adventurer started "a company for carrying on an undertaking of great advantage, but nobody to know what it is." Next morning this great man opened an office in Cornhill, and before three o'clock one thousand shares had been subscribed for at ten dollars a share, and the deposits paid. He put the ten thousand dollars in his pocket, set off the same evening for the Continent, and was never heard of again. He had assured them that nobody would know what the undertaking was, and he had kept his word.

The South Sea stock rose in one day from 130 per cent to 300, and finally to 1,000 per cent. It then became known that Sir John

Blount, the chairman, and some others had sold out, making vast fortunes. The price of stock began to fall, and at last the crisis brought ruin to thousands. The poet Gay, who had been given £20,000 of stock, and had thought himself rich, lost all, and was so ill in consequence that his life was in danger. Some men committed suicide on account of their losses, and some became insane. Prior said, "I am lost in the South Sea. The roaring of the waves and the madness of the people are justly put together." The people were now as wild with anger as they had been intoxicated with hope for gain. They demanded redress, and the punishment of the directors of the South Sea Company. Men high in position were thrown into the Tower after it was found that the books of the company had been tampered with or destroyed, and large amounts of stock used to bribe men in office. The directors were fined over ten million dollars, and their fortunes distributed among the sufferers. Sir John Blount was allowed but £5,000 out of a fortune of £183,000. The fortune of another, a million and a half pounds, was given to the losers. One man was treated with especial severity because he was reported to have said that "he would feed his carriage horses off gold."

Mr. Guy, fearing that there was trickery when the stock rose so rapidly, sold out when the prices were from three to six hundred, and thereby saved himself from financial ruin. He was now very rich, having always lived economically. When he was a bookseller it is said that he always ate his dinner on his counter, using a newspaper for a tablecloth.

The following story is told by Walter Thornbury in his "Old and New London:"—

"'Vulture' Hopkins, so called from his alleged desire to seize upon gains, and who had become rich in South Sea stock, once called upon Mr. Guy to learn a lesson, as he said, in the art of saving. Being introduced into the parlor, Guy, not knowing his visitor, lighted a candle; but when Hopkins said, 'Sir, I always thought myself perfect in the art of getting and husbanding money, but being informed that you far exceed me, I have taken the liberty of waiting upon you to be satisfied on this subject.' Guy replied, 'If that is all your business, we can as well talk it over in the dark,' and immediately put out the candle. This was evidence sufficient for Hopkins, who acknowledged Guy to be his master, and took his leave."

Notwithstanding Mr. Guy's penuriousness, he had the grace of gratitude. Thousands forget their helpers after prosperity comes to them. Not so Thomas Guy. The *Saturday Magazine* for Aug. 2, 1834, relates this incident: "The munificent founder of Guy's Hospital was a man of very humble appearance, and of a melancholy cast of countenance. One day, while pensively leaning over one of the bridges, he attracted the attention and commiseration of a bystander, who,

81

apprehensive that he meditated self-destruction, could not refrain from addressing him with an earnest entreaty not to let his misfortunes tempt him to commit any rash act; then, placing in his hand a guinea, with the delicacy of genuine benevolence he hastily withdrew.

"Guy, roused from his revery, followed the stranger, and warmly expressed his gratitude, but assured him that he was mistaken in supposing him to be either in distress of mind or of circumstances, making an earnest request to be favored with the name of the good man, his intended benefactor. The address was given, and they parted. Some years later Guy, observing the name of his friend in the bankrupt list, hastened to his house, brought to his recollection their former interview; found upon investigation that no blame could be attached to him under his misfortunes; intimated his ability and also his intention to serve him; entered into immediate arrangements with his creditors; and finally re-established him in a business which ever after prospered in his hands, and in the hands of his children's children, for many years in Newgate Street."

Those who knew Mr. Guy best declared that "his chief design in getting money seems to have been with a view of employing the same in good works." He gave five guineas to Mr. Bowyer, a printer, who had lost everything by fire, "not knowing," said Mr. Guy, "how soon it may be our own case." He also gave in 1717 to the Stationer's Company £1,000, to be distributed to poor members and widows at the rate of £50 per annum.

"Many of his poor though distant relations had stated allowances from him of £10 or £20 a year, and occasionally larger sums; and to two of them he gave £500 apiece to advance them in the world. He has several times given £50 for discharging insolvent debtors. He has readily given £100 at a time on application to him on behalf of a distressed family."

In 1704 Mr. Guy was asked to become the governor of St. Thomas's Hospital, partly because he was a prominent and able citizen, and partly because he might thus become interested and give some money. Mr. Guy accepted the office, and soon built three new wards at a cost of £1,000, and provided the hospital with £100 a year for the benefit of its poor. When patients left the hospital they were often unfit for work, and this money would provide food for them for a time. He had given already to the steward money and clothes for such cases of need. He also built, in 1724, a new entrance to St. Thomas's Hospital, improved the front, and erected two large brick houses, these works costing him £3,000.

Mr. Guy seems to have given constantly from his youth, and always with good sense in his gifts. He was growing old. He probably had meditated long and carefully as to what use he should put his wealth. Highmore, in his "History of the Public Charities of London," tells this rather improbable story: "For the application of this fortune to charitable uses the public are indebted to a trifling circumstance. He employed a female servant whom he had agreed to marry. Some days previous to the intended ceremony he had ordered the pavement before his door to be mended up to a particular stone which he had marked, and then left his house on business.

"The servant, in his absence, looking at the workmen, saw a broken stone beyond this mark which they had not repaired; and on pointing to it with that design, they acquainted her that Mr. Guy had not ordered them to go so far. She, however, directed it to be done, adding, with the security incidental to her expectation of soon becoming his wife, 'Tell him I bade you, and he will not be angry.' But she soon learnt how fatal it is for one in a dependent position to exceed the limits of his or her authority; for her master, on his return, was angered that they had gone beyond his orders, renounced his engagement to his servant, and devoted his ample fortune to public charity."

In 1721, when Mr. Guy was seventy-six years of age, he leased a large piece of ground of St. Thomas's Hospital for a thousand years at £30 a year, to erect upon it a great hospital for incurables; "to receive and entertain therein four hundred poor persons, or upwards, laboring under any distempers, infirmities, or disorders, thought capable of relief by physic or surgery; but who, by reason of the small hopes there may be of their cure, or the length of time which for that purpose may be required or thought necessary, are or may be adjudged or called incurable, and as such not proper subjects to be received into or continued in the present hospital, in and by which no provision has been made for distempers deemed or called incurable."

While Mr. Guy had primarily in mind the poor and incurable, and the insane as well, in his will he directed the trustees to use their judgment about the length of time patients should remain, either for life or for a short period. Mr. Guy at once procured a plan for his hospital, and in the spring of 1722 laid the foundations. He went to the work "with all the expedition of a youth of fortune erecting a house for his own residence." The original central building of stone cost £18,793. The eastern wing, begun in 1738, was completed at a cost of £9,300; the western wing, in 1780, at a cost of £14,537.

Mr. Guy lived to see his treasured gift roofed in before his death, which occurred Dec. 27, 1724, in his eightieth year. In a little more than a week afterwards, Jan. 6, 1725, his hospital was opened, and sixty patients were admitted.

After the death of Mr. Guy one thousand guineas were found in his iron chest; and as it was imagined that these were placed there to defray his funeral expenses, they were used for that purpose. His body lay in state at Mercer's Hall, Cheapside, and was taken with "great funeral pomp" to the Parish Church of St. Thomas, Southwark, to rest there till the chapel at the hospital should be completed. Two hundred blue-coat boys from Christ's Hospital walked in the procession, and sang before the hearse, which was followed by forty coaches, each drawn by six horses.

Mr. Guy had not forgotten these "blue-coat boys" in his will, and left a perpetual annuity of £400 to educate four children yearly, with preference for his own relatives. The boys from Christ's Hospital always interest tourists in London. They wear long blue gowns, yellow stockings, and knee-breeches. No cover is worn on their heads, even in winter.

This school was founded by the boy king, Edward VI., for poor boys, though his father, Henry VIII., gave the building, which belonged to the Grey Friars, to the city of London, but Edward caused the school to be established. It is a quaint and most interesting spot, where four queens and scores of lords and ladies are buried,—Margaret, second wife of Edward I.; Isabella, the infamous wife of Edward II.; Joan, daughter of Edward II., and wife of David Bruce, King of Scotland; and others. Twelve hundred boys study at the hospital. Lamb, Coleridge, and other famous men were among the blue-coats. The latter tells some interesting things about the school in his "Table-Talk." "The discipline at Christ's Hospital in my time was ultra-Spartan; all domestic ties were to be put aside. 'Boy!' I remember Boyer saying to me once when I was crying the first day of my return after the holidays, 'boy! the school is your father; boy! the school is your mother; boy! the school is your brother; the school is your sister; the school is your first cousin, and your second cousin, and all the rest of your relatives. Let's have no more crying!'

"No tongue can express good Mrs. Boyer. Val Le Grice and I were once going to be flogged for some domestic misdeed, and Boyer was thundering away at us by way of prologue, when Mrs. B. looked in and said, 'Flog them soundly, sir, I beg!' This saved us. Boyer was so nettled by the interruption that he growled out, 'Away, woman! away!' and we were let off."

While Mr. Guy remembered the blue-coat orphans, he seemed to have remembered everybody else in his will. So much were the people interested in the lengthy document with its numerous gifts, that the will went through three editions the first year of its publication. Mr. Guy gave to every living relative, even to distant cousins—in all over £75,000. These were mainly gifts of £1,000 each at four per cent, so that each one received £40 a year. These legacies were called "Guy's Thousands." If the recipients were under age, the interest was to be used for his or her education and apprenticeship.

One thousand pounds were given for the release of poor prisoners for debt in London, Middlesex, or Surrey, in sums not to exceed five pounds each. About six hundred persons were thus set at liberty. Another thousand pounds were left to the trustees to relieve "such poor people, being housekeepers, as in their judgments shall be thought convenient." The interest on more than £2,000 was left for "putting out children apprentices, nursing, or such like charitable deed."

Then followed the great gift of nearly a million and a half dollars for the hospital. After the buildings were erected, the remainder was to be used "in the purchase of lands or reversions in fee simple, so that the rents might be a perpetual provision for the sick." Considerably over a million dollars were thus expended in purchasing over 8,000 acres in Essex, a large estate of the Duke of Chandos, for £60,800, and other tracts of land and houses.

About six years after the death of the founder, a bronze statue of him by Scheymaker was erected in the open square in front of the hospital, costing five hundred guineas. On the pedestal are representations of the Good Samaritan, Christ healing the sick, and Mr. Guy's armorial bearings. In the chapel a marble statue of Mr. Guy, costing £1,000, was erected by Mr. Bacon in 1779. The founder is represented as holding out one hand to raise a poor invalid lying on the earth, and pointing with the other hand to a person carried on a litter into one of the hospital wards. On the pedestal is an inscription beginning with these words,—

UNDERNEATH ARE DEPOSITED THE REMAINS OF
THOMAS GUY,
CITIZEN OF LONDON, MEMBER OF PARLIAMENT, AND THE
SOLE
FOUNDER OF THIS HOSPITAL IN HIS LIFETIME.

In 1788 the noble John Howard visited Guy's Hospital; and while he found some of the wards too low, being only nine feet and a half high, in the new wards he praised the iron bedsteads and hair beds as being clean and wholesome.

For over one hundred and seventy years Guy's Hospital has done its noble work. Departments have been added for special treatment of the eye, the ear, the teeth, the throat, etc., while thousands of mothers are cared for at their homes at the birth of their children.

In 1829, at his death, another governor of Guy's Hospital, Mr. William Hunt, left £180,000 to the hospital. He was buried in the vault under the chapel by the side of Thomas Guy. After some years, Hunt's House, a large central block, with north and south wings of brick with stone facings, was erected, the whole costing nearly £70,000. From time to time other needed buildings have been added, such as laboratories, museums, etc. There are now in the hospital over seven hundred beds. Only a few beds are reserved for those who can afford to pay; with this exception patients are admitted to all parts of the hospital free of charge. "The Royal Guide to London Charities," compiled by Herbert Fry, says, "No recommendation is needed for admission to this hospital. Sickness allied to poverty is an all-sufficient qualification." A fund has been established for relieving the families of deserving and poor patients while they are in the hospital. This is not only a blessing to the dependent ones, but prevents the anxiety and worry of the suffering inmates.

Guy's Hospital now receives into its wards yearly over 6,000 patients, and affords medical relief to about 70,000. The annual income of the hospital is about £40,000. Saving, industrious Thomas Guy wrought even better things for humanity than he could have hoped. It paid him to use a newspaper on his counter instead of a tablecloth for his meals, if every year thousands of poor men and women could be cared for in sickness without money, walk about his pleasant six acres during convalescence, and bless forever the name of Thomas Guy. What a contrast such a life to that of one who spends his wealth in fine houses, parties, expensive yachts, and self-indulgence!

In 1825 Guy's Medical School was opened in connection with the hospital, and has proved a great success. "It has become world-famed," write Messrs. Wilks and Bettany, "and has received pupils from all English-speaking lands, and not a few foreigners." Of Guy's Hospital Reports which began to be published in 1836, they say, "Nothing, perhaps, has done more to establish the reputation of Guy's Hospital abroad than these Reports. They may be found in the best libraries in Europe and in America, and have been well perused by many of the leading men on the Continent."

Those who wish to study medicine at Guy's have to pass a preliminary examination in arts, and take a five years' course. During four years "the time is equally divided between the study of the elements of medical science and clinical instruction in the practice of the profession." The last year is chiefly devoted to hospital practice. With this amount of study it is easily seen why Guy's Medical School takes high rank.

On March 26, 1890, a college built of red brick was formally opened by Mr. Gladstone. It cost £21,000, and is for the resident staff and students. A gymnasium was built also in 1890.

Guy's Hospital has been fortunate in the noted men who have been connected with it. One of its early surgeons, John Belchier, lies buried in the same vault with Thomas Guy. He fell in his office; and his servant, not being able to lift him, as he was a heavy man, offered to go for assistance. "No, John, I am dying," he said. "Fetch me a pillow; I may as well die here as anywhere else." It is related of him that, seeing the vanity of all earthly riches, he desired to be buried in the hospital, with iron nails in his coffin, which was to be filled with sawdust.

The learned Dr. Walter Moxon, who has been called from his combination of tenderness and ability "the perfect physician," was associated with Guy's Hospital for twenty years. Dr. Wilks says, in the garden of Dr. Moxon, "In the winter lumps of suet and cocoanut sawn in rings were hung upon the arches and boughs for the benefit of the tits, and loaves of bread were broken up for the blackbirds, thrushes, finches, and sparrows. Always before taking his own breakfast on a winter's morning, Moxon first saw to the feeding of his feathered friends."

Dr. Richard Bright, whose name is given to the disease which he so carefully studied, was for years connected with Guy's Hospital. He wrote valuable books, and was an untiring student. "He was sincerely religious, both in doctrine and in practice, and of so pure a mind that he never was heard to utter a sentiment or to relate an anecdote that was not fit to be heard by the merest child or the most refined woman."

Sir Astley Paston Cooper was associated with Guy's for twenty-five years. His father was a clergyman, and his mother an author. It is said that he was first attracted towards surgery by an accident to one of his foster-brothers. The youth fell from a heavy wagon, the wheels of which passed over his body, tearing the flesh from the thigh and injuring an artery, from which the blood flowed freely. Nobody seemed to know how to stop the blood, when Astley, a boy scarcely more than twelve, took out his handkerchief, and tied it tightly around the thigh and above the wound, thus staying the blood till a surgeon could be brought. Sir Astley used to say this accident, which resulted so well, created in his mind a love for surgery. His uncle, William Cooper, was a surgeon at Guy's, and encouraged his nephew's inclination for the medical profession. At twenty-three Sir Astley married a lady of wealth, lecturing on surgery on the evening of his wedding-day without any of the pupils being aware of his marriage. The first year of his practice he received £5 5s.; the second year, £26; the third year, £54; the fourth year, £96; the fifth year, £100; the sixth year, £200; the seventh, £400; the eighth, £610; the ninth, £1,100. When he was in the zenith of his fame he received £21,000 in one year. One merchant paid him £600 yearly. For a successful operation he was sometimes paid one thousand guineas. Each year he is said to have given £2,000 or £3,000 to poor relations.

"In his busy years," writes Dr. Samuel Wilks, "he rose at six, dissected privately until eight, and from half-past eight saw large numbers of patients gratuitously. At breakfast he ate only two well-buttered hot rolls, drank his tea cool, at a draught, read his paper a few minutes, and then was off to his consulting-room, turning round with a sweet, benign smile as he left the room." At one o'clock he would scarcely see another patient. "Sometimes the people in the hall and the anteroom were so importunate that Mr. Cooper was driven to escape through his stables and into a passage by Bishopsgate Church. At Guy's he was awaited by a crowd of pupils on the steps, and at once went into the wards, addressing the patients with such tenderness of voice and expression that he at once gained their confidence. His few pertinent questions and quick diagnosis were of themselves remarkable, no less than the judicious, calm manner in which he enforced the necessity for operations when required."

At two o'clock Sir Astley Cooper went across the street to St. Thomas's Hospital to lecture on anatomy. "After the lecture, which was often so crowded that men stood in the gangways and passages near to gain such portion of his lecture as they might fortunately pick up, he went round the dissecting-room, and afterwards left the hospital to visit patients or to operate privately, returning home at half-past six or seven. Every spare minute in his carriage was occupied with dictating to his assistants notes or remarks on cases or other subjects on which he was engaged. At dinner he ate rapidly, and not very elegantly, talking and joking; after dinner he slept for ten minutes at will, and then started to his surgical lecture, if it were a lecture night. In the evening he was usually again on a round of visits till midnight."

Sir Astley received a baronetcy and a fee of £500 for successfully removing a small tumor from the head of George IV. He wrote several books, and was president of various societies. He was as famous abroad as at home. The king of the French bestowed upon him the decoration of the Legion of Honor. He died of dropsy in 1841 in his chair, surrounded by his friends, saying, as he passed away, "God bless you; adieu to you all," and was buried under the chapel near Thomas Guy. His only child died in infancy. There is a statue of Sir Astley in St. Paul's Cathedral, and a bust of him in the museum of Guy's. He said of himself: "My own success depended upon my zeal and industry; but for this I take no credit, as it was given to me from above." He is said to have left a fortune of half a million of dollars.

The beloved Frederick Denison Maurice was elected chaplain of Guy's Hospital in 1836, when he was thirty-one. He wrote to a friend, "If I could get any influence over the medical students I should indeed think myself honored; and though some who have had experience think such a hope quite a dream, I still venture to entertain it." There seems no reason why a medical student, or any student indeed, should be rough in manner or hard of heart. A true man will be a gentleman not less in the dissecting-room than in the parlor. He will be humane to the lowest animal, and tender and considerate in the presence of suffering.

Sir William Withey Gull, the son of a barge-owner and wharfinger in Essex, who rose to eminence by his power of work and will, was for twenty years physician and lecturer at Guy's Hospital.

Going there as a student when he was twenty-one, he was told by the treasurer, "I can help you if you will help yourself." He used to say that his real education was given him by his sweet-faced mother. He won many prizes, acted as tutor to gain the means of living, and made friends by his winsome manner as well as his knowledge. The lady to whom he was engaged died, but her father was so attached to young Gull that he left him a considerable legacy. Mr. Gull afterwards married a sister of his friend Dr. Lacy. He rose rapidly in his profession, and was made F.R.S. in 1869, having been made LL.D. of Oxford and Cambridge the previous year.

His knowledge was profound on many subjects,—poetry, philosophy, and of course medicine. His industry was astonishing to all, and his personal influence remarkable. "Not many years ago," says Dr. Wilks, "we heard an old student of Guy's descant on his beautiful lectures, and especially those on fever. On being questioned as to what Gull said which most struck him, he said he could not remember anything in particular, but he would come to London any day to hear Gull reiterate the words in very slow measure, 'Now typhoid, gentlemen.' ... When Gull left the bedside of his patient, and said in measured tones, 'You will get well,' it was like a message from above.... It was not penetration only which Gull possessed, but endurance. It was ever being remarked with what deliberate care he went over every case, as if that particular one was his sole charge for the day."

Dr. Gull attended the Prince of Wales in his very severe illness from typhoid fever in 1871, when his life was despaired of; and for this he was created a baronet, and Physician Extraordinary to the Queen. He died of apoplexy, Jan. 29, 1890, leaving a fortune of £344,000 (over a million and a half of dollars), largely earned by his own industry and ability. His son, Sir Cameron Gull, has founded a studentship of pathology at Guy's, worth about £150 per annum. Sir William was buried, by his own desire, in his native village, Thorpe-le-Soken, beside his father and mother.

Thomas Guy has slept for over a century in the midst of the great work which his fortune began and still carries forward. Who shall estimate the good done every year to six thousand suffering persons, mostly poor, who need the care and skill of a great hospital, and to seventy thousand, or two hundred daily, who come for medical treatment? The fact that Thomas Guy became rich through industry, economy, and business sagacity will be forgotten; the fact that he was a member of Parliament for thirteen years is of little moment; but the fact that he gave his wealth to bless the world will be remembered as long as England lasts, or humanity suffers.

SOPHIA SMITH
AND HER COLLEGE FOR WOMEN

Miss Sophia Smith, the founder of Smith College, came from a family of savers as well as givers. Self-indulgent persons rarely give.

She was the niece of Oliver Smith, whose unique charities have been a blessing to many towns. Mr. Smith, who died at Hatfield, Mass., Dec. 22, 1845, left to the towns of Northampton, Hadley, Hatfield, Amherst, and Williamsburg, in the county of Hampshire, and Deerfield, Greenfield, and Whately, in the county of Franklin, about a million dollars to a Board of Trustees, to be used as follows:—

To be set aside for sixty years from the time of his death, so as to double and treble itself, for an Agricultural School at Northampton, $30,000. In 1894, forty-nine years after Mr. Smith died, this fund had become $190,801.15, so rapidly does interest accumulate. This will be used to purchase two farms, one a Pattern Farm, to become a model to all farmers; the other an Experimental Farm, to aid the Pattern Farm in the art and science of husbandry and agriculture. Buildings are to be erected on the grounds suitable for mechanics, and workshops for the manufacture of implements of husbandry of the most approved models. If the income will warrant it, tools for other trades may be manufactured.

There is also to be a School of Industry on the farms for the benefit of the poor. The boys to be aided must be from the poorest in the town, are to receive a good common education, and be taught in agriculture or in some mechanic art in the shops on the premises. When twenty-one years of age they are to be loaned $200 each, and after paying interest for five years at five per cent are to receive the $200 as a gift, if they have proved themselves worthy. Three years before they are twenty-one, each is to have a portion of his time to earn for himself.

After a bequest of $10,000 to the American Colonization Society, Mr. Smith's will provided that his property should go to poor boys and girls, poor young women and widows. The boy, not under twelve, of good moral character, should be bound out to some respectable family, and receive at twenty-one, if he had been a faithful apprentice, a loan of $500, and after five years the gift in full to help him make a start in the world.

The girl so bound out, if maintaining a good moral character, should receive $300 as a marriage portion, if the man she was to marry seemed a worthy man. If he was unworthy, the girl was to be aided in sickness or mental derangement up to the full amount of the marriage portion.

Each young woman in indigent or moderate circumstances, if she were to marry a sober man, could, by applying to the trustees, receive a marriage portion of fifty dollars, to be expended for necessary articles of household furniture. Each widow, with a child or children dependent on her for support, could receive fifty dollars; and this might be given yearly if the trustees thought wise.

Mr. Smith lived and died unmarried; but he knew that the pathway of many struggling lovers would be made easier if the young woman had even fifty dollars, or, if the girl had been bound out with strangers, $300 would make many a little home after marriage comfortable.

Mr. Smith has been dead over half a century, but his quaint and beautiful gift has been doing its work. During the year 1894, 51 boys and 17 girls were placed in good homes, and reared for useful lives. Nine received their marriage portion, and sixteen were helped in sickness. Thirty boys received their loan of $500 each, and thirty their gift of a like amount. There are now apprenticed 137 boys and 38 girls. Marriage gifts were made to 118 young women, and $50 were paid to each of 116 widows. Last year 289 persons received gifts to the amount of $30,785. What happiness this money means to those for the most part just looking out into the cares and work of life! How many fortunes are built on that first $500 so difficult to accumulate! How many homes kept from dire poverty by that first $300 with which to make the place attractive as well as comfortable! What an incentive for a boy or girl to be industrious, saving, temperate, and upright! What a comfort to feel that after we are silent our work can speak for us through a whole State, and even a whole nation!

Mr. Oliver Smith depended much upon his nephew, Austin Smith, a successful and wealthy man, to carry out his wishes. Austin and his brother Joseph were members of the General Court of Massachusetts. When their father died, though he was not wealthy like Oliver, he left his two sons the larger part of his fortune, and his two daughters, Harriet and Sophia, enough to support them with close economy. The father was a soldier in the Revolutionary War; and the grandfather, Samuel Smith, was commissioned lieutenant in 1755 by Governor Phipps.

Sophia, who must have been a sweet-faced girl, judging from her appearance in later life, was eager for study; but there was little chance for a girl to obtain an education, and little sympathy, as a rule, with those girls who desired it. She was born in Hatfield, Mass., Aug. 27, 1796. When Sophia was a little girl, Abigail Adams, the noble wife of John Adams, our second president, wrote to a friend in England, "You need not be told how much, in this country, female education is neglected, nor how fashionable it is to ridicule female learning."

Mrs. Samuel D. (Locke) Stow, in a history of Mount Holyoke Seminary, shows how meagre were the early advantages for girls. "Boston did not permit girls to attend the public schools till 1790, and then only during the summer months, when there were not boys enough to fill them. This lasted till 1822, when Boston became a city. An aged resident of Hatfield used to tell of going to the schoolhouse when she was a girl, and sitting on the doorstep to hear the boys recite their lessons. No girl could cross the threshold as a scholar. The girls of Northampton were not admitted to the public schools till 1792. In the Centennial *Hampshire Gazette* it was stated: 'In 1788 the question was before the town, and it was voted not to be at any expense for schooling girls.' The advocates of the measure were persistent, however, and appealed to the courts; the town was indicted and fined for this neglect. In 1792 it was voted by a large majority to admit girls between the ages of eight and fifteen to the schools from May 1 to Oct. 31. It was not till 1802 that all restrictions were removed."

These summer schools from May to October were of comparatively little worth. All children brought their work, braiding, sewing, and knitting, and were taught to read and write, and to have "good manners," according to the accepted notions of the time. "At first arithmetic and geography were taught only in the winter, for a knowledge of numbers or ability to cast accounts was deemed quite superfluous for girls. When Colburn's Mental Arithmetic was introduced, some of our mothers who desired to study it were told derisively, 'If you expect to become widows, and have to carry pork to market, it may be well enough to study mental arithmetic.'

"The first school in New England," says Mrs. Stow, "designed exclusively for the instruction of girls in branches not taught in the common schools, is said to have been an evening school conducted by William Woodbridge, who was a graduate of Yale in 1780. His theme on graduation was, 'Improvement in Female Education.' Reducing his theory to practice, in addition to his daily occupation he gave his evenings to the instruction of girls in Lowth's Grammar, Guthrie's Geography, and the art of composition. The popular sentiment deemed him visionary. 'Who,' it said, 'shall cook our food and mend our clothes if the girls are to be taught philosophy and astronomy?' In Waterford, N.Y., in 1820, occurred the public examination of a young lady in geometry. It was the first instance of the kind in the State, and perhaps in the country, and called forth a storm of ridicule. Her teacher was Mrs. Emma Willard."

Sophia Smith's girlhood was passed during this indifference or opposition to education for women. When she was fourteen, in 1810, she went to school in Hartford, Conn., for twelve weeks; and four years later, at eighteen, she was for a short time a pupil in the Hopkins Academy in Hadley. She studied diligently with her quick, eager mind, and was thankful for these crumbs of knowledge, though she lamented through her life that her opportunities had been so limited.

Year by year went by in the quiet New England home, her sister Harriet taking upon herself the burden of household cares and business, as Sophia was frail, and at forty had become very deaf. Her mind had been broadened, and her heart kept tender to every sorrow, by her Christian faith and devotion to duty. The town of Hatfield had capable ministers, who were intellectual as well as spiritual helpers, and Sophia Smith enjoyed cultivated minds.

"By reading mostly," says the Rev. John M. Greene of Lowell, Mass., "she kept herself familiar with the common events and occurrences of the day. Probably what she and others called a calamity was a blessing to her. She had fortitude to bear the trial, and the wisdom to improve the reflective and meditative powers of her mind, far beyond what the fashionable and gossiping woman attains. Deafness is an admirable remedy for insincerity, shallowness, and foolish talking. It sifts what we hear, and compels us to try to say what is worth attention."

Miss Smith attended the services of the Congregational Church, of which she was a member; and though she could not hear a word of the sermon perhaps, she felt accountable for the influence of her presence. She loved the Bible, and would quote the words of Sir William Jones: "The Bible contains more true sublimity, more exquisite beauty, more pure morality, more important history, and finer strains of poetry and eloquence, than can be collected from all other books, in whatever age or language they have been written." She had the strength of character of the typical New England woman, yet possessing gentle manners and most refined tastes.

She loved nature; and in Hatfield, with its magnificent elms and beautiful river, Miss Smith had much to enjoy. Some of these great elms measure twenty-eight feet in circumference, three yards from the ground.

In this charming scenery, reading her books, and doing good as she had opportunity, Miss Smith was growing old. Her sister Harriet had died a little before the time of our Civil War, and the lonely woman bent her energies towards helping other aching hearts. She worked with her own hands to aid the soldiers and their families, and when she had the means used it generously.

Her brother Austin died March 8, 1861; and very unexpectedly Sophia Smith became the possessor, through his gift, of over $200,000. "God permitted him," says the Rev. Mr. Greene, to "gather the gold, preparing all the while the heart of a devout and Christlike sister to dispense it."

Miss Smith at once felt her great responsibility. Some persons living all their lives most carefully would have rejoiced at the opportunity to buy comforts,—a carriage for daily riding, attractive clothes, more books, or take a journey to the Old World or elsewhere. But Miss Smith said at once, "This is a large property put into my hands, but I am only the steward of God in respect to it." She very wisely sought the advice of her pastor, the Rev. John M. Greene, a man of broad scholarship and generous nature. Dr. Greene was a lover of books; and finding so much happiness for himself in a student's life, he rightly thought that woman should have the bliss of possessing knowledge for her own sake, as well as for her increased influence in the world.

Miss Smith desired so to give as would accord with the wishes of her brother Austin were he alive, but could not be sure what were his preferences. She wished to give the money for education; for that was her great joy, mingled with regret that her way, as that of every other woman at that time, had been so hedged up by mistaken public opinion.

She longed to build a college for women, even when learned doctors wrote books to show that girls would be ruined in health by study, and that they were mentally inferior to the other sex. It was said that women would not care for higher education; that if they went to college they would not marry, and would cease to be attractive to men; that in any event the intellectual standard would be lowered if women were admitted to any college.

Miss Smith said, "There is no justice in denying women equal educational advantages with men. Women are the natural educators and physicians of the race, and they ought to be fitted for their work." When the foolish and untrue argument was used, that educated women do not make good wives and mothers, Miss Smith would say, "Then they are wrongly educated—some law is violated in the process."

Miss Smith had read history, and she knew that the Aspasias and the De Maintenons are the women who have had the strongest power with men. She knew that an educated woman is the companion of her children and their intellectual guide. She knew that women ought to be interested in the welfare of the state, rather than in a round of parties and amusements. She had no love for display, though she had taste in dress and in her home; and she longed to see all women have a purpose in life other than frivolity and pleasure-seeking. But Miss Smith feared that $200,000 would not be sufficient to found a college for women, and gave up the idea. Two months after her brother died she made her will, giving $75,000 for an Academy at Hatfield, $100,000 to a Deaf Mute Institution in Hatfield, and $50,000 to a Scientific School in connection with Amherst College. Six years later Mr. John Clarke provided a deaf mute institution for the

94

Commonwealth, and Miss Smith was at liberty to turn her fortune into another channel.

The old idea of a *real college* for women, a project as dear to Dr. Greene as to herself, was again upon her mind. She read all she could find upon the subject. She loved and believed in her own sex, and knew the low intellectual standard of the ordinary boarding-school. She said, "We should educate the whole woman, physical, intellectual, moral, and spiritual." She insisted that the education given in the college which she hoped to found should be *equal* to that obtained in a college for men.

"There is a good deal that is heroic," says a writer in *Scribner's Monthly*, May, 1877, "in the spectacle of this lonely woman, shut out in a great measure by her infirmity and secluded life from so many human interests and pleasures, quietly elaborating a plan by which she could broaden and enrich the lives of multitudes of her sex, and give increased dignity and power to woman in the generations to come."

In July, 1868, Miss Smith made her last will, stating the object for which she wished her money to be used: "The establishment and maintenance of an institution for the higher education of young women, with the design to furnish them means and facilities for education equal to those which are afforded in our colleges for young men."

"The formal wording," says M. A. Jordan in the *New England Magazine* for January, 1887, "hardly tells the story of self-denial, painful industry, commonplace restriction and isolation, that lies behind it in the lives of this brother and sister."

Miss Smith wished the college to be Christian, "not Congregational," she said, "or Baptist, or Methodist, or Episcopalian, but *Christian*." She hoped the Bible would be studied in the Hebrew and Greek in her college, so that the students could know for themselves the truth of the translations which we have to-day.

Miss Smith gave about $400,000 for the founding of Smith College,—the fortune left by her brother had increased,—with the express condition that not more than half the amount should be used in buildings and grounds. It required much urging to allow the college to bear her name. After counselling with friends, Miss Smith decided that the college should be built at Northampton, which George Bancroft thought "the most beautiful town in New England, where no one can live without imbibing love for the place," with the provision that the town should raise $25,000, which was done. Northampton seemed preferable to Hatfield, because more easy of access, and possessed of a public library and other intellectual attractions. After her brother's money came into her hands, Miss Smith continued to economize for herself, but gave generously to others. Often in her journal she wrote, "I feel the responsibility of this great property."

She subscribed $5,000 to the Massachusetts Agricultural College if it should be located at Northampton, $300 for a library for the young people's Literary Association in Hatfield, $1,000 towards the organ in the church, $30,000 for the endowment of a professorship in Andover Theological Seminary, and to many other objects. "She gave to them *all*," says Dr. Greene, "Home Missions and Foreign Missions, the Bible Society and Tract Society, the Seamen and Freedmen,—to all the objects presented. In her journal she writes: 'I desire to give where duty calls.' ... Before her death she had great satisfaction and comfort in her Andover donation.... When she was considering whether or not to make her donation to Andover Theological Seminary, Professor Park asked her if he might consult a mutual friend, an eminent lawyer and business man, about it. With uplifted hands and almost a rebuking gesture she replied, 'No, no; I'll make up my mind myself.' One of her most intimate friends, a graduate of Mount Holyoke Seminary, remarked, 'I never was acquainted with a person who felt more deeply than Miss Smith her accountability to God.'"

Miss Smith's life declined pleasantly and happily. In 1866 she wrote in her journal: "Sunday afternoon. It is a most splendid day; have been to church, although I have not heard. I feel the presence of Him who is everywhere, and who is all love to him that seeketh Him and serves Him.... I resolve with His blessing to give myself unreservedly anew to Him, to watch over my thoughts and words, and to strive after a more perfect life in all my dealings with my fellow-men, and strive to make this great affliction [deafness] a means of sanctification, and make it a means of improvement in the divine life."

May 9, 1870, she made her last record in her journal: "I resolve to begin anew to strive to be better in everything; to guard against carelessness in talking; to strive for more patience and sense, and to strive for more earnestness, to do more good; to strive against selfishness, and to cultivate good feelings in all; to live to God's glory, that others, seeing our good works, may glorify our Father in heaven."

Such golden words might well be cut on the walls of Smith College, that the students might imitate the resolve of the founder, who believed, as she said in her will, "that all education should be for the glory of God and the good of man.... It is not my design to render my sex any the less feminine, but to develop as fully as may be the powers of womanhood, and furnish women with the means of usefulness, happiness, and honor, now withheld from them."

One month after writing in her journal, June 12, 1870, Sophia Smith passed to her reward, at the age of seventy-five. She was in her usual health till four days before her death, when she was prostrated by paralysis. She was buried in the Hatfield Cemetery under a simple monument of her own erecting. She had provided for a better and more enduring monument in Smith College, and she knew that no other was needed. The seventy-five-thousand-dollar academy at Hatfield would also keep her in blessed remembrance.

The thought of Miss Smith, after her death, began to shape itself into brick and stone. Thirteen acres of ground were purchased for the site of the college, commanding a view of the beautiful valley of the Connecticut River; and the main building, of brick and freestone, was erected in secular Gothic style, the interior finished in unpainted native woods. On the large stained-glass window over the entrance of the building is a copy of the college seal, a woman radiant with light, with the motto underneath in Greek which expressed the desire of the founder: "Add to your virtue knowledge."

The homestead which was on the estate when purchased was made over for a home for the students, as the plan of small dwellings to accommodate from twenty to fifty young women had been decided upon in preference to several hundreds gathered under one roof.

The right person for the right place had been chosen as president, the Rev. Dr. L. Clark Seelye, at that time a professor in Amherst College. He had made a careful inspection of the principal educational institutions both in this country and in Europe, and his plans as to buildings and courses of study were adopted.

Smith College was dedicated July 14, 1875, and opened to students in the following September. President Seelye in his admirable inaugural address said, "One hundred years ago a female college would have been simply an object of ridicule.... You have seen machines invented to do the work which formerly absorbed the greater portion of woman's time and strength. Factories have supplanted the spinning-wheel and distaff. Sewing-machines will stitch in an hour more than our grandmothers could in a day. I need not ask you what we are to do with force which has thus been set free. The answer comes clearly from an enlightened public opinion, saying, 'Put it to higher uses; train it to think correctly; to work intelligently; to do its share in bringing the human mind to the perfection for which it was designed.'"

Dr. Seelye emphasized the fact that this college was to give women "an education as high and thorough and complete as that which young men receive in Harvard, Yale, and Amherst." "I believe," he said, "this is the only female college that insists upon substantially the same requisites for admission which have been found practicable and essential in male colleges." He disapproved of a preparatory department, and other colleges for women have wisely followed the standard and example of Smith. Secondary schools have seen the necessity of a higher fitting for their students, that they may enter our best colleges.

Greek and the higher mathematics were made an essential part of the course. To this, exception was taken; and Dr. Seelye was frequently asked, "What use have young women of Greek?" He answered, "A study of Greek brings us into communion with the best scholarship and the acutest intellects of all European countries.... It would simply justify its place in our college curriculum upon the relation which it has had, and ever must have, to the growth of the human intellect."

Dr. Seelye favored the teaching of music and art, but not to the exclusion of other things, unless one had special gifts along those lines. "Musical entertainments," he said, "have generally been the grand parade-ground of female boarding-schools. All of us are familiar with the many wearisome hours which young ladies ordinarily are required to spend at the piano,—time enough to master most of the sciences and languages; and all of us are familiar with the remark, heard so frequently after school-days are over, 'I cannot play; I am out of practice.'"

President Seelye had to meet all sorts of objections to higher education for women. When he told a friend that Greek was to be studied in Smith College, the friend replied, "Nonsense! girls cannot bear such a strain;" "and yet his own daughters," says Dr. Seelye, "were going, with no remonstrance from him, night after night, through the round of parties and fashionable amusements in a great city. We question whether any greater expenditure of physical force is necessary to master Greek than to endure ordinary fashionable amusements. Woman's health is endangered far more by balls and parties than by schools. For one ruined by over-study, we can point to a hundred ruined by dainties and dances."

Another said to President Seelye, "Think of a wife who forced you to talk perpetually about metaphysics, or to listen to Greek and Latin quotations!" This would be much more agreeable conversation to some men than to hear about dress and servants and gossip.

When Smith College was opened in 1875, there were many applicants; but with requirements for admission the same as at Harvard, Yale, Brown, and Amherst, only fifteen could pass the examinations. The next year eighteen were accepted.

Each year the number has increased, till in the year 1895 there were 875 students at Smith College. The professorships are about equally divided between men and women. The chair of Greek, on the John M. Greene foundation, "is founded in honor of the Rev. John M. Greene, D.D., who first suggested to Miss Smith the idea of the college, and was her confidential adviser in her bequest," says the College Calendar.

There are three courses of study, each extending through four years,—the classical course leading to the degree of Bachelor of Arts, the scientific to Bachelor of Science, the literary to Bachelor of Letters. The maximum of work allowed to any student in a regular course is sixteen hours of recitation each week.

Year by year Miss Smith's noble gift has been supplemented by the gifts of others.

In 1878 the Lilly Hall of Science was dedicated, the gift of Mr. Alfred Theodore Lilly. This building contains lecture rooms, and laboratories for chemistry, physics, geology, zoölogy, and botany. In 1881 Mr. Winthrop Hillyer gave the money to erect the Hillyer Art Gallery, which now contains an extensive collection of casts, engravings, and paintings, and is provided with studios. One corridor of engravings and an alcove of original drawings were given by the Century Company. Mr. Hillyer gave an endowment of $50,000 for his gallery. A music-hall was also erected in 1881.

The observatory, given by two donors unknown to the public, has an eleven-inch refracting telescope, a spectroscope, siderial clock, chronograph, a portable telescope, and a meridian circle, aperture four inches.

The alumnæ gymnasium contains a swimming-bath, and a large hall for gymnastic exercises and in-door sport. A large greenhouse has been erected to aid in botanical work, with an extensive collection of tropical plants.

There are eight or more dwelling-houses for the students, each presided over by a competent woman, where the scholars find cheerful, happy homes. The Tenney House, bequeathed by Mrs. Mary A. Tenney, for experiments in co-operative housekeeping, enables the students to adapt their expenses to their means, if they choose to make the experiment together. Tuition is $100 a year, with $300 for board and furnished room in the college houses.

Smith College is fortunately situated. Opposite the grounds is the beautiful Forbes Library, with an endowment of $300,000 for books alone, and not far away a public library with several thousand volumes, and a permanent endowment of $50,000 for its increase. The students have access to the collections at Amherst College and the Massachusetts Agricultural College, also at Mount Holyoke College, about seven miles distant.

There are no secret societies at Smith. "Instead of hazing newcomers," says President Seelye, "the second or sophomore class will give them a reception in the art-gallery, introduce them to the older students with the courteous hospitality which good breeding dictates."

There are several literary and charitable societies in Smith College. Great interest is taken in the working-girls of New York, and in the college settlement of that city.

None of the evil effects predicted for young women in college have been realized. "Some of our best scholars," says President Seelye, "have steadily improved in health since entering college. Some who came so feeble that it was doubtful whether they could remain a term have become entirely well and strong.... We have had frequently professors from male institutions to give instruction; and their testimony is to the effect that the girls study better than the boys, and that the average scholarship is higher."

"The general atmosphere of the college is one of freedom," writes Louise Walston, in the "History of Higher Education in Massachusetts," by George Gary Bush, Ph.D. "The written code consists of one law,—Lights out at ten; the unwritten is that of every well-regulated community, and to the success of this method of discipline every year is a witness.

"This freedom is not license.... The system of attendance upon recitation at Smith is in this respect unique. It is distinctively a 'no-cut' system. In the college market that commodity known as indulgences is not to be found; and no student is expected to absent herself from lecture or recitation except for good reasons, the validity of which, however, is left to her own conscience. Knowledge is offered as a privilege, and is so received."

As Miss Smith directed in her will, "the Holy Scriptures are daily and systematically read and studied in the college." A chapel service is held in the morning of week-days, and a vesper service on Sunday. Students attend the churches of their preference in Northampton.

All honor to Sophia Smith, the quiet Christian woman, who, forgetting herself, became a blessing to tens of thousands by her gifts. At the request of the trustees of Smith College, Dr. Greene is preparing a volume on her life and character.

All honor, too, to the Rev. John M. Greene, who for twenty-five years has been the beloved pastor of the Eliot Church in Lowell, Mass. His quarter century of service was fittingly celebrated at Lowell, Sept. 26, 1895. Out of five hundred Congregational ministers in Massachusetts, only ten have held so long a pastorate as he over one church.

Among the hundreds of congratulations and testimonies to Dr. Greene's successful ministry, the able Professor Edwards A. Park of Andover, wrote to the congregation: "The city of Lowell has been favored with clergymen who will be remembered by a distant posterity, but not one of them will be remembered longer than the present pastor of Eliot Church. He was the father of Smith College, now so flourishing in Northampton, Mass. Had it not been for him that great institution would never have existed. For this great benefaction to the world, he will be honored a hundred years hence."

100

JAMES LICK
AND HIS TELESCOPE

James Lick, one of the great givers of the West, was born in Fredericksburg, Penn., Aug. 25, 1796. Little is known of his early life, except that his ancestors were Germans, and that he was born in poverty. His grandfather served in the Revolutionary War. James learned to make organs and pianos in Hanover, Penn., and in 1819 worked for Joseph Hiskey, a prominent piano manufacturer of Baltimore.

One day Conrad Meyer, a poor lad, came into the store and asked for work. Young Lick gave him food and clothing, and secured a place for him in the establishment. They became fast friends, and continued thus for life. Later Conrad Meyer was a wealthy manufacturer of pianos in Philadelphia.

James Lick in 1820, when he was twenty-four, went to New York, hoping to begin business for himself, but finding his capital too limited, in the following year, 1821, went to Buenos Ayres, South America, where he lived for ten years. At the end of that time he went to Philadelphia, and met his old friend Conrad Meyer. He had brought with him for sale $40,000 worth of hides and nutria skins. The latter are obtained from a species of otter found along the La Plata River.

He intended settling in Philadelphia, and rented a house on Eighth Street, near Arch, but soon abandoned his purpose, probably because the business outlook was not hopeful, and returned to Buenos Ayres to sell pianos. From the east side of South America he went to the west side, and remained in Valparaiso, Chili, for four years. He spent eleven years in Peru, making and selling pianos. Once, when his workmen left him suddenly to go to Mexico, rather than break a contract he did all the work himself, and accomplished it in two years.

In 1847 he went to San Francisco, which had only one thousand inhabitants. He was then about fifty years old, and took with him over $30,000, which, foreseeing California's wonderful prospects, he invested in land in San Francisco, and farther south in Santa Clara Valley.

In 1854, to the surprise of everybody, the quiet, parsimonious James Lick built a magnificent flour-mill six miles from San José. He tore down an old structure, and erected in its place a mill, finished within in solid mahogany highly polished, and furnished it with the best machinery possible. It was called "The Mahogany Mill," or more frequently "Lick's Folly." He made the grounds about the mill very attractive. "Upon it," says the San José *Daily Mercury*, June 28, 1888,

101

"he began early to set out trees of various kinds, both for fruit and ornament. He held some curious theories of tree-planting, and believed in the efficiency of a bone deposit about the roots of every young tree. Many are the stories told by old residents of James Lick going along the highway in an old rattletrap, rope-tied wagon, with a bearskin robe for a seat cushion, and stopping every now and then to gather in the bones of some dead beast. People used to think him crazy until they saw him among his beloved trees, planting some new and rare variety, and carefully mingling about its young roots the finest of loams with the bones he had gathered during his lonely rides.

"There is a story extant, and probably well-founded, which illustrates the odd means he employed to secure hired help at once trustworthy and obedient. One day while he was planting his orchard a man applied to him for work. Mr. Lick directed him to take the trees he indicated to a certain part of the grounds, and then to plant them with the tops in the earth and the roots in the air. The man obeyed the directions to the letter, and reported in the evening for further orders. Mr. Lick went out, viewed his work with apparent satisfaction, and then ordered him to plant the trees the proper way and thereafter to continue in his employ." Nineteen years after Mr. Lick built his mill, Jan. 16, 1873, he surprised the people of San José again, by giving it to the Paine Memorial Society of Boston, half the proceeds of sale to be used for a Memorial Hall, and half to sustain a lecture course. He had always been an admirer of Thomas Paine's writings. The mill was annually inundated by the floods from the Guadalupe River, spoiling his orchards and his roads, so that he tired of the property.

An agent of the Boston Society went to California, sold the mill for $18,000 cash, and carried the money back to Boston. Mr. Lick was displeased that the property which had cost him $200,000 should be sold at such a low price, and without his knowledge, as he would willingly have bought it in at $50,000.

It is said by some that Mr. Lick built his mill as a protest against the cheap and flimsy style of building on the Pacific Coast, but it is much more probable that he built it for another reason. In early life it is believed that young Lick fell in love with the daughter of a well-to-do miller for whom he worked. When the young man made known his love, which was reciprocated by the girl, the miller was angry, and is said to have replied, "Out, you beggar! Dare you cast your eyes upon my daughter, who will inherit my riches? Have you a mill like this? Have you a single penny in your purse?"

To this Lick replied "that he had nothing as yet, but one day he would have a mill beside which this one would be a pigsty."

Lick caused his elegant mill to be photographed without and within, and sent the pictures to the miller. It was, however, too late to win the girl, if indeed he ever hoped to do so; for she had long since

102

married, and Mr. Lick went through life a lonely and unresponsive man. He never lived in his palatial mill, but occupied for a time a humble abode near by.

After Mr. Lick disposed of his mill, he began to improve a tract of land south of San José known as "The Lick Homestead Addition." "Day after day," says the San José *Mercury*, "long trains of carts and wagons passed slowly through San José carrying tall trees and full-grown shrubbery from the old to the new location. Winter and summer alike the work went on, the old man superintending it all in his rattletrap wagon and bearskin robe. His plans for this new improvement were made regardless of expense. Tradition tells that he had imported from Australia rare trees, and in order to secure their growth had brought with them whole shiploads of their native earth. He conceived the idea of building conservatories superior to any on the Pacific Coast, and for that purpose had imported from England the materials for two large conservatories after the model of those in the Kew Gardens in London. His death occurred before he could have these constructed; and they remained on the hands of the trustees until a body of San Francisco gentlemen contributed funds for their purchase and donation to the use of the public in Golden Gate Park, where they now stand as the wonder and delight of all who visit that beautiful resort."

Mr. Lick also built in San Francisco a handsome hotel called the Lick House. With his own hands he carved some of the rosewood frames of the mirrors. He caused the walls to be decorated with pictures of California scenery. The dining-room has a polished floor made of many thousand pieces of wood of various kinds.

When Mr. Lick was seventy-seven years old, and found himself the owner of millions, with a laudable desire to be remembered after death, and a patriotism worthy of high commendation, he began to think deeply how best to use his property.

On Feb. 15, 1873, Mr. Lick offered to the California Academy of Sciences a piece of land on Market Street, the site of its present building. Professor George Davidson, then president of the academy, called to thank him, when Mr. Lick unfolded to him his purpose of giving a great telescope for future investigation of the heavenly bodies. He had become deeply interested from reading, it is said, about possible life on other planets. It is supposed by some that while Mr. Lick lived his lonely life in Peru, a priest, who gained his friendship, interested him in astronomy. Others think his mind was drawn towards it by reading about the Washington Observatory, completed in 1874, and noticed widely by the press.

Mr. Lick was not a scientist nor an astronomer; he had been too absorbed in successful business life for that; but he earned money that others might have the time and opportunity to devote their lives to science.

Mr. Lick appears to have had a passion for statuary, as shown by his gifts. At one time he thought of having expensive memorial statues of himself and family erected on the heights overlooking the ocean and the bay, but was dissuaded by one of his pioneer friends, according to Miss M. W. Shinn's account in the *Overland Monthly*, November, 1892.

"Mr. D. J. Staples felt it his duty to tell Mr. Lick frankly that his bequests for statues of himself and family would be utterly useless as a memorial; that the world would not be interested in them; and when Mr. Lick urged that such costly statues would be preserved for all time, as the statues of antiquity now remained the precious relics of a lost civilization, answered, almost at random, 'More likely we shall get into a war with Russia or somebody, and they will come around here with warships, and smash the statues to pieces in bombarding the city.'"

Mr. Lick conferred with his friends, but had his own decided wishes and plans which usually he carried out. On July 16, 1874, he conveyed all his property, real and personal, over $3,000,000, by deed of trust to seven men; but becoming dissatisfied with some members of the Board of Lick Trustees, he made a new deed, Sept. 21, 1875, under which his property has been used as he directed. A year later he changed some of the members, but the deed itself remained as before.

One of the first bequests under his deed of trust was for the telescope and observatory, $700,000. Another, to the Protestant Orphan Asylum of San Francisco, $25,000.

For an Orphan Asylum in San José, "free to all orphans without regard to creed or religion of parents," $25,000.

To the Ladies' Protective and Belief Society of San Francisco, $25,000.

To the Mechanics' Institute of San Francisco, "to be applied to the purchase of scientific and mechanical works for such Institute," $10,000.

To the Trustees of the Society for Prevention of Cruelty to Animals, of San Francisco, $10,000, with the hope expressed by him, "that the trustees of said society may organize such a system as will result in establishing similar societies in every city and town in California, to the end that the rising generations may not witness or be impressed with such scenes of cruelty and brutality as constantly occur in this State."

To found in San Francisco "an institution to be called The Old Ladies' Home," $100,000. For the erection and the maintenance of that extremely useful public charity, Free Public Baths, $150,000. These baths went into use Nov. 1, 1890.

For the erection of a monument to be placed in Golden Gate Park, "to the memory of Francis Scott Key, the author of 'The Star-Spangled Banner,'" $60,000. This statue was unveiled July 4, 1888.

To endow an institution to be called the California School of Mechanical Arts, "to be open to all youths born in California," $540,000.

For statuary emblematical of three important epochs in the history of California, to be placed in front of the San Francisco City Hall, $100,000.

To John H. Lick, his son, born in Pennsylvania, June 30, 1818, $150,000. The latter contested the will; and a compromise was effected whereby he received $533,000, the expense of the suit being a little over $60,000. This son, at his death, founded Lick College, Fredericksburg, Penn., giving it practically all his fortune. It is now called Schuylkill Seminary, and had 285 pupils in 1893, according to the Report of the Commissioner of Education. A family monument was erected at Fredericksburg, Penn., Mr. Lick's birthplace, at a cost of $20,000.

Mr. Lick set aside some personal property for his own economical use during his life. After all these bequests had been attended to, the remainder of his fortune was to be given in "equal proportions to the California Academy of Sciences and the Society of California Pioneers," to be expended in erecting buildings for them, and in the purchase of a "suitable library, natural specimens, chemical and philosophical apparatus, rare and curious things useful in the advancement of science, and generally in the carrying out of the objects and purposes for which said societies were respectively established." Each society has received about $800,000 from the Lick estate. These were very remarkable gifts from a man who had been a mechanic, brought up in narrow circumstances, and with limited education.

The California School of Mechanical Arts was opened in January, 1895, and now, in the spring of 1896, has 230 pupils. The substantial brick buildings are in Spanish architecture, and cost, with machinery and furniture, about $115,000, leaving $425,000 for endowment. The Academic Building is three stories high, and the shops one and two stories. The requirements for pupils in entering the school are substantially the same as for the last of the grammar grades of the public schools. There is no charge for tuition.

Mr. Lick in making this bequest stated its object: "To educate males and females in the practical arts of life, such as working in wood, iron, and stone, or any of the metals, and in whatever industry intelligent mechanical skill now is or can hereafter be applied."

In view of this desire on the part of the giver, a careful survey of industrial education was made; and it was decided to "give each student a thorough knowledge of the technique of some one industrial pursuit, from which he may earn a living."

The school course is four years. At the beginning of the third year the student must choose his field of work for the last year and a half, and give his time to it. Besides the ordinary branches, carpentry, forging, moulding, machine and architectural drawing, wood-carving, dressmaking, millinery, cookery, etc., are taught. It is expected that graduates will be able to earn good wages at once after leaving the school, and the teachers endeavor to find suitable situations for their pupils.

Miss Caroline Willard Baldwin, at the head of the science department, who is herself a Bachelor of Science from the University of California, and a Doctor of Science from Cornell University, writes me: "The grade of work is much the same as that given in the Pratt Institute in Brooklyn, and the entire equipment of the school is excellent."

The Lick Bronze Statuary at the City Hall in San Francisco was unveiled on Thanksgiving Day, Thursday, Nov. 29, 1894. Mr. Lick had specified in his deed of trust that it should "represent by appropriate designs and figures the history of California; first, from the early settlement of the Missions to the acquisition of California by the United States; second, from such acquisition by the United States to the time when agriculture became the leading interest of the State; third, from the last-named period to the first day of January, 1874." He knew that there is no more effective way to teach history and inculcate love of city and nation than by object-lessons. A great gift is a continual suggestion to others to give also. The statue of a noble man or woman is a constant educator and inspirer to good deeds.

The Lick Statuary is of granite, surmounted by bronze figures of heroic proportions. The main column is forty-six feet high, with a bronze figure twelve feet high, weighing 7,000 pounds, on the top, representing Eureka, a woman typical of California, with a grizzly bear by her side. Beneath are four panels, depicting a family of immigrants crossing the Sierras, a vaquero lassoing a steer, traders with the Indians, and California under American rule.

Below these panels are the heads in bronze of James Lick, Father Junipero Serra, Sir Francis Drake, and John C. Frémont; and below these, the names of men famous in the history of California,—James W. Marshall, the discoverer of gold at Sutter's mill, and others. There are granite wings to the main pedestal, the bronze figures of which represent early times,—a native Indian over whom bends a Catholic priest, and a Spaniard throwing his lasso; a group of miners in '49, and figures denoting commerce and agriculture. The artist was Mr. Frank Happersberger, a native of California. Members of the California Pioneers made eloquent addresses at the unveiling of the beautiful statue, the band played "The Star-Spangled Banner," and the children of the public schools sang "America."

"The benefactions of James Lick were not of a posthumous character," said the Hon. Willard B. Farwell in his address. "There was no indication of a desire to accumulate for the sake of accumulation alone, and to cling with greedy purpose and tenacity to the last dollar gained, until the heart had ceased its pulsations, and the last breath had been drawn, before yielding it up for the good of others. On the contrary, he provided for the distribution of his wealth while living.... There was no room for cavil then over the manner of his giving. He fulfilled in its broadest measure the injunction of the aphorism, 'He gives well who gives quickly.'"

The gift nearest to Mr. Lick's heart was his great telescope, to be, as he said in his deed of trust, "superior to and more powerful than any telescope yet made, with all the machinery appertaining thereto, and appropriately connected therewith."

This telescope with its building was to be conveyed to the University of California, and to be known as the "Lick Astronomical Department of the University of California."

Various sites were suggested for the great telescope. A gentleman relates the following story: "One of the sites suggested was a mountain north of San Francisco. Mr. Lick was ill, but determined upon visiting this mountain; so he was taken on a cot to the station; and on arriving at the town nearest the mountain, the cot was removed to a wagon, and they started towards the summit. By some accident the rear of the wagon gave way, and the cot containing the old gentleman slid out on the mountain-side. This so angered him that he said he would never place the telescope on a mountain that treated him in that way, and ordered the party to turn back towards San Francisco."

During the summer of 1875 Mr. Lick sent Mr. Fraser, his trusted agent, to report on Mount St. Helena, Monte Diablo, Mount Hamilton, and others. In many respects the latter, in sight of his old mill at San José, seemed the best situated of all the mountain peaks. "Yet the possibility that a complete astronomical establishment might one day be planted on its summit seemed more like a fairy-tale than like sober fact," says Professor Edward S. Holden, Director of the Lick Observatory. "It was at that time a wilderness. A few cattle-ranches occupied the valleys around it. Its slopes were covered with chaparral or thickets of scrub oak. Not even a trail led over it. The nearest house was eleven miles away." It was and is the home of many rattlesnakes. They live upon squirrels, and small birds and their eggs, and come up to the top of the mountain in quest of water.

Sir Edwin Arnold, who visited Mount Hamilton, tells this incident of the "road-runner," the bird sometimes called "chaparral cock," as it was told to him. "The rattlesnake is the deadly enemy of its species, always hunting about in the thickets for eggs and young birds, since the 'road-runner' builds its nest on the ground. When, therefore, the 'chaparral cocks' find a 'rattler' basking in the sun, they gather, I was assured, leaves of the prickly cactus, and lay them in a circle all around the serpent, which cannot draw its belly over the sharp needles of these leaves. Thus imprisoned, the reptile is set upon by the birds, and pecked or spurred to death."

Mount Hamilton, fifty miles southeast of San Francisco, is near San José, twenty-six miles eastward, and thus easy of access, save the difficulty of reaching its summit, 4,300 feet above the sea. This was overcome by the willingness of Santa Clara County to construct a road to its top; which road was completed in December, 1876, at a cost of about $78,000. The road rises 4,000 feet in twenty-two miles; and the grade nowhere exceeds six and one-half feet in one hundred, or 343 feet to the mile. Towards the top it winds round and round the flanks of the mountain itself.

The view from the top of the mountain is most inspiring. "The lovely valley of Santa Clara and the Santa Cruz mountains to the west, a bit of the Pacific and the Bay of Monterey to the southwest, the Sierra Nevada (13,000-14,000 feet) with countless ranges between to the southeast, the San Joaquin valley with the Sierras beyond to the east, while to the north lie many lower ranges of hills, and on the horizon Mount Shasta, or Lassens' Butte (14,400 feet), 175 miles away. The Bay of San Francisco lies flat before you, and beyond it is Mount Tamalpais at the entrance to the Golden Gate."

"One of the gorges in the vicinity of Mount Hamilton," writes Taliesin Evans in the May, 1886, *Century*, "is reputed to have been a favorite retreat of Joaquin Murietta, the famous bandit, whose name was a terror to the early settlers of the State. A spring, situated a mile and a half east of Observatory Peak, at which he is said to have drawn water, now bears the name of 'Joaquin's Spring.'"

On June 7, 1876, Congress gave the land for the site, 1,350 acres; and other land was given and purchased, till the Observatory now has 2,581 acres. It was necessary to remove 72,000 tons of solid rock from the mountain summit, which was lowered as much as thirty-two feet in places, that the buildings might have a level foundation. Clay for making the brick was found about two and one-half miles below the Observatory (by the road), thus saving over $46,000 in the 2,600,000 bricks used. Springs also were fortunately discovered about 340 feet below the present level of the summit.

In 1879, after the site had been decided upon, Professor S. W. Burnham of Chicago was asked by the Lick trustees to test it for astronomical purposes. He took his telescope, and remained there during August, September, and October. Out of sixty nights he found forty-two were of the very highest class for making observations, while eleven were foggy or cloudy. He discovered forty-two new double stars while on the top of the mountain.

Professor Burnham said in his Report, "The remarkable steadiness of the air, and the continued succession of nights of almost perfect definition, are conditions not to be hoped for in any place with which I am acquainted, and judging from the previous reports of the various observatories, are not to be met with elsewhere."

Meantime, even before Congress gave the land in 1876, Mr. D. O. Mills, one of the first trustees, had visited Professor Holden and Professor Newcomb at Washington to determine about the general plans for the Observatory. It was agreed that the latter should go to Europe to investigate the matter of procuring the glass necessary for a large reflector or refractor. It was finally decided that a refracting telescope was the best for the study of double stars and nebulæ, the moon's surface, etc., giving more distinctness and brilliancy, and being less subject to atmospheric disturbance.

Professor Newcomb experienced much difficulty in Europe in finding a firm ready to undertake to make a glass for a telescope larger and more powerful than any yet made. The firm of M. Feil & Sons, Paris, was finally chosen. Professor Newcomb wrote an interesting report of the process of making the glass.

"The materials," he said, "are mixed and melted in a clay pot holding from five hundred pounds to a ton, and are constantly stirred with an iron rod until the proper combination is obtained. The heat is then slowly diminished until the glass becomes too stiff to be stirred longer. Then the mass, pot and all, is placed in the annealing furnace. Here it must remain undisturbed for a period of a month or more, when it is taken out; the pot and the outside parts of the glass are broken away to find whether a lump suitable for the required disk can be found in the interior.

"If the interior were perfectly solid and homogeneous, there would be no further difficulty; the lump would be softened by heat, pressed into a flat disk, and reannealed, when the work would be complete. But in practice, the interior is always found to be crossed in every direction by veins of unequal density, which will injure the performance of the glass; and the great mechanical difficulty in the production of the disk is to cut these veins out and still leave a mass which can be pressed into a disk without any folding of the original surface."

The glass for a telescope is usually composed of a double convex lens of crown glass, and a plano-concave lens of flint glass. M. Feil & Sons made and shipped the latter, which weighed three hundred and seventy-five pounds, but broke the crown glass in packing it. Then during three years they made twenty unsuccessful trials before obtaining a perfect glass.

The cutting away of the clay pot and outside glass is a tedious process, requiring weeks and even months. No ordinary tools can be used. The pieces are "sawed by a wire working in sand and water.... When it is done," says Professor Newcomb, "the mass must be pressed into the shape of a disk, like a very thin grindstone, and in order to do this the lump must first be heated to the melting-point, so as to become plastic. But when Feil began to heat this large mass it flew to pieces." He took more and more time for heating, and finally succeeded.

The noted firm of Alvan Clark & Sons of Cambridge, Mass., did the polishing and shaping of the lenses, a labor requiring great skill and delicacy of workmanship. The objective glass was ordered in 1880, and reached Mount Hamilton late in 1886, having cost $51,000. It weighs with its cell 638 pounds. The Clarks would not undertake any larger objective than thirty-six inches. This was six inches larger than the great glass which they had made for the Imperial Observatory at Pulkowa, near St. Petersburg in Russia.

The glass, though an important part of the telescope, was only one of many things to be obtained. In 1876 Captain Richard S. Floyd, president of the Lick trustees, himself a graduate of the United States Naval Academy, met Professor Holden in London; and the latter became the planner and adviser, throughout the construction of the buildings and the telescope. Captain Floyd visited many observatories, and carried on a vast correspondence, amounting to several thousand letters, with astronomers and opticians all over the world.

Professor Holden was a graduate of West Point, had been a professor of mathematics in the navy, one of the astronomers at the Washington Observatory, in charge of several eclipse expeditions sent out by the government for observation, a member of various scientific societies in Europe as well as America, and associate member of the Royal Astronomical Society of England, and well-fitted for the position he was afterwards called to fill,—the directorship of the Lick Observatory. For some time he was also president of the University of California.

Between the years 1880 and 1888 the large astronomical buildings were erected on the top of Mount Hamilton. The main building of red brick consists of two domes, one twenty-five feet and six inches in diameter; the other seventy-six feet in diameter, connected by a hall over one hundred and ninety-one feet long. This hall is paved and wainscoted with marble. The rooms for work and study open towards the east into this hall. The library, a handsome room with white polished ash cases and tables, also opens into it. Near the main entrance is the visitors' room, where the visitors register their names, among them many noted scientists from various parts of the world. J. H. Fickel in the *Chautauquan*, June, 1893, says, "In this room stands the workbench which Mr. Lick used in his trade, that of piano-making, while in Peru. Though not an elaborate affair, nothing attracts the attention of visitors more than this article of furniture."

The large rotating dome at the south end of the building, made by the Union Iron Works of San Francisco, is covered with sheet steel, and the movable parts weigh about eighty-nine tons. It is easily

110

handled by means of a small engine in the basement. The small dome weighs about eight tons.

Near the main building are the meridian circle house, with its instrument for measuring the declination of stars, the transit house, the astronomers' dwellings, the shops, etc.

In the smaller dome is a twelve-inch equatorial telescope made by Alvan Clark & Sons, mounted at the Lick Observatory in October, 1881. There are also at Mount Hamilton, a six-and-one-half-inch equatorial telescope, a six-and-one-half-inch meridian circle, a four-inch transit and zenith telescope, a four-inch comet-seeker, a five-inch horizontal photoheliograph, the Crocker photographic telescope, and numerous clocks, spectroscopes, chronographs, meteorological instruments, and seismometers for measuring the time and intensity of earthquake shocks.

The buildings and instruments at Mount Hamilton are imbedded in the solid rock, so as not to be affected by the high winds on the top of the mountain.

In the *Century* for March, 1894, Professor Holden gives an interesting account of earthquakes, and the instruments for measuring them at the Lick Observatory. In the Charleston earthquake of 1886, it is computed that 774,000 square miles trembled, besides a vast ocean area. The effects of the shock were noted from Florida to Vermont, and from the Carolinas to Ontario, Iowa, and Arkansas.

The science of the measurement of earthquakes had its birth in Tokio, Japan, in which country there are, on an average, two earthquake shocks daily. "Every part of the upper crust of the earth is in a state of constant change," says Professor Holden. "These changes were first discovered by their effects on the position of astronomical instruments.... The earthquake of Iquique, a seaport town of South America, in 1877, was shown at the Imperial Observatory near St. Petersburg, an hour and fourteen minutes later, by its effects on the delicate levels of an astronomical instrument. I myself have watched the changes in a hill (100 feet above a frozen lake which was 700 feet distant) as the ice bent and buckled, and changed the pressure on the adjacent shore. The level would faithfully indicate every movement: ...

"In Italy and in Japan microphones deeply buried in the earth make the earth tremors audible in the observatory telephones. During the years 1808-1888 there were 417 shocks recorded in San Francisco. The severest earthquake felt within the city of San Francisco was that of 1868. This shock threw down chimneys, broke glass along miles of streets, and put a whole population in terror." The Lick Observatory has a complete set of Professor Ewing's instruments for earthquake measurements.

Accurate time signals are sent from the Observatory every day at noon, and are received at every railway station between San Francisco and Ogden, and many other cities. The instrumental equipment of the Observatory is declared to be unrivalled.

Interest centres most of all in the great telescope under the rotating dome, for which the 36-inch objective was made with so much difficulty. The great steel tube, a little over 56 feet long, holding the lens, and weighing with all its attachments four and one-half tons, the iron pier 38 feet high, the elaborate yet delicate machinery, were all made by Warner & Swasey of Cleveland, Ohio, whose skill has brought them well-deserved fame. The entire weight of the instrument is 40 tons. Its magnifying power ranges from 180 to 3,000 diameters.

On June 1, 1888, the Observatory, with its instruments, was transferred by the Lick trustees to the University of California. The whole cost was $610,000, leaving $90,000 for endowment out of the $700,000 given by Mr. Lick.

Fourteen years had passed since Mr. Lick made his deed of trust. He lived long enough to see the site chosen and the plans made for the telescope, but died at the Lick House, Oct. 1, 1876, aged eighty. The body lay in state in Pioneer Hall, and on Oct. 4 was buried in Lone Mountain Cemetery, having been followed to the grave by a long procession of State and city officials, faculty and students of the University, and members of the various societies to which Mr. Lick had given so generously.

He had expressed a desire to be buried on Mount Hamilton, either within or near the Observatory. Therefore a tomb was made in the base of the pier of the great 36-inch telescope; "such a tomb," says Professor Holden, "as no Old World emperor could have commanded or imagined."

On Sunday, Jan. 9, 1887, the body of James Lick having been removed from the cemetery, the casket was enclosed in a lead-lined white maple coffin, and laid in the new tomb with appropriate ceremonies, witnessed by a large gathering of people. A memorial document stating that "this refracting telescope is the largest which has ever been constructed, and the astronomers who have used it declare that its performance surpasses that of all other telescopes," was engrossed on parchment in India ink, and signed by the officials. It was then placed between two finely tanned skins, backed by black silk, and soldered in a leaden box eighteen inches in length, the same in width, and one inch in thickness. This was placed upon the iron coffin, and the outer casket was soldered up air-tight. After the vault had been built up to the level of the foundation stone, a great stone weighing two and one-half tons was let down slowly upon the brick-work, beneath which was the casket. Three other stones were placed in position, and then one section was laid of the iron pier, which weighs 25 tons.

Sir Edwin Arnold, who in 1892 went to see the great telescope, and "by a personal pilgrimage to do homage to the memory of James

Lick," writes: "With my hand upon the colossal tube, slightly managing it as if it were an opera-glass, and my gaze wandering around the splendidly equipped interior, full of all needful astronomical resources, and built to stand a thousand storms, I think with admiration of its dead founder, and ask to see his tomb. It is placed immediately beneath the big telescope, which ascends and descends directly over the sarcophagus wherein repose the mortal relics of this remarkable man,—a marble chest, bearing the inscription, 'Here lies the body of James Lick.'

"Truly James Lick sleeps gloriously under the bases of his big glass! Four thousand feet nearer heaven than any of his dead fellow-citizens, he is buried more grandly than any king or queen, and has a finer monument than the pyramids furnished to Cheops and Cephrenes."

Mr. Lick wished both to help the world and to be remembered, and his wish has been gratified.

From 1888 to 1893 the Lick telescope, with its 36-inch object-glass, was the largest refracting telescope in the world. The Yerkes telescope, with its 40-inch object-glass, is now the largest in the world. It is on the shore of Lake Geneva, Wis., seventy-five miles from Chicago, and belongs to the Chicago University. It will be remembered by those who visited the World's Fair at Chicago, and saw it in the Manufactures and Liberal Arts Building. Professor George E. Hale is the director of this great observatory. The glass was furnished by Mantois of Paris, from which the lenses were made by Alvan G. Clark, the sole survivor of the famous firm of Alvan Clark & Sons. The crown-glass double convex lens weighs 200 pounds; the plano-concave lens of flint glass, nearest the eye end of the telescope, weighs over 300 pounds.

The telescope and dome were made by Warner & Swasey, who made also the 26-inch telescope at Washington, the 18-inch at the University of Pennsylvania, the 10½-inch at the University of Minnesota, the 12-inch at Columbus, Ohio, and others. Of this firm Professor C. A. Young, in the *North American Review* for February, 1896, says, "It is not too much to say that in design and workmanship their instruments do not suffer in comparison with the best foreign make, while in 'handiness' they are distinctly superior. There is no longer any necessity for us to go abroad for astronomical instruments, which are fully up to the highest standards."

The steel tube of the Yerkes telescope is 64 feet long, and the 90-foot rotating dome, also of steel, weighs nearly 150 tons. The observatory, of gray Roman brick with gray terra-cotta and stone trimmings, is in the form of a Roman cross, with three domes, the largest dome at the western end covering the great telescope. Of the two smaller domes, one will contain a 12-inch telescope, and the other a 16-inch. Professor Young says of the Yerkes telescope, "It gathers three times as much light as the 23-inch instrument at Princeton; two and three-eighths as much as the 26-inch telescopes of Washington and Charlottesville; one and four-fifths as much as the 30-inch at Pulkowa; and 23 per cent more than the gigantic, and hitherto unrivalled, 36-inch telescope of the Lick Observatory. Possibly in this one quality of 'light,' the six-foot reflector of Lord Rosse, and the later five-foot reflector of Mr. Common, might compete with or even surpass it; but as an instrument for seeing things, it is doubtful whether either of them could hold its own with even the smallest of the instruments named above, because of the reflector's inherent inferiority in distinctness of definition."

Professor Young thinks the Yerkes telescope can hardly hope for the exceptional excellence of the "seeing" at Mount Hamilton, Nice, or Ariquipa, at least at night. The magnifying power of the Yerkes telescope is so great, being from 200 to 4,000, that the moon can be brought optically within sixty miles of the observer's eye. "Any lunar object five or six hundred feet square would be distinctly visible,—a building, for instance, as large as the Capitol at Washington."

Since the death of Mr. Lick others have added to his generous gifts for the purchase of special instruments, for sending expeditions to foreign countries to observe total solar eclipses, and the like. Mrs. Phœbe Hearst has given the fund which will yield $2,000 or more each year for Hearst Fellowships in astronomy or other special work. Colonel C. F. Crocker has given a photographic telescope and dome, and provided a sum sufficient to pay the expenses of an eclipse expedition to be sent from Mount Hamilton to Japan, in August, 1896, under charge of Professor Schæberle.

Mr. Edward Crossley, a wealthy member of Parliament for Halifax, England, has given a reflector and forty-foot dome, which reached Mount Hamilton from Liverpool in the latter part of 1895.

Mr. Lick's gift of the telescope has stimulated a love for astronomical study and research, not only in California, but throughout the world. The Astronomical Society of the Pacific was founded Feb. 7, 1889; and any man or woman with genuine interest in the science was invited to join. It has a membership of over five hundred, and its publications are valuable. The society holds its summer meetings on Mount Hamilton. Very wisely, for the sake of diffusing knowledge, visitors are made welcome to Mount Hamilton every Saturday evening between the hours of seven and ten o'clock, to look through the big telescope and through the smaller ones when not in use. In five years, from June 1, 1889, to June 1, 1894, there were 33,715 visitors. Each person is shown the most interesting celestial objects, and the whole force of the Observatory is on duty, and spares no pains to make the visits both interesting and profitable.

James Lick planned wisely when he thought of his great telescope, even if he had no other wish than to be remembered and honored. Undoubtedly he did have other motives; for Professor Holden says, "A very extensive course of reading had given him the generous idea that the future well-being of the race was the object for a good man to strive to forward. Towards the end of his life, at least, the utter futility of his money to give any inner satisfaction oppressed him more and more."

The results of scientific work of the Lick Observatory have been most interesting and remarkable. Professor Edward E. Barnard discovered, Sept. 9, 1892, the fifth satellite of Jupiter, one hundred miles in diameter. He discovered nineteen comets in ten years, and has been called the "comet-seeker." He has also, says Professor Holden, made a very large number of observations "upon the physical appearance of the planets Venus, Jupiter, and Saturn; upon the zodiacal light, etc.; upon meteors, lunar eclipses, double stars, occultations of stars, etc.; and he has discovered a considerable number of new nebulæ also." Professor Barnard resigned Oct. 1, 1895, to accept the position of professor of astronomy in the University of Chicago, and is succeeded by Professor Wm. J. Hussey of the Leland Stanford Junior University.

Sir Edwin Arnold, during his visit to the Observatory, at the suggestion of Professor Campbell, looked through the great telescope upon the nebula in Orion. "I saw," he writes, "in the well-known region of 'Beta Orionis,' the vast separate system of that universe clearly outlined,—a fleecy, irregular, mysterious, windy shape, its edges whirled and curled like those of a storm-cloud, with stars and star clusters standing forth against the milky white background of the nebula like diamonds lying upon silver cloth. The central star, which to the naked eye or to a telescope of lower power looks single and of no great brilliancy, resolved itself, under the potent command of the Lick glass, into a splendid trapezium of four glittering worlds, arranged very much like those of the Southern Cross.

"At the lower right-hand border of the beautiful cosmic mist, there opens a black abyss of darkness, which has the appearance of an inky cloud about to swallow up the silvery filigree of the nebula; but this the great glass fills up with unsuspecting worlds when the photographic apparatus is fitted to it. I understood Professor Holden's views to be that we were beholding, in that almost immeasurably remote silvery haze, an entirely separated system of worlds and clusters, apart from all others, as our own system is, but inconceivably grander, larger, and more populous with suns and planets and their starry allies."

Professor John M. Schæberle, formerly of Michigan University, has discovered two or more comets, written much on solar eclipses, the "canals" of Mars, and the sun's corona. He, with Professor S. W. Burnham, went to South America to observe the solar eclipse of Dec. 21-22, 1889; and the former took observations on the solar eclipse April 16, 1893, at Mina Bronces, Chili.

Professor Burnham catalogued over one hundred and ninety-eight new double stars, which he discovered while at Mount Hamilton. He, with Professor Holden and others, have taken remarkable photographs of the moon; and the negatives have been sent to Professor Weinek of Prague, who makes enlarged drawings and photographs of them. Astronomers in Copenhagen, Vienna, Great Britain, and other parts of Europe, are working with the Lick astronomers. Star maps, in both northern and southern hemispheres, have been made at the Lick Observatory, and photographs of the milky way, the sun and its spots, comets, nebulæ, Mars, Jupiter, etc. Professor Holden has written much in the magazines, the *Century*, *McClure's*, *The Forum*, and elsewhere, concerning these photographs, "What we really know about Mars," and kindred topics.

Professor Perrine discovered a new comet in February, 1896, which for some time travelled towards the earth at the rate of 1,600,000 miles per day. Professor David P. Todd of Amherst College was enabled to make at the Lick Observatory the finest photographs ever made of the transit of Venus, Dec. 6, 1882. As there will not be another transit of Venus till Jan. 8, 2004, so that no living astronomer will ever behold another, this transit was of special importance. The transit of Mercury was also observed in 1881 by Professor Holden and others.

The equipment at the Lick Observatory is admirable, and the sight excellent; but the income from the $90,000 endowment is too small to allow the desired work. There are but seven observers at Mount Hamilton, while at Greenwich, at Paris, and other observatories, there are from forty to fifty men. The total income for salaries and all other expenses is $22,000 at the Lick Observatory; at Paris, Greenwich, Harvard College, the United States Naval Observatory at Washington, etc., from $60,000 to $100,000 is spent yearly, and is all useful. Fellowships producing $600 a year are greatly needed, to be named after the givers, and the money to provide a larger force of astronomers. Mr. Lick's great gift has been nobly begun, but funds are necessary to carry on the work.

LELAND STANFORD
AND HIS UNIVERSITY

"The biographer of Leland Stanford will have to tell the fascinating story of a career almost matchless in the splendor of its incidents. It was partly due to the circumstances of his time, but chiefly due to the largeness and boldness of his nature, that this plain, simple man succeeded in cutting so broad a swath. He lived at the top of his possibilities." Thus wrote Dr. Albert Shaw in the *Review of Reviews*, August, 1893.

Leland Stanford, farmer-boy, lawyer, railroad builder, governor, United States Senator, and munificent giver, was born at Watervliet, N.Y., eight miles from Albany, March 9, 1824. He was the fourth son in a family of seven sons and one daughter, the latter dying in infancy.

His father, Josiah Stanford, was a native of Massachusetts, but moved with his parents to the State of New York when he was a boy. He became a successful farmer, calling his farm by the attractive name of Elm Grove. He had the energy and industry which it seems Leland inherited. He built roads and bridges in the neighborhood, and was an earnest advocate of DeWitt Clinton's scheme of the Erie Canal, connecting the great lakes with New York City by way of the Hudson River.

"Gouverneur Morris had first suggested the Erie Canal in 1777," says T. W. Higginson, "and Washington had indeed proposed a system of such waterways in 1774. But the first actual work of this kind in the United States was that dug around Turner's Falls in Massachusetts soon after 1792. In 1803 DeWitt Clinton again proposed the Erie Canal. It was begun in 1817, and opened July 4, 1825, being cut mainly through a wilderness. The effect produced on public opinion was absolutely startling. When men found that the time from Albany to Buffalo was reduced one-half, and that the freight on a ton of merchandise was cut down from $100 to $10, and ultimately to $3, similar enterprises sprang into being everywhere."

People were not excited over canals only; everybody was interested about the coming railroads. George Stephenson, in the midst of the greatest opposition, landowners even driving the surveyors off their grounds, had built a road from Liverpool to Manchester, England, which was opened Sept. 15, 1830. The previous month, August, the Mohawk and Hudson River Railroad from Albany to Schenectady, sixteen miles, was commenced, a charter having been granted sometime before this. Josiah Stanford was greatly interested in this enterprise, and took large contracts for grading. Men at the Stanford home talked of the great future of railroads in America, and even prophesied a road to Oregon. "Young as he was when the question of a railroad to Oregon was first agitated," says a writer, "Leland Stanford took a lively interest in the measure. Among its chief advocates at that early day was Mr. Whitney, one of the engineers in the construction of the Mohawk and Hudson River Railway. On one occasion, when Whitney passed the night at Elm Grove, Leland being then thirteen years of age, the conversation ran largely on this overland railway project; and the effect upon the mind of such a boy may be readily imagined. The remembrance of that night's discussion between Whitney and his father never left him, but bore the grandest fruits."

The cheerful, big-hearted boy worked on his father's farm with his brothers, rising at five o'clock, even on cold winter mornings, that he might get his work done before school hours. He himself tells how he earned his first dollar. "I was about six years old," he said. "Two of my brothers and I gathered a lot of horseradish from the garden, washed it clean, took it to Schenectady, and sold it. I got two of the six shillings received. I was very proud of my money. My next financial venture was two years later. Our hired man came from Albany, and told us chestnuts were high. The boys had a lot of them on hand which we had gathered in the fall. We hurried off to market with them, and sold them for twenty-five dollars. That was a good deal of money when grown men were getting only two shillings a day."

Perhaps the boy felt that he should not always like to work on the farm, for he had made up his mind to get an education if possible. When he was eighteen his father bought a piece of woodland, and told him if he would cut off the timber he might have the money received for it. He immediately hired several persons to help him, and together they cut and piled 2,600 cords of wood, which Leland sold to the Mohawk and Hudson River Railroad at a profit of $2,600.

After using some of this money to pay for his schooling at an academy at Clinton, N.Y., he went to Albany, and for three years studied law with the firm of Wheaton, Doolittle, & Hadley. He disliked Greek and Latin, but was fond of science, particularly geology and chemistry, and was a great reader, especially of the newspapers. He attended all the lectures attainable, and was fond of discussion upon all progressive topics. Later in life he studied sociological matters, and read John Stuart Mill and Herbert Spencer.

Young Stanford determined to try his fortune in the West. He went as far as Chicago, and found it low, marshy, and unattractive. This was in 1848, when he was twenty-four years old. The town had been organized but fifteen years, and did not have much to boast of. There were only twenty-eight voters in Chicago in 1833. In 1837 the entire population was 4,470. Chicago had grown rapidly by 1848; but mosquitoes were abundant, and towns farther up Lake Michigan gave better promise for the future. Mr. Stanford finally settled at Port Washington, Wis., above Milwaukee, which place it was thought would prove a rival of Chicago. Forty years later, in 1890, Port Washington had a population of 1,659, while Chicago had increased to 1,099,850.

Mr. Stanford did well the first year at Port Washington, earning $1,260. He remained another year, and then, at twenty-six, went back to Albany to marry Miss Jane Lathrop, daughter of Mr. Dyer Lathrop, a respected merchant. They returned to Port Washington, but Mr. Stanford did not find the work of a country lawyer congenial. He had chosen his profession, however, and would have gone on to a measure of success in it, probably, had not an accident opened up a new field.

He had been back from his wedding journey but a year or more, when a fire swept away all his possessions, including a quite valuable law library. The young couple were really bankrupt, but they determined not to return to Albany for a home.

Several of Mr. Stanford's brothers had gone to California in 1849, after the gold-fields were discovered, and had opened stores near the mining-camps. If Leland were to join them, it would give him at least more variety than the quiet life at Port Washington. The young wife went back to Albany to care for three years for her invalid father, who died in April, 1855. The husband sailed from New York, spending twelve days in crossing the isthmus, and in thirty-eight days reached San Francisco, July 12, 1852. For four years he had charge of a branch store at Michigan Bluffs, Placer County, among the miners.

He engaged also in mining, and was not afraid of the labor and privations of the camp. He said some years later, "The true history of the Argonauts of the nineteenth century has to be written. They had no Jason to lead them, no oracles to prophesy success nor enchantments to avert dangers; but, like self-reliant Americans, they pressed forward to the land of promise, and travelled thousands of miles, when the Greek heroes travelled hundreds. They went by ship and by wagon, on horseback and on foot; a mighty army, passing over mountains and deserts, enduring privations and sickness; they were the creators of a commonwealth, the builders of states."

Mr. Stanford had the energy of his father; he had learned how to work while on the farm, and he had a pleasant and kindly manner to all. Said a friend of his, after Mr. Stanford had become the governor of a great State, and the possessor of many millions, "The man who held the throttle of the locomotive, he who handled the train, worked the brake, laid the rail, or shovelled the sand, was his comrade, friend, and equal. His life was one of tender, thoughtful compassion for the man less fortunate in life than himself."

The young lawyer was making money, and a good reputation as well, in the mining-camps. Says an old associate, "Mr. Stanford in an unusual degree commanded the respect of the heterogeneous lot of men who composed the mining classes, and was frequently referred to by them as a sort of arbitrator in settling their disputes for them. While at Michigan Bluffs he was elected a justice of the peace, which office was the court before which all disputes and contentions of the miners and their claims were settled. It is a singular fact, with all the questions that came before him for settlement, not one of them was appealed to a higher court.

"Leland Stanford was at this time just as gentle in his manner and as cordial and respectful to all as in his later years. Yet he was possessed of a courage which, when tested, as occasion sometimes required, satisfied the rough element that he was not a man who could be imposed upon. His principle seemed to be to stand up for the right at all times. He never indulged in profanity or coarse words of any kind, and was as considerate in his conduct when holding intercourse with the rough element as though in the midst of the highest refinement."

Mr. Stanford had prospered so well that in 1855 he purchased the business of his brothers in Sacramento, and went East to bring his wife to the Pacific Coast. He studied his business carefully. He made himself conversant with the statistics of trade, the tariff laws, the best markets and means of transportation. He read and thought, while some others idled away their hours. He was deeply interested in the new Republican party, which was then in the minority in California. He believed in it, and worked earnestly for it. When the party was organized in the State in 1856, he was one of the founders of it. He became a candidate for State treasurer, and was defeated. Three years later he was nominated for governor; "but the party was too small to have any chance, and the contest lay between opposing Democratic factions." Mr. Stanford was to learn how to win success against fires and political defeats.

A year later he was a delegate at large to the Republican National Convention; and instead of supporting Mr. Seward, who was from his own State of New York, he worked earnestly for Abraham Lincoln, with whom he formed a lasting friendship. After Mr. Lincoln was inaugurated, Mr. Stanford remained in Washington several weeks, at the request of the president and Secretary Seward, to confer with them about the surest means of keeping California loyal to the Union.

Mr. Blaine says of California and Oregon at this time: "Jefferson Davis had expected, with a confidence amounting to certainty, and based, it is believed, on personal pledges, that the Pacific Coast, if it did not actually join the South, would be disloyal to the Union, and would, from its remoteness and its superlative importance, require a large contingent of the national forces to hold it in subjection.

"It was expected by the South that California and Oregon would give at least as much trouble as Kentucky and Missouri, and would thus indirectly, but powerfully, aid the Southern cause."

120

In the spring of 1861 Mr. Stanford was again nominated by the Republicans for governor. Though he declined at first, after he had consented, with his usual vigor, earnestness, and perseverance, with faith in himself and his fellow-men as well, he and his friends made a thorough and spirited canvass; and Mr. Stanford received 56,036 votes, about six times as many as were given him two years before.

"The period," says the San Francisco *Chronicle*, "was one of unexampled difficulty of administration; and to add to the embarrassments occasioned by the Civil War, the city of Sacramento and a vast area of the valley were inundated. On the day appointed for the inauguration the streets of Sacramento were swept by a flood, and Mr. Stanford and his friends were compelled to go and return to the Capitol in boats. The messages of Governor Stanford, and indeed all his state papers, indicated wide information, great common-sense, and a comprehensive grasp of State and national affairs, remarkable in one who had never before held office under either the State or national government. During his administration he kept up constant and cordial intercourse with Washington, and had the satisfaction of leaving the chair of state at the close of his term of office feeling that no State in the Union was more thoroughly loyal."

There was much disloyalty in California at first, but Mr. Stanford was firm as well as conciliatory. The militia was organized, a State normal school was established, and the indebtedness of the State reduced one-half under his leadership as governor.

After the war was over, Governor Stanford cherished no animosities. When Mr. Lamar's name was sent to the Senate as associate justice of the Supreme Court, and many were opposed, Mr. Stanford said, "No man sympathized more sincerely than myself with the cause of the Union, or deprecated more the cause of the South. I would have given fortune and life to have defeated that cause. But the war has terminated, and what this country needs now is absolute and profound peace. Lamar was a representative Southern man, and adhered to the convictions of his boyhood and manhood. There never can be pacification in this country until these war memories are obliterated by the action of the Executive and of Congress."

Mr. Stanford declined a re-election to the governorship, because he wished to give his time to the building of a railroad across the continent. He had never forgotten the conversation in his father's home about a railroad to Oregon. When he went back to Albany for Mrs. Stanford, after being a storekeeper among the mines, and she was ill from the tiresome journey, he cheered her with the promise, "Never mind; a time will come when I will build a railroad for you to go home on."

Every one knew that a railroad was needed. Vessels had to go around Cape Horn, and troops and produce had to be transported over

121

the mountains and across the plains at great expense and much hardship. Some persons believed the building of a road over the snow-capped Sierra Nevada Mountains was possible; but most laughed the project to scorn, and denounced it as "a wild scheme of visionary cranks."

"The huge snow-clad chain of the Sierra Nevadas," says Mr. Perkins, the senator from California who succeeded Mr. Stanford, "whose towering steeps nowhere permitted a thoroughfare at an elevation less than seven thousand feet above the sea, must be crossed; great deserts, waterless, and roamed by savage tribes, must be made accessible; vast sums of money must be raised, and national aid secured at a time in which the credit of the central government had fallen so low that its bonds of guaranty to the undertaking sold for barely one-third their face value."

In the presence of such obstacles no one seemed ready to undertake the work of building the railroad. One of the persistent advocates of the plan was Theodore J. Judah, the engineer of the Sacramento Valley and other local railroads. He had convinced Mr. Stanford that the thing was possible. The latter first talked with C. P. Huntington, a hardware merchant of Sacramento; then with Mark Hopkins, Mr. Huntington's partner, and later with Charles Crocker and others. A fund was raised to enable Mr. Judah and his associates to perfect their surveys; and the Central Pacific Railroad Company was formed, June 28, 1861, with Mr. Stanford as president.

In Mr. Stanford's inaugural address as governor he had dwelt upon the necessity of this railroad to unite the East and the West; and now that he had retired from the gubernatorial office, he determined to push the enterprise with all his power. Neither he nor his associates had any great wealth at their command, but they had faith and force of character. The aid of Congress was sought and obtained by a strictly party vote, Republicans being in the majority; and the bill was signed by President Lincoln, July 1, 1862.

The government agreed to give the company the alternate sections of 640 acres in a belt of land ten miles wide on each side of the railroad, and $16,000 per mile in bonds for the easily constructed portion of the road, and $32,000 and $48,000 per mile for the mountainous portions. The company was to build forty miles before it received government aid.

It was so difficult to raise money during the Civil War that Congress made a more liberal grant July 2, 1864, whereby the company received alternate sections of land within a belt twenty miles on each side of the road, or the large amount of 12,800 acres per mile, making for the company nearly 9,000,000 acres of land. The government was to retain, to apply on its debt, only half the money it owed the company for transportation instead of the whole. The most important provision of the new Act was the authority of the company to issue its own first-mortgage bonds to an amount not exceeding those of the United States, and making the latter take a second mortgage.

There is no question but the United States has given lavishly to railroads, as the cities have given their streets free to street railroads; but during the Civil War the need of communication between East and West seemed to make it wise to build the road at almost any sacrifice. Mr. Blaine says, "Many capitalists who afterwards indulged in denunciations of Congress for the extravagance of the grants, were urged at the time to take a share in the scheme, but declined because of the great risk involved."

Mr. Stanford broke ground for the railroad by turning the first shovelful of earth early in 1863. "At times failure seemed inevitable," says the New York *Tribune*, June 22, 1893. "Even the stout-hearted Crocker declared that there were times when he would have been glad to 'lose all and quit;' but the iron will of Stanford triumphed over everything. As president of the road he superintended its construction over the mountains, building 530 miles in 293 days. On the last day, Crocker laid the rails on more than ten miles of track. That the great railroad builders survived the ordeal is a marvel. Crocker, indeed, never recovered from the effects of the terrific strain. He died in 1888. Hopkins died twelve years before, in 1876."

With a silver hammer Governor Stanford drove a golden spike at Promontory Point, Utah, May 10, 1869, which completed the line of the Central Pacific, and joined it with the Union Pacific Railroad, and the telegraph flashed the news from the Atlantic to the Pacific. The Union Pacific was built from Omaha, Neb., to Promontory Point, though Ogden, Utah, fifty-two miles east of Promontory Point, is now considered the dividing line.

After this road was completed, Mr. Stanford turned to other labors. He was made president or director of several railroads,—the Southern Pacific, the California & Oregon, and other connecting lines. He was also president of the Oriental and Occidental Steamship Company, which plied between San Francisco and Chinese ports, and was interested in street railroads, woollen mills, and the manufacture of sugar.

Foreseeing the great future of California, he purchased very large tracts of land, including Vina with nearly 60,000 acres, the Gridley Ranch with 22,000 acres, and his summer home, Palo Alto, thirty miles from San Francisco, with 8,400 acres. He built a stately home in San Francisco costing over $1,000,000, and in his journeys abroad collected for it costly paintings and other works of art.

But his chief delight was in his Palo Alto estate. Here he sought to plant every variety of tree, from the world over, that would grow in

California. Many thousands were set out each year. He was a great lover of trees, and could tell the various kinds from the bark or leaf.

He loved animals, especially the horse, and had the largest horse farm for raising horses in the world. Some of his remarkable thoroughbreds and trotters were Electioneer, Arion, Palo Alto, Sunol, "the flying filly," Racine, Piedmont that cost $30,000, and many others. He spent $40,000, it is said, in experiments in instantaneous photography of the horse; and a book resulted, "The Horse in Motion," which showed that the ideas of painters about a horse at high speed were usually wrong. No one was ever allowed to kick or whip a horse or destroy a bird on the estate. Mr. George T. Angell of Boston tells of the remark made to General Francis A. Walker by Mr. Stanford. The horses of the latter were so gentle that they would put their noses on his shoulder, or come up to visitors to be petted. "How do you contrive to have your horses so gentle?" asked General Walker. "I never allow a man to *speak* unkindly to one of my horses; and if a man *swears* at one of them, I discharge him," was the reply. There were large greenhouses and vegetable gardens at Palo Alto, and acres of wheat, rye, oats, and barley. But the most interesting and beautiful and highly prized of all the charms at Palo Alto was an only child, a lad named Leland Stanford, Jr. He was never a rugged boy; but his sunny, generous nature and intellectual qualities gave great promise of future usefulness. Mrs. Sallie Joy White, in the January, 1892, *Wide Awake*, tells some interesting things about him. She says, "His chosen playmate was a little lame boy, the son of people in moderate circumstances, who lived near the Stanfords in San Francisco. The two were together almost constantly, and each was at home in the other's house. He was very considerate of his little playfellow, and constituted himself his protector."

When Mrs. Sarah B. Cooper was making efforts to raise money for the free kindergarten work in San Francisco suggested by Felix Adler in 1878, she called on Mrs. Stanford, and the boy Leland heard the story of the needs of poor children. Putting his hand in his mother's, he said, "Mamma, we must help those children."

"Well, Leland," said his mother, "what do you wish me to do?"

"Give Mrs. Cooper $500 now, and let her start a school, then come to us for more." And Leland's wish was gratified.

"Between this time, 1879, and 1892," says Miss M. V. Lewis in the *Home Maker* for January, 1892, "Mrs. Leland Stanford has given $160,000, including a permanent endowment fund of $100,000 for the San Francisco kindergartens." She supports seven or more, five in San Francisco, and two at Palo Alto.

A writer in the press says, "Her name is down for $8,000 a year for these schools, and I am told she spends much more. I attended a reception given her by the eight schools under her patronage; and it was a very affecting sight to watch these four hundred children, all under four years of age, marching into the hall and up to their benefactor, each tiny hand grasping a fragrant rose which was deposited in Mrs. Stanford's lap. These children are gathered from the slums of the city. It is far wiser to establish schools for the training of such as these, than to wait until sin and crime have done their work, and then make a great show of trying to reclaim them through reformatory institutions."

Leland, Jr., was very fond of animals. Mrs. White tells this story: "One day, when he was about ten years of age, he was standing looking out of the window, and his mother heard a tumult outside, and saw Leland suddenly dash out of the house, down the steps, into a crowd of boys in front of the house. Presently he reappeared covered with dust, holding a homely yellow dog in his arms. Quick as a flash he was up the steps and into the house with the door shut behind him, while a perfect howl of rage went up from the boys outside.

"Before his mother could reach him he had flown to the telephone, and summoned the family doctor. Thinking from the agonized tones of the boy that some of the family had been taken suddenly and violently ill, the doctor hastened to the house.

"He was a stately old gentleman, who believed fully in the dignity of his profession; and he was somewhat disconcerted and a good deal annoyed at being confronted with a very dusty, excited boy, holding a broken-legged dog that was evidently of the mongrel family. At first he was about to be angry; but the earnest, pleading look on the little face, and the perfect innocence of any intent of discourtesy, disarmed the dignified doctor, and he explained to Leland that he did not understand the case, not being accustomed to treating dogs, but that he would take him and the dog to one who was. So they went, doctor, boy, and dog, in the doctor's carriage to a veterinary surgeon, the leg was set, and they returned home. Leland took the most faithful care of the dog until it recovered, and it repaid him with a devotion that was touching."

Leland, knowing that he was to be the heir of many millions, was already thinking how some of the money should be used. He had begun to gather materials for a museum, to which the parents devoted two rooms in their San Francisco home. He was fitting himself for Yale College, was excellent in French and German, and greatly interested in art and archæology. Before entering upon the long course of study at college, he travelled with his parents abroad. In Athens, in London, on the Bosphorus, everywhere, with an open hand, his parents allowed him to gather treasures for his museum, and for a larger institution which he had in mind to establish sometime.

While staying for a while in Rome, symptoms of fever developed in young Leland, and he was taken at once to Florence. The best medical skill was of no avail; and he soon died, March 13, 1884, two

125

months before his sixteenth birthday. His parents telegraphed this sad message home, "Our darling boy went to heaven this morning."

The story is told that while watching by the bedside of his son, worn with care and anxiety, Governor Stanford fell asleep, and dreamed that his son said to him, "Father, don't say you have nothing to live for; you have a great deal to live for. Live for humanity, father," and that this dream proved a comforter.

The almost prostrated parents brought home their beloved boy to bury him at Palo Alto. On Thanksgiving Day, Thursday, Nov. 27, 1884, the doors of the tomb which had been prepared near the house were opened at noon, and Leland Stanford, Jr., was laid away for all time from the sight of those who loved him. The bearers were sixteen of the oldest employees on the Palo Alto farm. The sarcophagus in which Leland, Jr., sleeps is eight feet four inches long, four feet wide, and three feet six inches high, built of pressed bricks, with slabs of white Carrara marble one inch thick firmly fastened to the bricks with cement. In the front slab of this sarcophagus are cut these words:—

BORN IN MORTALITY
MAY 14, 1868,
LELAND STANFORD, JR.
PASSED TO IMMORTALITY
MARCH 13, 1884.

Electric wires were placed in the walls of the tomb, in the doors of iron, and even in the foundations, so that no sacrilegious hand should disturb the repose of the sleeper without detection. Memorial services for young Leland were held in Grace Church, San Francisco, on the morning of Sunday, Nov. 30, 1884, the Rev. Dr. J. P. Newman of New York preaching an eloquent sermon. The floral decorations were exquisite; one bower fifteen feet high with four floral posts supporting floral arches, a cross six feet high of white camellias, lilies, and tuberoses, relieved by scarlet and crimson buds, and pillows and wreaths of great beauty.

"Nature had highly favored him for some noble purpose," said Dr. Newman. "Although so young, he was tall and graceful as some Apollo Belvidere, with classic features some master would have chosen to chisel in marble or cast in bronze; with eyes soft and gentle as an angel's, yet dreamy as the vision of a seer; with broad, white forehead, home of a radiant soul.... He was more than a son to his parents,—he was their companion. He was as an angel in his mother's sick room, wherein he would sit for hours and talk of all he had seen, and would cheer her hope of returning health by the assurance that he had prayed on his knees for her recovery on each of the twenty-four steps of the Scala Santa in Rome, and that when he was but eleven years old...."

126

"He had selected, catalogued, and described for his projected museum seventeen cases of antique glass vases, bronze work, and terra-cotta statuettes, dating back far into the centuries, and which illustrate the creative genius of those early ages of our race."

Such a youth wasted no time in foolish pleasures or useless companions. Like his father he loved history, and sought out, says Dr. Newman, the place where Pericles had spoken, and Socrates died; "reverently pausing on Mars Hill where St. Paul had preached 'Jesus and the Resurrection;' and lingering with strange delight in the temple of Eleusis wherein death kissed his cheek into a consuming fire."

At the close of Dr. Newman's memorial address the favorite hymn of young Leland was sung, "Tell Me the Old, Old Story." From this crushing blow of his son's death Mr. Stanford never recovered. For years young Leland's room in the San Francisco home was kept ready and in waiting, the lamp dimly lighted at night, and the bedclothes turned back by loving hands as if he were coming back again. The horses the boy used to ride were kept unused in pasture at Palo Alto, and cared for, for the sake of their fair young owner. The little yellow dog whose broken leg was set was left at Palo Alto when the boy went to Europe with his parents. When he was brought back a corpse, the dog knew all too well the story of the bereavement. After the body was placed in the tomb, the faithful creature took his place in front of the door. He could not be coaxed away even for his food, and one morning he was found there dead. He was buried near his devoted human friend.

"Toots," an old black and tan whom young Leland had brought from Albany, was much beloved. "Mr. Stanford would not allow a dog in the house save this one," says a writer in the San Francisco *Chronicle*. "'Toots' was an exception, and he had full run of the house. He was the envy of all the dogs, even of the noble old Great Dane. 'Toots' would climb upon the sofa alongside of Mr. Stanford, and forgetting a well-known repugnance he would pet him and say, 'There is always a place for you; always a place for you.'"

The year following the death of young Leland, on Nov. 14, 1885, Mr. Stanford and his wife founded and endowed their great University at Palo Alto. In conveying the estates to the trustees, Mr. Stanford said, "Since the idea of establishing an institution of this kind for the benefit of mankind came directly and largely from our son and only child, Leland, and in the belief that had he been spared to advise us as to the disposition of our estate he would have desired the devotion of a large portion thereof to this purpose, we will that for all time to come the institution hereby founded shall bear his name, and shall be known as the 'Leland Stanford, Jr., University.'"

Mr. Stanford and his wife visited various institutions of learning throughout the country, and found consolation in raising this noble monument to a noble son—infinitely to be preferred to shafts or statues of marble and bronze.

This same year, 1885, Mr. Stanford's friends, fearing the effect of his sorrow, and hoping to divert him somewhat from it, secured his election by the California Legislature to the United States Senate. He took his seat March 4, 1885, just a year after the death of his son. He did not make many speeches, but he proved a very useful member from his good sense and counsel and kindly leaning toward all helpful legislation for the poor and the unfortunate. He was re-elected March 3, 1891, for a second term of six years.

He will be most remembered in Congress for his Land-Loan Bill which he originated and presented to the Senate. "The bill proposed that money should be issued upon land to half the amount of its value, and for such loan the government was to receive an annual interest of two per cent per annum."

"Whatever may be thought by some of the practical utility of his financial scheme," says Mr. Mitchell, a senator from Oregon, "which he so earnestly and ably advocated, and which was approved by millions of his countrymen, for the loaning of money by the United States direct to the people at a low rate of interest, taking mortgages on farms as security, all will now agree it indicated in unmistakable terms a philanthropic spirit, an earnest desire to aid, through the instrumentality of what he regarded as constitutional and proper governmental influence, not the great moneyed institutions of the country, not the vast corporations of the land, with several of which he was prominently identified in a business way, but rather the great masses of producers,—the farmers, the planters, and the wage-workers of his country."

In this connection the suggestion of Professor Richard T. Ely in his book on "Socialism and Social Reform," page 334, might well be heeded. After showing that Germany and other countries have used government credit to some extent in behalf of the farming community, and that New York State has been making loans to farmers for a generation or more, he says, "A sensible demand on the part of farmers' organizations would be that Congress should appoint a commission of experts to investigate thoroughly the use of government credit in various countries and at different times, in behalf of the individual citizen, especially the farmer, and to make a full and complete report, in order that anything which is done should be based upon the lessons to be derived from actual experience."

Mr. and Mrs. Stanford were much beloved in Washington for their cordiality and generosity. They gave an annual dinner to the Senate pages, with a gift for each boy of a gold scarf-pin, or something attractive, and at Christmas a five-dollar gold-piece to each. Also a luncheon each winter, and gifts of money, gloves, etc., to the telegraph and messenger boys. Every orphan asylum and charity hospital in Washington was remembered at Christmas. Mr. Sibley, representative for Pennsylvania, relates this incident showing Mr. Stanford's habit of giving. "My partner and myself had purchased a young colt of him, for which we paid him $12,500. He took out his check-book, drew two checks of $6,250 each, and sent them to two different city homes for friendless children; and with a twinkle in his eye, and broadly beaming benevolence in his features, said, 'Electric Bell ought to make a great horse; he starts in making so many people happy in the very beginning of his life.'"

Mr. Daniels of Virginia tells how Mr. Stanford was observed one day by a friend to give $2,000 to an inventor who was trying to apply an electric motor to the sewing-machine. Mr. Stanford remarked, "This is the thirtieth man to whom I have given a like sum to develop that idea."

After Mr. Stanford had been in the Senate two years, on May 14, 1887, he and Mrs. Stanford laid the corner-stone of their University at Palo Alto, on the 19th anniversary of the birthday of Leland Stanford, Jr. In less than four years, on October 1, 1891, the doors of the University were opened to receive five hundred students, young men and women; for Mr. Stanford had written in his grant of endowment "to afford equal facilities and give equal advantages in the University to both sexes." In his address to the trustees he said, "The rights of one sex, political or otherwise, are the same as those of the other sex, and this equality of rights ought to be fully recognized."

Mrs. Stanford said to Mrs. White as they sat in her library at Palo Alto, "Whatever the boys have, the girls have as well. We mean that the girls of our country shall have a fair chance. There shall be no dividing line in the studies. If a girl desires to become an electrician, she shall have the opportunity, and that opportunity shall be the same as the young men's. If she wishes to study mechanics, she may do it."

Mr. Stanford said in his address on the day of opening, "I speak for Mrs. Stanford as well as for myself, for she has been my active and sympathetic coadjutor, and is co-grantor with me in the endowment and establishment of this University."

They had been urged to give their fortune in other directions, as some persons believed that much education would unfit people for labor. "We do not believe," said Mr. Stanford, and the world honors him for his belief, "there can be superfluous education. As man cannot have too much health and intelligence, so he cannot be too highly educated. Whether in the discharge of responsible or humble duties he will ever find the knowledge he has acquired through education, not only of practical assistance to him, but a factor in his personal happiness, and a joy forever."

Mr. Stanford desired that the students should "not only be

scholars, but have a sound practical idea of commonplace, every-day matters, a self-reliance that will fit them, in case of emergency, to earn their own livelihood in an humble as well as an exalted sphere." To this end he provided, besides the usual studies in colleges, for "mechanical institutes, laboratories, etc." There are departments of civil engineering, mechanical engineering, electrical engineering, besides shorthand and typewriting, agriculture, and other practical work.

He wished to have taught in the University "the right and advantages of association and co-operation. ... Laws should be formed to protect and develop co-operative associations. Laws with this object in view will furnish to the poor man complete protection against the monopoly of the rich; and such laws, properly administered and availed of, will insure to the workers of the country the full fruits of their industry and enterprise."

He gave directions that "no drinking saloons shall be opened upon any part of the premises." He "prohibited sectarian instruction," but wished "to have taught in the University the immortality of the soul, the existence of an all-wise and benevolent Creator, and that obedience to His laws is the highest duty of man." Mr. Stanford said, "It seems to us that the welfare of man on earth depends on the belief in immortality, and that the advantages of every good act and the disadvantages of every evil one follow man from this life into the next, there attaching to him as certainly as individuality is maintained."

The object of the University is, he said, "to qualify students for personal success and direct usefulness in life." Again he said, "The object is not alone to give the student a technical education, fitting him for a successful business life, but it is also to instil into his mind an appreciation of the blessings of this government, a reverence for its institutions, and a love for God and humanity."

Mr. Stanford wished plain and substantial buildings, "built as needed and no faster," urging the trustees to bear in mind "that extensive and expensive buildings do not make a university; that it depends for its success rather upon the character and attainments of its faculty."

Mr. Stanford chose for the president of his University David Starr Jordan, well-known for his scientific work and his various books. Though a comparatively young man, being forty years of age, Dr. Jordan had had wide experience. He was graduated from Cornell University in 1872, and for two years was professor at institutions in Illinois and Wisconsin. In 1874 he was lecturer in marine botany at the Anderson School at Penikese, and the following year at the Harvard Summer School at Cumberland Gap. During the next four years, while holding the chair of biology in Butler University, Indianapolis, he was the naturalist of two geological surveys in Indiana and Ohio. For six years he was professor of zoölogy in Indiana University, and for the six years following its president. For fourteen years he had been assistant to the United States Fish Commission, exploring many of our rivers, and part of that time agent for the United States Census Bureau in investigating the marine industries of the Pacific Coast. He had studied also in the large museums abroad.

Dr. Albert Shaw tells this interesting incident. "President Jordan had once met the young Stanford boy on the seashore, and won the lad's gratitude by telling him of shells and submarine life. It was a singular coincidence that the parents afterwards heard Dr. Jordan make allusions in a public address which gave them the knowledge that this was the interesting stranger who had taught their son so much, and had so enkindled the boy's enthusiasm. His choice as president was an eminently wise one."

Mr. Stanford wished ten acres to be set aside "as a place of burial and of last rest on earth for the bodies of the grantors and of their son, Leland Stanford, Jr., and, as the board may direct, for the bodies of such other persons who may have been connected with the University."

Mr. Stanford lived to see his University opened and doing successful work. The plan of its buildings, suggested by the old Spanish Missions of California, was originally that of Richardson, the noted architect of Boston; but as he died before it was completed, the work was done by his successors, Shepley, Rutan, & Coolidge.

The plan contemplates a number of quadrangles in the midst of 8,400 acres. "The central group of buildings will constitute two quadrangles, one entirely surrounding the other," says the *University Register* for 1894—1895. "Of these the inner quadrangle, with the exception of the chapel, is now completed. Its twelve one-story buildings are connected by a continuous open arcade, facing a paved court 586 feet long by 246 feet wide, or three and a quarter acres. The buildings are of a buff sandstone, somewhat varied in color. The stonework is of broken ashlar, with rough rock face, and the roofs are covered with red tile." Within the quadrangle are several circular beds of semi-tropical trees and plants.

Miss Milicent W. Shinn, in the *Overland Monthly* for October, 1891, says, "I should think it hard to say too much of the simple dignity, the calm influence on mind and mood, of the great, bright court, the deep arcade with its long vista of columns and arches, the heavy walls, the unchanging stone surfaces. They seemed to me like the rock walls of nature; they drew me back, and made me homesick for them when I had gone away."

Behind the central quadrangle are the shops, foundry, and boiler-house. On the east side is Encina Hall, a dormitory for 315 men, provided with electric lights, steam heat, and bathrooms on each floor. It is four stories high, and, like the quadrangle, of buff Almaden sandstone.

131

On the west side of the quadrangle is Roble Hall, for one hundred young women, and is built of concrete. There are two gymnasiums, called Encina and Roble gymnasiums.

Perhaps the most interesting of all the buildings, the especial gift of Mrs. Stanford, is the Leland Stanford Junior Museum, of concrete, in Greek style of architecture, 313 by 156 feet, including wings, situated a quarter of a mile from the quadrangle, and between the University and the Stanford residence. The collection made by young Leland is placed here, and his own arrangement reproduced. The collection includes Egyptian bronzes, Greek and Roman glass and statues. The Cesnola collection contains five thousand pieces of Greek and Roman pottery and glass. The Egyptian collection, made by Brugsch Bey, Curator of the Gizeh Museum, for Mrs. Stanford, comprises casts of statuary, mummies, scarabees, etc. Mr. Timothy Hopkins of San Francisco, one of the trustees, has given for the Egyptian collection embroideries dating from the sixth to the twenty-first dynasty. He has also given a collection of ancient and modern coins and costumes, household goods, etc., from Corea. There are stone implements from Copenhagen, Denmark, and relics from the mounds of America. Mrs. Stanford is making the collection of fine arts, and a very large number of copies of great paintings is intended. Much attention will be given to local history, Indian antiquities, and Spanish settlements of early California.

The library has 23,000 volumes and 6,000 pamphlets. Mr. Hopkins has given a valuable collection of railway books, unusually rich in the early history of railways in Europe and America, with generous provision for its increase. Mr. Hopkins has also founded the Hopkins Seaside Laboratory at Pacific Grove, two miles west of Monterey, to provide for investigations in marine biology, as a branch of the biological work of the University.

Students are not received into the University under sixteen years of age, and if special students, not under twenty, and must present certificates of good moral character. If from other colleges they must bring letters of honorable dismissal. They are offered a choice of twenty-two subjects for entrance examination, and must pass in twelve subjects. *Tuition in all departments is free.*

"The degree of Bachelor of Arts is granted to students who have satisfactorily completed the equivalent of four years' work of 15 hours of lecture or recitation weekly, or a total of 120 hours, and who have also satisfied the requirements in major and minor subjects."

President Jordan says, in the *Educational Review* for June, 1892: "In the arrangement of the courses of study two ideas are prominent: first, that every student who shall complete a course in the University must be thoroughly trained in some line of work. His education must have as its central axis an accurate and full knowledge of something. The second is that the degree to be received is wholly a subordinate matter, and that no student should be compelled to turn out of his way in order to secure it. The elective system is subjected to a single check. In order to prevent undue scattering, the student is required to select the work in general of some one professor as major subject or specialty, and to pursue this subject or line of subjects as far as the professor in charge may deem it wise or expedient. In order that all courses and all departments may be placed on exactly the same level, the degree of Bachelor of Arts is given in all alike for the equivalent of the four years' course. Should his major subject, for instance, be Greek, then the title is given that of Bachelor of Arts in Greek; should the major subject be chemistry, Bachelor of Arts in chemistry, and so on."

In 1895 there were 1,100 students in the University, of whom 728 were men, and 372 women. Several of the students are from the New England States.

Mr. Stanford spent over a million dollars in the University buildings, and gave as an endowment over 89,000 acres of land valued at more than five million dollars. The Palo Alto estate has 8,400 acres; the Vina estate, 59,000 acres, with over 4,000 acres planted to grapes which are made into wine—those of us who are total abstainers regret such use; and the Gridley estate 22,000 acres, one of California's great wheat farms. In years to come it is hoped that these properties, which are never to be sold, will so increase in value that they will be worth several times five millions.

Mr. and Mrs. Stanford made their wills, giving to the University "additional property," that the endowment, as Mr. Stanford said, "will be ample to establish and maintain a university of the highest grade." It has been stated, frequently, that the "full endowment" in land and money will be $20,000,000 or more.

Senator Stanford's death came suddenly at the last, at Palo Alto, Tuesday, June 20-21, 1893. He had not been well for some time; but Tuesday he had driven about the estate, with his usual interest and good cheer. He retired to rest about ten o'clock; and at midnight his wife, who occupied an adjoining apartment, heard a movement as if Mr. Stanford were making an effort to rise. She spoke to him, but received no answer. His breathing was unnatural; and in a few minutes he passed away, apparently without pain.

Mr. Stanford was buried at Palo Alto, Saturday, June 24. The body lay in the library of his home, in a black cloth-covered casket, with these words on the silver plate:—

LELAND STANFORD.
BORN TO MORTALITY MARCH 9, 1824.
PASSED TO IMMORTALITY, JUNE 21, 1893.
AGED 69 YRS., 3 MOS., 12 DAYS.

Flowers filled every part of the library. The Union League Club sent a floral piece representing the Stars and Stripes worked in red and white in "everlasting," with star lilies on a ground of violets. There was a triple arch of white and pink flowers representing the central arch of the main University building. There were wreaths and crosses and a broken wheel of carnations, hollyhocks, violets, white peas, and ferns.

At half-past one, after all the employees had taken their last look of the man who had always been their friend,—one, seventy-six years old, who had worked with Mr. Stanford in the mine, broke down completely,—the body was borne to the quadrangle of the University by eight of the oldest engineers in point of service on the Southern Pacific Railroad. The funeral *cortège* passed through a double line of the two hundred or more employees at Palo Alto, several Chinese laborers being at the end of the line. Senator Stanford was always opposed to any legislation against the Chinese.

The body was placed on a platform at one end of the quadrangle, the remaining space being filled with several thousand persons. About sixteen hundred chairs were provided, but these could accommodate only a small portion of those present. The platform was decorated with ferns, smilax, white sweet peas, and thousands of St. Joseph's lilies. The temporary chancel was flanked by two remarkable flower pieces: on the left, a *fac-simile* of the first locomotive ever purchased and operated on the Central Pacific Railroad, the "Governor Stanford," sent by the employees of the company. The boiler and smoke-stack were of mauve-colored sweet peas; the headlight and bell were of yellow pansies; the cab of white sweet peas bordered by yellow pansies; the tender of white sweet peas edged by pansies and lined with ivy; on the side of the cab, in heliotrope, the name Governor Stanford. On the right of the bier was the gift of the employees of the Palo Alto stock-farm, a representation in sweet peas of the senator's favorite bay horse.

After the burial service of the Episcopal Church, a solo, "O sweet and blessed country," and address by Dr. Horatio Stebbins of the First Unitarian Church of San Francisco, the choir sang "Lead Kindly Light," and the body of Senator Stanford was conveyed through the cypress avenue to the mausoleum in the ten acres adjoining the residence grounds. The tomb is in the form of a Greek temple lined with white marble, guarded by a sphinx on either side of the entrance.

Here beside the open doors stood another beautiful floral tribute, a shield eight feet high, of roses, lilies, and other flowers sent by the employees of the Sacramento Railroad shops. Worked in violets were the words "The Laborers' Tribute to the Laborers' Friend." The choir sang, "Abide with Me," the body was laid in the tomb, and the bronze doors were closed. A few days later the body of Leland Stanford, Junior, the boy whose death, as Dr. Stebbins said at the senator's funeral, "drew the sunbeams out of the day," was laid beside that of his father. Some time the mother will sleep here with her precious dead.

Mr. Stanford's heart was bound up in his University. He said, after his son died, "The children of California shall be our children." Mr. Sibley of Pennsylvania tells how, three years after Leland Junior died, he and Mr. Stanford "went together to the tomb of the boy, and the father told amid tears and sobs how, since the death of his son, he had adopted and taken to his heart and love every friendless boy and girl in all the land, and that, so far as his means afforded, they should go to make the path of every such an one smoother and brighter."

Mr. Stanford told Dr. Stebbins, in speaking of the University: "We feel [he always used the plural, thus including that womanly heart from whose fountains his life had ever been refreshed] that we have good ground for hope. We are very happy in our work. We do not feel that we are making great sacrifices. We feel that we are working with and for the Almighty Providence."

By the will of Mr. Stanford the University receives two and a half million dollars, but this bequest is not yet available. He always felt, and rightly, that his wife owned all their large fortune equally with himself; therefore he placed no restrictions upon her disposal of it. Inasmuch as she is a co-founder of the University, she will doubtless add largely to its endowment. Should she do this, the power of Leland Stanford Junior University for good will be almost unlimited.

Even granite mausoleums crumble away; but great deeds last forever, and make their doers immortal.

CAPTAIN THOMAS CORAM
AND HIS FOUNDLING ASYLUM

One of the best of England's charities is the Foundling Asylum in London, founded in 1739 by Captain Thomas Coram. He was not a man of family or means, but he had a warm heart and great perseverance. For seventeen years he labored against indifference and prejudice, till finally his home for little waifs and outcasts became a visible fact, and for more than a century has been doing its noble work.

Captain Coram was born at Lyme Regis, in Dorsetshire, in 1668, a seaport town which carried on some trade with Newfoundland. It is probable that his father was a seafaring man, as the lad early followed that occupation. When he was twenty-six years old we hear of him in the New World at Taunton, Mass., earning his living as a shipwright.

He did not wait to become rich—as indeed he never was—before he began to plan good works. He had saved some money by the year 1703, when he was thirty-five; for we see by the early records that he conveyed to the governor and other authorities in Taunton, fifty-nine acres to be used whenever the people so desired, for an Episcopal church or a schoolhouse. This gift, the deed alleges, was made "in consideration of the love and respect which the donor had and did bear unto the said church, as also for divers other good causes and considerations him especially at that present moving."

Later he gave to Taunton a quite valuable library, a portion of which remains at present. A Book of Common Prayer is now in the church, on whose title-page it is stated that it was the gift "by the Right Honorable Arthur Onslow, Speaker of the Honourable House of Commons of Great Britain, one of His Majesty's most Honourable Privy Council, and Treasurer of His Majesty's Navy, etc., to Thomas Coram, of London, Gentleman, for the use of a church, lately built at Taunton, in New England."

About this time, 1703, Mr. Coram moved to Boston, and became the master of a ship. He was deeply interested in the colonies of the mother country, and though in a comparatively humble station, began to project plans for their increase in commerce, and growth in wealth. In 1704 he helped to procure an Act of Parliament for encouraging the making of tar in the northern colonies of British America by a bounty to be paid on the importation. Before this all the tar was brought from Sweden. The colonies were thereby saved five million dollars.

In 1719, when on board the ship Sea Flower for Hamburgh, that he might obtain supplies of timber and other naval stores for the royal navy, Captain Coram was stranded off Cuxhaven and his cargo plundered.

Some years later, in 1732, having become much interested in the settlement of Georgia, Captain Coram was appointed one of the trustees by a charter from George II.

Three years after this, in 1735, the energetic Captain Coram addressed a memorial to George II., about the settlement of Nova Scotia, as he had found there "the best cod-fishing of any in the known parts of the world, and the land is well adapted for raising hemp and other naval stores." One hundred laboring men signed this memorial, asking for free passage thither, and protection after reaching Nova Scotia.

Captain Coram was so interested in the project that he appeared on several occasions before the Lords Commissioners for Trade and Plantations, and was, says Horace Walpole, "the most knowing person about the plantations I ever talked with." For several years nothing was done about his memorial, but before his death England took action about her now valuable colony.

About 1720 Captain Coram lived in Rotherhithe, and going often to London early in the morning and returning late at night, became troubled about the infants whom he saw exposed or deserted in the public streets, sometimes dead, or dying, or perhaps murdered to avoid publicity. Sometimes these foundlings, if not deserted, were placed in poor families to whom a small sum was paid for their board; and often they were blinded or maimed as they grew older, and sent on the streets to beg.

The young mother, usually homeless and friendless, was almost as helpless as her child if she tried to keep it and earn a living. People scorned her, or arrested her and threw her into prison: the shipmaster tried to find a remedy for the evil.

He talked with his friends and acquaintances, but no one seemed to care. He besought those high in authority, but few seemed to think that foundlings were worth saving. The poor and the disgraced should bear their sorrows alone. Some from all ranks thought the charity a noble one, and wondered that it had been so long neglected; but none gave a penny, or put forth any effort.

"His arguments," wrote Coram's most intimate friend, Dr. Brocklesby, "moved some, the natural humanity of their own temper more, his firm but generous example most of all; and even people of rank began to be ashamed to see a man's hair become gray in the course of a solicitation by which he was to get nothing. Those who did not enter far enough into the case to compassionate the unhappy infants for whom he was a suitor, could not help pitying him."

Captain Coram finally turned to woman for aid, and obtained the names of "twenty-one ladies of quality and distinction" who were

137

willing to help in his project of a foundling asylum. Not all "ladies of quality" were willing to help, however; for in the Foundling Hospital may be seen this note, attached to a memorial addressed to "H.R.H., the Princess Amelia."

"On Innocents' Day, the 28th December, 1737, I went to St. James' Palace to present this petition, having been advised first to address the lady of the bedchamber in waiting to introduce it. But the Lady Isabella Finch, who was the lady in waiting, gave me rough words, and bid me gone with my petition, which I did, without opportunity of presenting it."

Finally Captain Coram's incessant labors bore fruit. On Tuesday, Nov. 20, 1739, at Somerset House, London, a meeting of the nobility and gentry was held, appointed by his Majesty's royal charter to be governors and guardians of the hospital. Captain Coram, now seventy-one years of age, addressed the president, the Duke of Bedford, with great feeling. "My Lord," he said, "although my declining years will not permit me to hope seeing the full accomplishment of my wishes, yet I can now rest satisfied; and it is what I esteem an ample reward of more than seventeen years' expensive labor and steady application, that I see your Grace at the head of this charitable trust, assisted by so many noble and honorable governors."

The house for the foundlings was opened in Hatton Garden in 1741, no child being received over two months old. No questions as to parentage were to be asked; and when no more infants could be taken in, the sign, "The house is full," was hung over the door. Sometimes one hundred women would be at the door with babies in their arms; and when only twenty could be received, the poor creatures would fight to be first at the door, that their child might find a home. Finally the infants were admitted by ballot, by means of balls drawn by the mothers out of a bag. If they drew a white ball, the child was received; if a black ball, it was turned away.

The present Foundling Hospital was begun in 1740, and the western wing finished and occupied in 1745, on the north side of Guilford Street, London, the governors having bought the land, fifty-five acres, from the Earl of Salisbury.

Hogarth, the painter, was deeply interested in Captain Coram's benevolent object. He painted for the hospital some of his finest pictures, and influenced his brother artists to do the same. Hogarth's "March to Finchley" was intended to be dedicated to George II. A proof print was accordingly presented to the king for his approval. The picture gives "a view of a military march, and the humors and disorders consequent thereon."

The king was indignant, and exclaimed, "Does the fellow mean to laugh at my guards?"

"The picture, please your Majesty," said one of the bystanders, "must be considered as a burlesque."

"What! a painter burlesque a soldier? He deserves to be picketed for his insolence," replied the king.

The picture was returned to the mortified artist, who dedicated it to "the king of Prussia, an encourager of the arts."

So many fine paintings were presented to the hospital,—one of Raphael's cartoons, a picture by Benjamin West, and others,—and such a crowd of people came daily to see them in splendid carriages and gilt sedan chairs, that the institution "became the most fashionable morning lounge in the reign of George II."

This exhibition of pictures of the united artists was the precursor of the Royal Academy, founded in 1768. Before this time the artists had their annual reunion and dinner together at the Foundling Hospital, the children entertaining them with music.

Hogarth, notwithstanding his busy life, requested that several of the infants should be sent to Chiswick, where he resided; and he and Mrs. Hogarth looked carefully after their welfare. It was the custom to send the babies into the country to be nursed by some mother, as soon as they were received at the hospital.

Handel, as well as Hogarth, was interested in the foundlings. The chapel had been erected by subscription in 1847. George II subscribed £2,000 towards its erection, and £1,000 towards supplying a preacher. Handel offered a performance in vocal and instrumental music to raise money in building the chapel. The most distinguished persons in the realm came to hear the music. Over a thousand were present, the tickets being half a guinea each.

Each year, as long as Handel was able to do so, he superintended the performance of his great Oratorio of the Messiah in the chapel, which netted the treasury £7,000. When he died he made the following bequest: "I give a fair copy of the Score, and all the parts of my Oratorio called the Messiah, to the Foundling Hospital."

A singular gift to the hospital was from Omychund, a black merchant of Calcutta, who bequeathed to that and the Magdalen Hospital 37,500 current rupees, to be equally divided between them.

Captain Coram lived ten years after his good work was begun. He loved to visit the hospital, and looked upon the children as if they were his own. He rejoiced in every gift, although he had no money of his own to give. He had buried his wife, Eunice, after whom the first girl at the hospital was named. The first boy was called Thomas Coram, after the founder.

During the last two years of Captain Coram's life, when it was known by his friends that he was without funds, Dr. Brocklesby called to ask him if a subscription in his behalf would offend him. He replied, "I have not wasted the little wealth of which I was formerly possessed in self-indulgence and vain expenses, and am not ashamed to confess that, in this my old age, I am poor."

Mr. Gideon, his friend, obtained various sums from those interested. The late Prince of Wales subscribed twenty guineas yearly.

Captain Coram, content with supplying his barest needs, turned his thoughts to more benevolence. He desired to unite the Indians in North America more closely to British interests, by establishing among them a school for girls. He lived long enough to make some progress in this work, but he was too old to be very active.

He died at his lodgings near Leicester Square, on Friday, March 29, 1751, at the age of eighty-four, his last request being that he might be buried in the chapel of his Foundling Hospital. He was buried there April 3, at the east end of the vault, in a lead coffin enclosed in stone. His funeral was attended by a great concourse of people. The choir of St. Paul's Cathedral, with many notables, were at the hospital to receive the body, and pay it suitable honors. The shipmaster had won renown, not by learning or wealth, but by disinterested benevolence. Seventeen years of patient and persistent labor brought its reward.

In the southern arcade of the chapel one may read a long inscription to the memory of

CAPTAIN THOMAS CORAM,
WHOSE NAME WILL NEVER WANT A MONUMENT AS
LONG AS THIS HOSPITAL SHALL SUBSIST.

In front of the hospital is a fine statue of the founder by William Calder Marshall, R.A.; and within, in the girls' dining-room, is Coram's portrait by Hogarth.

After fifteen years from the time of opening the hospital, the governors, their land having risen in value so that their income was larger, and Parliament having given £10,000, determined that their institution should be carried on in an unrestricted manner, as is the case in Russia and some other countries on the Continent.

In Moscow the Foundling Hospital admits 13,000 children yearly. The mother may reclaim her child at any time before it is ten years of age. The state knows that the child has received a better start in life than it could have done with the poor mother.

The Foundling Asylum at St. Petersburg, established by Catherine the Great, is the largest and finest in the world. The buildings cover twenty-eight acres, and the institution has an annual revenue from the government and from private sources of nearly $5,000,000. Thirteen thousand babies are sometimes brought in one year, who but for this blessed charity would probably have been put out of the way. Twenty-five thousand foundlings are constantly enrolled. In Russia infanticide is said to be almost unknown.

Married people, if poor, may bring their child for one year. If not able to provide for it at the end of that time, then it belongs to the state. The boys become mechanics, or enter the army and navy; and the girls become teachers, nurses, etc.

The Foundling Hospital in London determined to welcome all deserted or destitute infants, and save as many as possible from sin and want. A basket was hung outside the gate of the hospital, and one hundred and seventeen infants were put in it the first day.

Abuses of this kind intention soon crept in. Parents too poor to care for their children sent them from the country to London, and they died often on the way thither. One man, who carried five infants in a basket, got drunk on the journey, lay all night on a common, and three out of the five babies were found dead in the morning. Often the carriers stole all the clothing of the little ones, and they were thrown into the basket naked. Within four years about fifteen thousand babies were received, but only forty-four hundred lived to be sent out into homes. The mothers hated to part with their infants, and would often follow them for miles on foot. The poor mother would leave some token by which her child could be identified. Sometimes it was a coin or a ribbon, or possibly the daintiest cap the poverty of the mother would permit her to make. Sometimes a verse of poetry was pinned on the dress:—

"If Fortune should her favors give,
That I in better plight might live,
I'd try to have my boy again,
And train him up the best of men."

"The court-room of the Foundling," says a writer in "Chambers's Journal," "has probably witnessed as painful scenes as any chamber in Great Britain; and again, when the children, at five years old, are brought up to London, and separated from their foster-mothers, these scenes are renewed."

"The stratagems resorted to by women to identify their children," says "Old and New London," "and to assure themselves of their well-being, are often singularly touching. Sometimes notes are found pinned to the infant's garments, beseeching the nurse to tell the mother her name and residence, that the latter may visit the child during its stay in the country. They will also attend the baptism in the chapel, in the hope of hearing the name conferred upon the infant; for, if they succeed in identifying the child during its stay at nurse, they can always preserve its identification during its subsequent abode in the hospital, since the children appear in chapel twice on Sunday, and dine in public on that day, which gives opportunity of seeing them from time to time, and preserving the recollection of their features."

141

So many children were brought to the hospital after all restrictions were removed, in 1756, the death-roll was so large, and the expenses so great, that after four years different methods were adopted. There are now about five hundred children in the Foundling Hospital, who remain till they are fifteen years old, when they are apprenticed till of age at some kind of labor. None are received at the hospital except when a vacancy occurs, as the size of the buildings and funds will not permit more inmates. Usually about forty are received, one-sixth of those who apply. There is a fund provided to help those in later life who prove idiotic or blind, or unfitted to earn their support.

Sundays visitors in London go often to hear the trained voices of the foundlings. The girls, in their white caps and white kerchiefs, sit on one side of the organ, a gift from the great Handel, and the boys, neatly dressed, on the other side. There is a juvenile band of musicians among the boys; and so well do they play, that, on leaving the institution, they often find positions in the bands of Her Majesty's Household Troops or in the navy. Lieutenant-Colonel James C. Hyde presented the boys with a set of brass instruments, and some valuable drawings of native artists of India, for the adornment of their walls.

Some time ago I visited with much interest the New York Foundling Hospital, on Sixty-eighth Street, six stories high, founded by and in charge of the Sisters of Charity. During the year 1895 there were cared for 3,109 infants and little children, and 516 needy and homeless mothers. On one side of the Foundling Hospital is the Maternity Hospital, and on the other side the Children's Hospital.

The cradle to receive the baby is placed within the vestibule, so that the Sister, when the bell is rung, may talk kindly with the person bringing it, and often persuades her to remain for some months and care for her child. No information is sought as to names, family, etc. Other infants are taken into the country to be nursed by foster-mothers, and the institution does not lose its close oversight of the little ones.

When these infants are unclaimed, they are usually sent to homes in the West to be adopted. Since the opening of the Foundling Hospital in 1869, twenty-six years ago, 27,171 waifs have been received and cared for.

The "Nursery and Child's Hospital," Fifty-first Street and Lexington Avenue, carries on a work similar to the Foundling Asylum, and, though under Protestant control, is not a denominational enterprise.

In Cleveland, Ohio, one of the most interesting charities is the "Lida Baldwin Infants' Rest," for which Mr. H. R. Hatch has given an admirable building, at 1416 Cedar Avenue, costing $17,000 or $18,000. Babies, if over two years old, are taken to the Protestant Orphan Asylum on St. Clair Street. The "Rest" is named after the first wife of

Mr. Hatch, an enterprising and philanthropic merchant, who, among other gifts, has just presented a handsome granite library building, costing nearly $100,000, to Adelbert College of Western Reserve University.

When Reuben Runyan Springer died in Cincinnati, Ohio, Dec. 10, 1884, at the age of eighty-four years, he did not forget to give the Sisters of Charity $20,000 for a foundling asylum. His family were originally from Sweden. When a youth he was clerk on a steamboat from Cincinnati to New Orleans, and soon acquired an interest in the boat, and began his fortune. Later, he was partner in a grocery house. Mr. Springer gave to the Little Sisters of the Poor $35,000, Good Samaritan Hospital $30,000, St. Peter's Benevolent Society $50,000, besides many other gifts. To music and art he gave $420,000. To his two faithful domestics and friends, he gave $7,500 each, and to his coachman his horses, carriages, harness, and $5,000. His various charities amounted to a million dollars or more.

Most cities have, or ought to have, a foundling asylum, though often it bears a different name. The Roman Catholics seem to be wiser in this respect, and more careful to save infant life, than we of the Protestant faith.

HENRY SHAW
AND HIS BOTANICAL GARDEN

It is rare that a poor boy comes to America from a foreign land, with almost no money in his pocket, and leaves to his adopted town and State a million four hundred thousand dollars to beautify a city, to elevate its taste, and to help educate its people.

Henry Shaw of St. Louis, Mo., was born in Sheffield, England, July 24, 1800. He was the oldest of four children, having had a brother who died in infancy and two sisters. His father, Joseph Shaw, was a manufacturer of grates, fire-irons, etc., at Sheffield.

The boy obtained his early education at Thorne, a village not far from his native town, and used to get his lessons in an arbor, half hidden by vines, and surrounded by trees and flowers. From childhood he had a passion for a garden, and worked with his two little sisters in planting anemones and buttercups.

From the school at Thorne the lad was transferred to Mill Hill, about twenty miles from London, to a "Dissenting" school, the father being a Baptist. Here he studied for six years, Latin, French, and probably other languages, as he knew in later life German, Italian, and Spanish. He became especially fond of French literature, and in manhood read and wrote French as easily and correctly as English. He was for a long time regarded as the best mathematician in St. Louis.

In 1818, when Henry was eighteen, he and the rest of the family came to Canada. The same year his father sent him to New Orleans to learn how to raise cotton; but the climate did not please him, and he removed to a small French trading-post, called St. Louis, May 3, 1819.

The youth had a little stock of cutlery with him, the capital for which his uncle, Mr. James Hoole, had furnished. His nephew was always grateful for this kind act. He rented a room on the second floor of a building, and cooked, slept, ate, and sold his goods in this one room. He went out very little in the evening, preferring to read books, and sometimes played chess with a friend. It is thought that he rather avoided meeting young ladies, as he perhaps naturally preferred to marry an English girl, when able to support her; but when the fortune was earned he was wedded to his gardens, his flowers, and his books, so that he never married. The young man showed great energy in his hardware business, was very economical, honest, and always punctual. He had little patience with persons who were not prompt, and failed to keep an engagement.

Though usually self-poised, possessing almost perfect control over a naturally quick temper, a gentleman relates that he once saw him angry because a man failed to keep an appointment; but Mr. Shaw regretted that he had allowed himself to speak sharply, and asked the offending person to dine with him. His head-gardener, Mr. James Gurney, from the Royal Botanical Garden in Regent's Park, London, said many years ago of Mr. Shaw, "In twenty-three years I never heard him speak a harsh or an irritable word. No matter what went wrong,— and on such a place, and with so many men, things will go wrong occasionally,—he was always pleasant and cheerful, making the best of what could not be helped."

Mr. Shaw gave close attention to business in the growing town of St. Louis, and in 1839, after he had been there twenty years, was astonished to find that his annual profits were $25,000. He said, "this was more money than any man in my circumstances ought to make in a single year;" and he resolved to go out of business as soon as a good opportunity presented itself. This occurred the following year, in 1840; and at forty years of age, Mr. Shaw retired from business with a fortune of $250,000, equivalent to a million, probably, at the present day.

After twenty years of constant labor he determined to take a little rest and change. In September, 1840, he went to Europe, stopping in Rochester, N.Y., where his parents and sisters then resided, and took his younger sister with him.

He was absent two years, and coming home in 1842, soon arranged for another term of travel abroad. He remained in Europe three years, travelling in almost all places of interest, including Constantinople and Egypt. He kept journals, and wrote letters to friends, showing careful observation and wide reading. He made a third and last visit to Europe in 1851, to attend the first World's Fair, held in London. During this visit he conceived the plan of what eventually became his great gift. While walking through the beautiful grounds of Chatsworth, the magnificent home of the Duke of Devonshire, Mr. Shaw said to himself, "Why may not I have a garden too? I have enough land and money for something of the same sort in a smaller way."

The old love for flowers and trees, as in boyhood, made the man in middle life determine to plant not so much for himself as for posterity. He had finished a home in the suburbs of St. Louis, Tower Grove, in 1849; and another was in process of building in the city on the corner of Seventh and Locust Streets, when Mr. Shaw returned from Europe in 1851.

For five or six years he beautified the grounds of his country home, and in 1857 commissioned Dr. Engelmann, then in Europe, to examine botanical gardens and select proper books for a botanical library. Correspondence was begun with Sir William J. Hooker, the distinguished director of the famous Kew Gardens in London, our own beloved botanist, Professor Asa Gray of Harvard College, and others. Dr. Engelmann urged Mr. Shaw to purchase the large herbarium of the then recently deceased Professor Bernhardi of Erfurt, Germany, which was done, Hooker writing, "The State ought to feel that it owes you much for so much public spirit, and so well directed."

March 14, 1859, Mr. Shaw secured from the State Legislature an Act enabling him to convey to trustees seven hundred and sixty acres of land, "in trust, upon a portion thereof to keep up, maintain, and establish a botanic garden for the cultivation and propagation of plants, flowers, fruit and forest trees, and for the dissemination of the knowledge thereof among men, by having a collection thereof easily accessible; and the remaining portion to be used for the purpose of maintaining a perpetual fund for the support and maintenance of said garden, its care and increase, and the museum, library, and instruction connected therewith."

For the next twenty-five years Mr. Shaw gave his time and strength to the development of his cherished garden and park. "He lived for them," says Mr. Thomas Dimmock, "and, as far as was practicable, in them; walking or driving every day, when weather and health allowed, and permitting no work of importance to go on without more or less of his personal inspection and direction. The late Dr. Asa Gray, than whom there can be no higher authority, once said, 'This park and the Botanical Garden are the finest institutions of the kind in the country; in variety of foliage the park is unequalled.'"

Once when Mr. Shaw was escorting a lady through his gardens, she said, "I cannot understand, sir, how you are able to remember all these different and difficult names."—"Madam," he replied, with a courtly bow, "did you ever know a mother who could forget the names of her children? These plants and flowers are my children. How can I forget them?"

So devoted was Mr. Shaw to his work, that he did not go out of St. Louis for nearly twenty years, except for a drive to the neighboring village of Kirkwood to dine with a friend.

Nine years after the garden had been established, in 1866, Mr. Shaw began to create Tower Grove Park, of two hundred and seventy-six acres, planting from year to year over twenty thousand trees, all raised in the arboretum of the garden. Walks were gravelled, flower-beds laid out, ornamental water provided, and artistic statues of heroic size, made by Baron von Mueller of Munich, of Shakespeare, Humboldt, and Columbus. The niece of Humboldt, who saw the statue of her uncle at Munich, wrote to Mr. Shaw, saying that "Europe had done nothing comparable to it for the great naturalist."

Mr. Shaw used to say, when setting out these trees, that he was "planting them for posterity," as he did not expect to live to see them reach maturity. They were, however, of good size when he died in his ninetieth year, Sunday, Aug. 25, 1889.

"The death, peaceful and painless," says Mr. Dimmock, "occurred

146

in his favorite room on the second floor of the old homestead, by the window of which he sat nearly every night for more than thirty years until the morning hours, absorbed in the reading which had been the delight of his life. This room was always plainly furnished, containing only a brass bedstead, tables, chairs, and the few books he loved to have near him. The windows looked out upon the old garden which was the first botanical beginning at Tower Grove.

"On Saturday, Aug. 31, after such ceremonial as St. Louis never before bestowed upon any deceased citizen, Henry Shaw was laid to rest in the mausoleum long prepared in the midst of the garden he had created—not for himself merely, but for the generations that shall come after him, and who, enjoying it, will 'rise up and call him blessed.'"

Mr. Shaw was beloved by his workmen for his uniform kindness to them. Once when a young boy who was visiting him, and walking with him in the garden, passed a lame workman, and did not speak, although Mr. Shaw said "Good-morning, Henry," the courteous old gentleman said, "Charles, you did not speak to Henry. Go back and say 'Good-morning' to him." Mr. Shaw employed many Bohemians, because he said, "They do not seem to be very popular with us, and I think I ought to help them all I can."

Mr. Shaw was always simple in his tastes and economical in his habits. He drove his one-horse barouche till his friends, owing to his infirmities from increasing age, prevailed upon him to have a carriage and a driver.

Four years before the death of Mr. Shaw he endowed a School of Botany as a department of Washington University, giving improved real estate yielding over $5,000 annually. He desired "to promote education and investigation in that science, and in its application to horticulture, arboriculture, medicine, and the arts, and for the exemplification of the Divine wisdom and goodness as manifested throughout the vegetable kingdom."

Dr. Asa Gray had been deeply interested in this movement, and twice visited St. Louis to consult with Mr. Shaw. By the recommendation of Dr. Gray, Mr. William Trelease, Professor of Botany in Wisconsin University at Madison, a graduate of Cornell University, and associated for some time with Professor Gray in various labors, was made Englemann Professor in the Henry Shaw School of Botany.

Professor Trelease was also made director of the Missouri Botanical Garden, and has proved his fitness for the position by his high rank in scholarship, his contributions to literature, and his devotion to the work which Mr. Shaw felt satisfaction in committing to his care. His courtesy as well as ability have won him many friends. Mr. Shaw left by will various legacies to relatives and institutions, his property, invested largely in land, having become worth over a million

147

dollars. He gave to hospitals, several orphan asylums, Old Ladies' Home, Girls' Industrial Home, Young Men's Christian Association, etc., but by far the larger part to his beloved garden. He wished it to be open every day of the week to the public, except on Sundays and holidays, the first Sunday in June and the first Sunday in September being exceptions to the rule. When the garden was opened the first Sunday of June, 1895, there were 20,159 visitors, and in September, though showery, 15,500.

Mr. Shaw bequeathed $1,000 annually for a banquet to the trustees of the garden, and literary and scientific men whom they choose to invite, thus to spread abroad the knowledge of the useful work the garden and schools of botany are doing; also $400 for a banquet to the gardeners of the institution, with the florists, nurserymen, and market-gardeners of St. Louis and vicinity. Each year $500 is to be used in premiums at flower-shows, and $200 for an annual sermon "on the wisdom and goodness of God as shown in the growth of flowers, fruits, and other products of the vegetable kingdom."

The Missouri Botanical Garden, Shaw's Garden as it is more commonly called, covering about forty-five acres, is situated on Tower Grove Avenue, about three miles southwest of the New Union Station. The former city residence of Mr. Shaw has been removed to the garden, in which are the herbarium and library, with 12,000 volumes. The herbarium contains the large collection of the late Dr. George Engelmann, about 100,000 specimens of pressed plants; and the general collection contains even more than this number of specimens from all parts of the world. The palms, the cacti, the tree-ferns, the fig-trees, etc., are of much interest. There is an observatory in the centre of the garden; and south of this, in a grove of shingle-oaks and sassafras-trees, is the mausoleum of Henry Shaw, containing a life-like reclining marble statue of the founder of the garden, with a full-blown rose in his hand.

During the past year several ponds have been made in the garden for the Victoria Regia, or Amazon water-lily, and other lilies. On the approach of winter, over a thousand plants are taken from the ground, potted, and distributed to charitable institutions and poor homes in the city.

Much practical good has resulted from the great gift of Henry Shaw. According to his will, there are six scholarships provided for garden pupils. Three hundred dollars a year are given to each, with tuition free, and lodging in a comfortable house adjacent to the garden. So many persons have applied for instruction, that as many are received as can be taught conveniently, each paying $25 yearly tuition fee.

The culture of flowers, small fruits, orchards, house-plants, etc., is taught; also landscape-gardening, drainage, surveying, and kindred subjects. "It is safe to predict," says the Hon. Wm. T. Harris, Commissioner of Education, "that the future will see a large representation of specialists resorting to St. Louis to pursue the studies necessary for the promotion of agricultural industry."

Dr. Trelease gives two courses of evening lectures at Washington University each year, and at the garden he gives practical help to his learners. He investigates plant diseases and the remedies, and aids the fruit-grower, the florist, and the farmer, in the best methods with grasses, seeds, trees, etc. He deprecates the reckless manner in which troublesome weeds are scattered from farm to farm with clover and grass seed. He and his assistants are making researches concerning plants, flowers, etc., which are published annually.

The memory of Henry Shaw, "the first great patron of botanical science in America," is held in honor and esteem by the scientific world. The flowers and trees which he loved and found pleasure in cultivating, each year make thousands happier.

Nature was to him a great teacher. In his garden, over a statue of "Victory," these words are engraved in stone: "O Lord, how manifold are thy works: in wisdom hast thou made them all."

The seasons will come and go; the flowers will bud and blossom year after year, and the trees spread out their branches: they will be a continual reminder of the white-haired man who planted them for the sake of doing good to others.

Harvard College received a valuable gift May, 1861, through the munificence of the late Benjamin Bussey of Roxbury, Mass., in property estimated at $413,092.80, "for a course of instruction in practical agriculture, and the various arts subservient thereto." The superb estate is near Jamaica Plain. The students of the Bussey Institute generally intend to become gardeners, florists, landscape-gardeners, and farmers. The Arnold Arboretum occupies a portion of the Bussey farm in West Roxbury. The fund given by the late James Arnold of New Bedford, Mass., for this purpose now amounts to $156,767.97.

JAMES SMITHSON
AND THE SMITHSONIAN INSTITUTION

Another Englishman besides Henry Shaw to whom America is much indebted is James Smithson, the giver of the Smithsonian Institution at Washington. Born in 1765 in France, he was the natural son of Hugh, third Duke of Northumberland, and Mrs. Elizabeth Macie, heiress of the Hungerfords of Audley, and niece of Charles, Duke of Somerset.

At Pembroke College, Oxford, he was devoted to science, especially chemistry, and spent his vacations in collecting minerals. He was graduated May 26, 1786, and thereafter gave his time to study and original research. In 1790 he was elected a Fellow of the Royal Society, and became the friend of many distinguished men, both in England and on the Continent, where he lived much of the time. Among his friends and correspondents, were Sir Humphry Davy, Berzelius (the noted chemist of Sweden), Gay-Lussac the chemist, Thomson, Wollaston, and others.

He wrote and published in the *Philosophical Transactions of the Royal Society*, and also in Thomson's *Annals of Philosophy*, many valuable papers on the "Composition of Zeolite," "On a Substance Procured from the Elm Tree, called Ulmine," "On a Saline Substance from Mount Vesuvius," "On Facts Relating to the Coloring Matter of Vegetables," etc. At his death he left about two hundred manuscripts. He was deeply interested in geology, and made copious notes in his journal on rocks and mining. His life seems to have been a quiet one, devoted to intellectual pursuits.

Professor Henry Carrington Bolton, in the *Popular Science Monthly* for January and February, 1896, relates this incident of Smithson: "It is said that he frequently narrated an anecdote of himself which illustrated his remarkable skill in analyzing minute quantities of substances, an ability which rivalled that of Dr. Wollaston. Happening to observe a tear gliding down a lady's cheek, he endeavored to catch it on a crystal vessel. One-half the tear-drop escaped; but he subjected the other half to reagents, and detected what was then called microcosmic salt, muriate of soda, and some other saline constituents held in solution."

When Mr. Smithson was over fifty years of age, in 1818 or 1819, he had a misunderstanding with the Royal Society, owing to their refusal to publish one of his papers. It is said that prior to this he intended to leave all his wealth, over $500,000 to the society.

About three years before his death, he made a brief will, giving the income of his fortune to his nephew, Henry James Hungerford, and the whole fortune to the children of his nephew, if he should marry. In case he did not marry, Smithson bequeathed the whole of his property "to the United States of America, to found at Washington, under the name of the Smithsonian Institution, an establishment for the increase and diffusion of knowledge among men."

Mr. Smithson, says Professor Simon Newcomb, "is not known to have had the personal acquaintance of an American, and his tastes were supposed to have been aristocratic rather than democratic. We thus have the curious spectacle of a retired English gentleman bequeathing the whole of his large fortune to our Government, to found an establishment which was described in ten words, without a memorandum of any kind by which his intentions could be divined, or the recipient of the gift guided in applying it."

Mr. Smithson died June 27, 1829, in Genoa, Italy, at the age of sixty-four. His nephew survived him only six years, dying unmarried at Pisa, Italy, June 5, 1835. He used the income from his uncle's estate while he lived, and upon his death it passed to the United States. Hungerford's mother, who had married a Frenchman, Madame Théodore de la Batut, claimed a life-interest in the estate of Smithson, which was granted till her death in 1861. To meet this annuity $26,210 was retained in England until she died.

For several years it was difficult to decide in what way Congress should use the money "for the increase and diffusion of knowledge among men." John Quincy Adams desired a great astronomical observatory; Rufus Choate of Massachusetts urged a grand library; a senator from Ohio wished a botanical garden; another person a college for women; another a school for indigent children of the District of Columbia; still another a great agricultural school.

After seven years of indecision and discussion the Smithsonian Institution was organized by act of Congress, Aug. 10, 1846, which provided for a suitable building to contain objects of natural history, a chemical laboratory, a library, gallery of art, and geological and mineralogical collections. The minerals, books, and other property of James Smithson, were to be preserved in the Institution.

Professor Joseph Henry, whose interesting life I have sketched in my "Famous Men of Science," was called to the headship of the new Institution. For thirty-three years he devoted his life to make Smithson's gift a blessing to the world and an honor to the name of the generous giver. The present secretary is the well-known Professor Samuel P. Langley.

The library was after a time transferred to the Library of Congress, the art department to the Corcoran Art Gallery, and the Smithsonian Institution began to do its specific work of helping men to make original scientific research, to aid in explorations, and to send scientific publications all over the world. Its first publication was a work on the mounds and earthworks found in the Mississippi Valley. Much time has also been given to the study of the character and pursuits of the earliest races on this continent.

The Smithsonian Institution now owns two large buildings, one completed in 1855, costing about $314,000, and the great National Museum, which Congress helped to build. This building has a floor space of 100,000 square feet, and contains over three and one-half million specimens of birds, fishes, Oriental antiquities, minerals, fossils, etc. So much of value has been gathered by government surveys, as well as by contributions from other nations by way of exchange, that halls twice as large as those now built could be filled by the specimens. So popular is the museum as a place to visit, that in the year ending June 30, 1893, over 300,000 persons enjoyed its interesting accumulations.

Correspondence is carried on with learned societies and men of science all over the world. The official list of correspondents is over 24,000. The transactions of learned societies and some other scientific works are exchanged with those abroad. The weight of matter sent abroad by the Smithsonian Institution at the end of the first decade was 14,000 pounds for 1857; at the end of the third decade 99,000 pounds for the year 1877. The official documents of Congress, or by the government bureaus, are exchanged for similar works of foreign nations. In one year, 1892-1893, over 100 tons of books were handled.

The "Smithsonian Contributions to Knowledge" now number over thirty volumes, and are valuable treatises on various branches of science. The scholarly William B. Taylor said these books "distributed over every portion of the civilized or colonized world constitute a monument to the memory of the founder, James Smithson, such as never before was builded on the foundation of £100,000."

The Smithsonian Institution has been a blessing in many ways. It organized a system of telegraphic meteorology, and gave to the world "that most beneficent national application of modern sciences,—the storm warnings."

In the year 1891 the Institution received valuable aid from Mr. Thomas G. Hodgkins of Setauket, N.Y., by the gift of $200,000. The income from $100,000 is to be used in prizes for essays relating to atmospheric air. Mr. Hodgkins, also an Englishman, died Nov. 25, 1892, nearly ninety years old. He gave $100,000 to the Royal Institution of Great Britain, and $50,000 each to the Society for Prevention of Cruelty to Children, and to Animals. He made his fortune, and having no family, spent it for "the diffusion of knowledge among men."

A very interesting feature was added to the work of the Smithsonian Institution in 1890, when Congress appropriated

$200,000 for the purchase of land for the National Zoölogical Park. As no native wild animals in America seem safe from the cupidity of the trader, or the slaughter of the pleasure-loving sportsman, it became necessary to take measures for their preservation. About 170 acres were purchased on Rock Creek, near Washington; and there are already more than 500 animals—bisons, etc.—in these picturesque grounds. These will be valuable object-lessons to the people, and help still further to carry out James Smithson's idea, "the increase and diffusion of knowledge among men."

PRATT, LENOX, MARY MACRAE STUART, NEWBERRY, CRERAR, ASTOR, REYNOLDS, AND THEIR LIBRARIES

ENOCH PRATT

Enoch Pratt was born in North Middleborough, Mass., Sept. 10, 1808. He graduated at Bridgewater Academy when he was fifteen; and a position was found for him in a leading house in Boston, where he remained until he was twenty-one years of age. He had written to a friend in Boston two weeks before his school closed, "I do not want to stay at home long after it is out."

The eager, ambitious boy, with good habits, constant application to business, the strictest honesty, and good common-sense, soon made himself respected by his employers and his acquaintances.

He removed to Baltimore in 1831, when he was twenty-three years old, without a dollar at his command, and established himself as a commission merchant. He founded the wholesale iron house of Pratt & Keith, and subsequently that of Enoch Pratt & Brother. "Prosperity soon followed," says the Hon. George Wm. Brown, "not rapidly but steadily, because it was based on those qualities of honesty, industry, sagacity, and energy, which, mingled with thrift, although they cannot be said to insure success, are certainly most likely to achieve it."

Six years after coming to Baltimore, when he was twenty-nine years old, Mr. Pratt married Maria Louisa Hyde, Aug. 1, 1837. Her paternal ancestors were among the earliest settlers of Massachusetts; her maternal, a German family who settled in Baltimore over a century and a half ago.

As years went by, and the unobtrusive, energetic man came to middle life, he was sought to fill various positions of honor and trust in Baltimore. He was made director and president of a bank, which position he has held for over twoscore years, director and vice-president of railroads and steamboat lines, president of the House of Reformation at Cheltenham (for colored children), and of the Maryland School for the Deaf and Dumb at Frederick. He has also taken active interest in the Maryland Institute for the Promotion of the Mechanic Arts, and is treasurer of the Peabody Institute.

For years he has been one of the finance commissioners elected by the city council, without regard to his political belief, but on account of his ability as a financier, and his wisdom. He is an active member of the Unitarian Church.

For several years Mr. Pratt had thought about giving a free public library to the people of Baltimore. In 1882, when he was seventy-four, Mr. Pratt gave to the city $1,058,000 for the establishing of his library, the building to cost about $225,000, and the remainder, a little over $833,000, to be invested by the city, which obligated itself to pay $50,000 yearly forever for the maintenance of the free library. Mr. Pratt also provided for four branch libraries, which cost $50,000, located wisely in different parts of the city.

The main library was opened Jan. 4, 1886, with appropriate ceremonies. The Romanesque building of Baltimore County white marble is 82 feet frontage, with a depth of 140 feet. A tower 98 feet high rises in the centre of the front. The floor of the vestibule is in black and white marble, and the wainscoting of Tennessee and Vermont marbles, principally of a dove color. The reading-room in the second story is 75 feet long, 37 feet wide, and 25 feet high. The walls are frescoed in buff and pale green tints, the wainscoting is of marble, and the floor is inlaid with cherry, pine, and oak. The main building will hold 250,000 volumes.

The Romanesque branch libraries are 40 by 70 feet, one story in height, built of pressed brick laid with red mortar, with buff stone trimmings. The large reading-room in each is light and cheerful, and the book-room has shelving for 15,000 volumes.

The librarian's report shows that in nine years, ending with Jan. 1, 1895, over 4,000,000 books have been circulated among the people of Baltimore. Over a half-million books are circulated each year. The library possesses about 150,000 volumes. "The usefulness of the branch libraries cannot be stated in too strong terms," says the librarian, Mr. Bernard C. Steiner. Fifty-seven persons are employed in the library,—fourteen men and forty-three women.

Mr. Pratt is now eighty-eight years old, and has not ceased to do good works. In 1865 he founded the Pratt Free School at Middleborough, Mass., where he was born. Ex-Mayor James Hodges tells this incident of Mr. Pratt: "Some years ago he sold a farm in Virginia to a worthy but poor young man for $20,000. The purchaser had paid from time to time one-half the purchase money, when a series of bad seasons and failure of crops made it impossible to meet the subsequent payments. Mr. Pratt sent for him, and learned the facts.

"After expressing sympathy for the young man's misfortunes, and encouraging him to persevere and hope, he cancelled his note for the balance due,—$10,000,—and handed him a valid deed for the property. Astonished and overwhelmed by this princely liberality, the recipient uttered a few words, and retired from his benefactor's presence. Not until he had reached his Virginia home was he able to find words to express his gratitude."

The great gift of Enoch Pratt in his free library has stimulated like gifts all over the country; and in his lifetime he is enjoying the fruits of his generosity.

JAMES LENOX

The founder of Lenox Library on Seventy-second Street, overlooking Central Park, was born in New York City, Aug. 19, 1800, and died there Feb. 17, 1880. His father, Robert, was a wealthy Scotch merchant of New York, who left to his only son and seven daughters several million dollars.

Robert purchased from the corporation of New York a farm of thirty acres of land in Fourth and Fifth Avenues, near Seventy-second Street. For twelve acres on one side he gave $500, and for the rest on the other side, $10,700. He thought the land might "at no distant day be the site of a village," and left it to his son on condition that it be kept from sale for several years.

The son was educated at Princeton and Columbia Colleges, studied law, but, being devoted to literary matters, spent much time abroad in collecting valuable books and works of art. The only lady to whom he was ever attached, it is stated, refused him, and both remained single.

He was a quiet, retiring man, a member of the Presbyterian Church, and a most generous giver, though his benefactions were kept from publicity as much as possible. He once sent $7,000 to a lady for a deserving charity, and refused her second application because she had told of his former gift.

He built Lenox Library of Lockport limestone, and gave to it $735,000 in cash, and ten city lots of great value, on which the building stands. The collection of books, marbles, pictures, etc., which he gave is valued at a million dollars.

He gave probably a million in money and land to the Presbyterian Hospital, of which he was for many years the president. He was also president of the American Bible Society, to which he gave liberally. To the Presbyterian Home for Aged Women he gave land assessed at $64,000. He gave to Princeton College and Theological Seminary, to his own church, and to needy men of letters.

After his death, his last surviving sister, Henrietta Lenox, in 1887 gave to the library ten valuable adjoining lots, and $100,000 for the purchase of books.

The nephew of Mr. Lenox, Robert Lenox Kennedy, who succeeded his uncle as president of the Board of Trustees of the library, presented to the institution, in 1879, Munkacsy's great picture of "Blind

156

Milton dictating 'Paradise Lost' to his Daughter." He died at sea, Sept. 14, 1887.

The Lenox Library has a remarkable collection of works, which will always be an honor to America. Its early American newspapers bear dates from 1716 to 1800, and include examples of nearly every important gazette of the Colonial and Revolutionary times. The library received in 1894 over 45,000 papers. The *Boston News Letter*, the first regular newspaper printed in America, is an object of interest. Several of the newspapers appeared in mourning on account of the Stamp Act in October, 1765.

The library has large collections in American history, Bibles, early educational books, and old English literature. "The Souldier's Pocket Bible" is one of two known copies—the other being in the British Museum—of the famous pocket Bible used by Cromwell's soldiers. Many of the Bibles are extremely rare, and of great value. There are five copies of Eliot's Indian Bible. There are 2,200 English Bibles from 1493, and 1,200 Bibles in other languages.

One of the oldest American publications in the library is "Spiritual Milk for Boston Babes in Either England," by John Cotton, B.D., in 1656. An old English work has this title: "The Boke of Magna Carta, with divers other statutes, etc., 1534 (Colophon:) Thus endyth the boke called Magna Carta, translated out of Latyn and Frenshe into Englyshe by George Ferrers."

There are several interesting books concerning witchcraft. The original book of testimony taken in the trial of Hugh Parsons for witchcraft at Springfield, in 1651, is mostly in the handwriting of William Pynchon, but with some entries by Secretary Edward Rawson. The library possesses the manuscript of Henry Harrisse's work on the "Discovery of America," forming ten folio volumes. The library of the Hon. George Bancroft was purchased by the Lenox Library in 1893.

The Milton collection in the library contains about 250 volumes, nearly every variety of the early editions. Several volumes have Milton's autograph and annotations. There are about 500 volumes of Bunyan's "Pilgrim's Progress," and books relating to the writer, containing nearly 350 editions in many languages. There are also about 200 volumes of Spanish manuscripts relating to America. The set of "Jesuit Relations," the journals of the early Jesuit missionaries in this country, is the most complete in existence.

Many thousands of persons come each year to see the books and pictures, as well as to read, and all are aided by the courteous librarian, Mr. Wilberforce Eames, who loves his work, and has the scholarship necessary for it.

MARY MACRAE STUART

At her death in New York City, Dec. 30, 1891, gave the Robert L. Stuart fine-art collections valued at $500,000, her shells, minerals, and library, to the Lenox Library, on condition that they should never be exhibited on Sunday. To nine charitable institutions in New York she gave $5,000 each; to Cooper Union, $10,000; to the Cancer Hospital, $25,000; and about $5,000,000 to home and foreign missions of the Presbyterian Church, hospitals, disabled ministers, freedmen, Church Extension Society, aged women, etc., of the same church, and also the Young Men's Christian Association, Woman's Hospital, Society for Prevention of Cruelty to Children, Society for Relief of Poor Widows with Small Children, City Mission and Tract Society, Bible Society, Colored Orphans, Juvenile Asylum, and other institutions in New York.

Mrs. Stuart was the daughter of a wealthy New York merchant, Robert Macrae, and married Robert L. Stuart, the head of the firm of sugar-refiners, R. L. & A. Stuart. Both brothers were rich, and gave away before Alexander's death a million and a half. Robert left an estate valued at $6,000,000 to his wife, as they had no children; and she, in his behalf, gave away his fortune and also her own. She would have given largely to the Museum of Natural History and Museum of Art in New York, but from a fear that they would be opened to the public on Sundays.

WALTER L. NEWBERRY

Chicago has been recently enriched by two great gifts, the Newberry and Crerar Libraries. Walter Loomis Newberry was born at East Windsor, Conn., Sept. 18, 1804. He was educated at Clinton, N.Y., and fitted for the United States Military Academy, but could not pass the physical examination. After a time spent with his brother in commercial life in Buffalo, N.Y., he removed to Detroit in 1828, and engaged in the dry-goods business. He went to Chicago in 1834, when that city had but three thousand inhabitants, and became first a commission merchant, and later a banker. He invested some money which he brought with him in forty acres on the "North Side," which is now among the best residence property in the city, and of course very valuable.

Mr. Newberry helped to found the Merchants' Loan & Trust Companies' Bank, and was one of its directors. He was also the president of a railroad.

He was always deeply interested in education; was for many

158

years on the school-board, and twice its chairman. He was president of the Chicago Historical Society, and was the first president of the Young Men's Library Association, which he helped to found.

Mr. Newberry died at sea, Nov. 6, 1868, at the age of sixty-four, leaving about $5,000,000 to his wife and two daughters.

If these children died unmarried, half the property was to go to his brothers and sisters, or their descendants, after the death of his wife, and half to the founding of a library.

Both daughters died unmarried,—Mary Louisa on Feb. 18, 1874, at Pau, France; and Julia Rosa on April 4, 1876, at Rome, Italy. Mrs. Julia Butler Newberry, the wife, died at Paris, France, Dec. 9, 1885.

The Newberry Library building, 300 feet by 60, of granite, is on the north side of Chicago, facing the little park known as Washington Square. It is Spanish-Romanesque in style, and has room for 1,000,000 books. There will be space for 4,000,000 volumes when the other portions of the library are added. A most necessary part of the work of the trustees was the choosing of a librarian with ability and experience to form a useful reference library, which it was decided that the Newberry Library should be, the Public Library, with its annual income of over $70,000, seeming to meet the needs of the people at large. Dr. William Frederick Poole, for fourteen years the efficient librarian of the Chicago Public Library, was chosen librarian of the Newberry Library.

Dictionaries, bibliographies, cyclopædias, and the like, were at once purchased. The first gift made to the library was the Caxton Memorial Bible, presented Sept. 29, 1877, by the Oxford University Press, through the late Henry Stevens, Esq., of London. The edition was limited to one hundred copies, and the copy presented to the Newberry Library is the ninety-eighth. Mr. George P. A. Healey, the distinguished artist, also gave about fifty of his valuable paintings to the library. Several thousand volumes on early American and local history, collected by Mr. Charles H. Guild of Somerville, Mass., were purchased by Dr. Poole for the library. A collection of 415 volumes of bound American newspapers, covering the period of the Civil War, 1861-1865, were procured. An extremely useful medical library has been given by Dr. Nicholas Senn, Professor of Surgery in Rush Medical College. A valuable collection on fish, fish culture, and angling, made during forty years by the publisher, Robert Clarke of Cincinnati, has been bought for the library. A very interesting collection of early books and manuscripts was purchased from Mr. Henry Probasco of Cincinnati. The collection of Bibles is very rich; also of Shakespeare, Homer, Dante, Horace, and Petrarch. There were in 1895 over 125,600 volumes in the library, and over 30,000 pamphlets.

To the great regret of scholars everywhere, Dr. Poole died March 1, 1894. Born in Salem, Mass., Dec. 24, 1821, descended from an old

English family, young Poole attended the common school in Danvers till he was twelve, helped his father on the farm, and learned the tanner's trade. He loved his books, and his good mother determined that he should have an opportunity to go back to his studies.

In 1842 he entered Yale College, at the close of the Freshman year, spent three years in teaching, and was graduated in 1849. While in college, he was appointed assistant librarian of his college society, the "Brothers in Unity," which had 10,000 volumes. He soon saw the necessity of an index for the bound sets of periodicals in the library, if they were to be of practical use, and began to make such an index. The little volume of one hundred and fifty-four pages appeared in 1848, and the edition was soon exhausted. A volume of five hundred and thirty-one pages appeared in 1853; and "Poole's Index" at once secured fame for its author, both at home and abroad.

Dr. Poole was the librarian of the Boston Athenæum for thirteen years, and accepted a position in Chicago, October, 1873, to form the public library. In 1882 Dr. Poole issued the third edition of his famous "Index to Periodical Literature," having 1,469 pages. In this work he had the co-operation of the American Library Association, the Library Association of Great Britain and Ireland, and the able assistance of Wm. I. Fletcher, M.A., librarian of Amherst College. Since Dr. Poole's death, Mr. Fletcher and Mr. R. R. Bowker have carried forward the Index, aided by many other librarians.

Dr. Poole was president of the American Historical Society, 1887, of the American Library Association 1886-1888, and had written much on historical and literary topics. The Boston *Herald* says, "Dr. Poole was a bibliographer of world-wide reputation, and one whose extended knowledge of books was simply wonderful." His "Index to Periodical Literature," invaluable to both writers and readers, will perpetuate his name. Dr. Poole was succeeded by the well-known author, Mr. John Vance Cheney, who had been eight years at the head of the San Francisco public library.

JOHN CRERAR

Was born in New York City, the son of John Crerar, his parents both natives of Scotland.

He was educated in a common school, and at the age of eighteen became a clerk in a mercantile house. In 1862 he went to Chicago, and associated himself with J. McGregor Adams in the iron business. He was also interested in railroads, and was the president of a company. He was an upright member of the Second Presbyterian Church, and his first known gift was $10,000 to that church.

Unmarried, he lived quietly at the Grand Pacific Hotel until his death, Oct. 19, 1889. In his will he said, "I ask that I may be buried by the side of my honored mother, in Greenwood Cemetery, Brooklyn, N.Y., in the family lot, and that some of my many friends see that this request is complied with. I desire a plain headstone, similar to that which marks my mother's grave, to be raised over my head." The income of $1,000 was left to care for the family lot. He left various legacies to relatives. To first cousins he gave $20,000 each; to second cousins, $10,000; and to third cousins, $5,000 each. To one second cousin, on account of kindness to his mother, an additional $10,000; to the widow of a cousin, $10,000 for kindness to his only brother, Peter, then dead. To several other friends sums from $50,000 to $5,000 each.

To his partner he gave $50,000, and the same to his junior partner. To his own church, $100,000, and a like amount to the missions of the church. To the church in New York to which his family formerly belonged, and where he was baptized, $25,000. To the Chicago Orphan Asylum, the Chicago Nursery, the American Sunday-school Union, the Chicago Relief Society, the Illinois Training-School for Nurses, the Chicago Manual Training-School, the Old People's Home, the Home for the Friendless, the Young Men's Christian Association, each $50,000.

To the Chicago Historical Society, the St. Luke's Free Hospital, and the Chicago Bible Society, each $25,000. To St. Andrew's Society of New York and of Chicago, each $10,000. To the Chicago Literary Club, $10,000. For a statue of Abraham Lincoln, $100,000.

All the rest of the property, about three millions, was to be used for a free public library, to be called "The John Crerar Library," located on the South Side, inasmuch as the Newberry was to be on the North Side.

Mr. Crerar said in his will, "I desire the books and periodicals selected with a view to create and sustain a healthy moral and Christian sentiment in the community. I do not mean by this that there shall not be anything but hymn-books and sermons; but I mean that dirty French novels, and all sceptical trash, and works of questionable moral tone, shall never be found in this library. I want its atmosphere that of Christian refinement, and its aim and object the building up of character."

Mr. Crerar was fond of reading the best books. His liberality and love of literature helped to bring Thackeray to this country to lecture.

Some of the cousins of Mr. Crerar tried to break the will on the grounds put forth for breaking Mr. Tilden's will, whereby New York City failed to receive five or six millions for a public library. Fortunately the courts accepted the plain intention of the giver, and the property is now devoted to the public good through a great library largely devoted to science.

161

JOHN JACOB ASTOR

From the little village of Waldorf, near Heidelberg, Germany, came the head of the Astor family to America when he was twenty years old. Born July 17, 1763, the fourth son of a butcher, he helped his father until he was sixteen, and then determined to join an elder brother in London, who worked in the piano and flute factory of their uncle.

Having no money, he set out on foot for the Rhine; and resting under a tree, he made this resolution, which he always kept, "to be honest, industrious, and never gamble." Finding employment on a raft of timber, he earned enough money to procure a steerage passage from Holland to London, where he remained till 1783, helping his brother, and learning the English language. Having saved about seventy-five dollars at the end of three or four years, John Jacob invested about twenty-five in seven flutes, purchased a steerage ticket across the water for a like amount, and put about twenty-five in his pocket.

On the journey over he met a furrier, who told him that money could be made in buying furs from the Indians and men on the frontier, and selling them to large dealers. As soon as he reached New York, he entered the employ of a Quaker furrier, and learned all he could about the business, meantime selling his flutes, and using the money to buy furs from the Indians and hunters. He opened a little shop in New York for the sale of furs and musical instruments, walked nearly all over New York State in collecting his furs, and finally went back to London to sell his goods.

He married, probably in 1786, Sarah Todd, who brought as her marriage portion $300, and what was better still, economy, energy, and a willingness to share her husband's constant labors. As fast as a little money was saved he invested it in land, having great faith in the future of New York City. He lived most simply in the same house where he carried on his business, and after fifteen years found himself the owner of $250,000.

In 1809 he organized the American Fur Company, and established trade in furs with France, England, Germany, and Russia, and engaged in trade with China. He used to say in his old age, "The first hundred thousand dollars—that was hard to get; but afterward it was easy to make more."

He died March 29, 1848, leaving a fortune estimated at $20,000,000, much of it the result of increased values of land, on which he had built houses for rent. By will Mr. Astor conveyed the large sum, at that time, of $400,000 to found a public library; his friends, Washington Irving, Dr. Joseph G. Cogswell, and Fitz-Greene Halleck, the poet, who was his secretary for seventeen years, having advised the gift of a library when he expressed a desire to do something helpful for the city of New York. He also left $50,000 for the benefit of the poor in his native town of Waldorf.

John Jacob Astor's eldest son, and third of his seven children, William B. Astor, left and gave during his lifetime $550,000 to Astor Library. His estate of $45,000,000 was divided between his two sons, John Jacob and William. The son of John Jacob, William Waldorf Astor, a graduate of Columbia College, ex-minister to Italy, is a scholarly man, and the author of several books. The son of William Astor, John Jacob Astor, a graduate of Harvard, lives on Fifth Avenue, New York. He has also written one or more books.

In 1879 John Jacob, the grandson of the first Astor in this country, a graduate of Columbia College, a student of the University of Göttingen, and a graduate of the Harvard Law School, erected a third structure for the library similar to those built by his father and grandfather, and gave in all $850,000 to Astor Library. The entire building now has a frontage of two hundred feet, with a depth of one hundred feet. It is of brown-stone and brick, and is Byzantine in style of architecture. In 1893 its total number of volumes was 245,349.

Astor Library possesses some very rare and valuable books. "Here is one of the very few extant copies of Wyckliffe's translation of the New Testament in manuscript," writes Frederick K. Saunders, the librarian, in the *New England Magazine* for April, 1890, "so closely resembling black-letter type as almost to deceive even a practised eye. It is enriched with illuminated capitals, and its supposed date is 1390. It is said to have been once the property of Duke Humphrey. There is an Ethiopic manuscript on vellum, the service book of an Abyssinian convent at Jerusalem. There are two richly illuminated Persian manuscripts on vellum which once belonged to the library of the Mogul Emperors of Delhi; also two exquisitely illuminated missals or books of Hours, the gift of the late Mr. J. J. Astor. One of the glories of the collection is the splendid Salisbury Missal, written with wonderful skill, and profusely emblazoned with burnished gold. Here also may be found the second printed Bible, on vellum, folio, 1462, which cost $9,000."

Mrs. Astor gave a valuable collection of autographs of eminent persons; and the family also gave "a magnificent manuscript written with liquid gold, on purple vellum, entitled 'Evangelistarium,' of almost unrivalled beauty, but no less remarkable for its great age, the date being A.D. 870. This is probably the oldest book in America." Ptolemy's Geography is represented by fifteen editions, the earliest printed in 1478.

John Jacob Astor, the grandson of the first John Jacob, died in New York, Feb. 22, 1890. He presented to Trinity Church the reredos and altar, costing $80,000, as a memorial of his father, William B.

Astor. Through his wife, who was a Miss Gibbs of South Carolina, he virtually built the New York Cancer Hospital, and gave largely to the Woman's Hospital. He gave $100,000 to St. Luke's Hospital, $50,000 to the Metropolitan Museum of Art, with his wife's superb collection of laces after her death in 1887. The paintings of John Jacob Astor costing $75,000 were presented to Astor Library by his son, William Waldorf Astor, after his father's death.

MORTIMER FABRICIUS REYNOLDS

"On the 2d of December, 1814, there was born, in the narrow clearing that skirted the ford of the Genesee River, the first child of white parents to see the light upon that 'Hundred-Acre Tract' which was the primitive site of the present city of Rochester. Mortimer Fabricius Reynolds was the name given, for family reasons, to the first-born of this backwoods settlement." Thus states the "Semi-Centennial History of the City of Rochester, N.Y.," published in 1888.

This boy, grown to manhood and engaged in commerce, was the sole survivor of the six children of his father, Abelard Reynolds. He was proud of the family name; but "his childlessness, and the consciousness that with him the name was to be extinct, had come to weigh with a painful gravity." Abelard Reynolds had made a fortune from the increase in land values, and both he and his son William had interested themselves deeply in the intellectual and moral advance of the community in which they lived.

Mortimer F. Reynolds desired to leave a memorial of his father, of his brother, William Abelard Reynolds, and of himself. He wisely chose to found a library, that the name might be forever remembered. He died June 13, 1892, leaving nearly one million to found and endow the Reynolds Library of Rochester, N.Y., Alfred S. Collins, librarian.

It is stated in the press that President Seth Low of Columbia College has given over a million dollars for the new library in connection with that college.

In "Public Libraries of America," page 144, a most useful book by William I. Fletcher, librarian of Amherst College, may be found a suggestive list of the principal gifts to libraries in the United States. Among the larger bequests are Dr. James Rush, Philadelphia, $1,500,000; Henry Hall, St. Paul, Minn., $500,000; Charles E. Forbes, Northampton, Mass., $220,000; Mr. and Mrs. Converse, Malden, Mass., $125,000; Hiram Kelley, Chicago, to public library, $200,000; Silas Bronson, Waterbury, Conn., $200,000; Dr. Kirby Spencer, Minneapolis, Minn., $200,000; Mrs. Maria C. Robbins of Brooklyn, N.Y., to her former home, Arlington, Mass., for public library building and furnishing, $150,000.

FREDERICK H. RINDGE
AND HIS GIFTS

Mr. Rindge, born in Cambridge, Mass., in 1857, but at present residing in California, has given his native city a public library, a city hall, a manual training-school, and a valuable site for a high school.

The handsome library, Romanesque in style, of gray stone with brown stone trimmings, was opened to the public in 1889. One room of especial interest on the first floor contains war relics, manuscripts, autographs and pictures of distinguished persons, and literary and historical matter connected with the history of Cambridge. The European note-book of Margaret Fuller is seen here, the lock, key, and hinges of the old Holmes mansion, removed to make way for the Law School, etc.

The library has six local stations where books may be ordered by filling out a slip; and these orders are gathered up three times a day, and books are sent to these stations the same day.

The City Hall, a large building also of gray stone with brown stone trimmings, is similar to the old town halls of Brussels, Bruges, and others of mediæval times. Its high tower can be seen at a great distance.

The other important gift to Cambridge from Mr. Rindge is a manual training-school for boys. Ground was broken for this school in the middle of July, 1888, and pupils were received in September. The boys work in wood, iron, blacksmithing, drawing, etc. The system is similar to that adopted by Professor Woodward at St. Louis. The boys, to protect their clothes, wear outer suits of dark brown and black duck, and round paper caps.

The fire-drill is especially interesting to strangers. Hose-carriages and ladders are kept in the building, and the boys can put streams of water to the top in a very brief time. Mr. Rindge supports the school. *The instruction is free*, and is a part of the public-school work. The pupils may take in the English High School a course of pure head-work, or part head-work and part hand-work. If they elect the latter, they drop one study, and in its place take three hours a day in manual training. The course covers three years.

Mr. Rindge inherited his wealth largely from his father. He made these gifts when he was twenty-nine years of age. Being an earnest Christian, he made it a condition of his gifts that verses of Scripture and maxims of conduct should be inscribed upon the walls of the various buildings. These are found on the library building; and the inscription on the City Hall reads as follows: "God has given commandments unto men. From these commandments men have framed laws by which to be governed. It is honorable and praiseworthy to faithfully serve the people by helping to administer these laws. If the laws are not enforced, the people are not well governed."

ANTHONY J. DREXEL
AND HIS INSTITUTE

The Drexel family, like a majority of the successful and useful families in this country, began poor. Anthony J. Drexel's father, Francis Martin Drexel, was born at Dornbirn, in the Austrian Tyrol, April 7, 1792. When he was eleven years old, his father, a merchant, sent him to a school near Milan. Later, when there was a war with France, he was obliged to go to Switzerland to avoid conscription.

He earned a scanty living at whatever he could find to do, but his chief work and pleasure was in portrait painting. When he was twenty-five, in 1817, he determined to try his fortune in the New World, and reached the United States after a voyage of seventy-two days.

He settled in Philadelphia as an artist, with probably little expectation of any future wealth. After nine years of work he went to Peru, Chili, and Mexico, and seems to have had good success in painting the portraits of noted people, General Simon Bolivar among them.

Returning to Philadelphia, he surprised his acquaintances by starting a bank in 1837. There were fears of failure from what seemed an inadequate capital and lack of knowledge of business; but Mr. Drexel was economical, strictly honest, energetic, and devoted to his work.

He opened a little office in Third Street, and placed his son Anthony, born Sept. 13, 1826, in the small bank. "While waiting on customers," says *Harper's Weekly*, "the boy was in the habit of eating his cold dinner from a basket under the counter." He was but a lad of thirteen, yet he soon showed a special fitness for the place by his quickness and good sense.

The bank grew in patrons, in reputation, and in wealth; and when Francis Drexel died, June 5, 1863, he had long been a millionnaire, had retired from business, and left the bank to the management of his sons.

Besides the bank in Philadelphia, branch houses were formed in New York, Paris, and London. "As a man of affairs," wrote his very intimate friend, George W. Childs, "no one has ever spoken ill of Anthony J. Drexel; and he spoke ill of no one. He did not drive sharp bargains; he did not profit by the hard necessities of others; he did not exact from those in his employ excessive tasks and give them inadequate pay. He was a lenient, patient, liberal creditor, a generous employer, considerate of and sympathetic with every one who worked for him...."

"He was a devoted husband, a loving parent, a true friend, a generous host, and in all his domestic relations considerate, just, and kind. His manners were finely courteous, manly, gentle, and refined. His mind was as pure as a child's; and during all the years of our close companionship I never knew him to speak a word that he might not have freely spoken in the presence of his own children. His religion was as deep as his nature, and rested upon the enduring foundations of faith, hope, and charity.

"He observed always a strict simplicity of living; he walked daily to and from his place of business, which was nearly three miles distant from his home. I was his companion for the greater part of the way every morning in these long walks; and as he passed up and down Chestnut Street, he was wont to salute in his cordial, pleasant, friendly manner, large numbers of all sorts and conditions of people. His smile was especially bright and attractive, and his voice low and sweet."

Mr. Drexel inherited his father's artistic tastes, and in his home at West Philadelphia, and at his country place, "Runnymede," near Lansdowne, he had many beautiful works of art, statuary, books, paintings, bronzes, and the like. He was also especially fond of music.

He was a great friend of General Grant, and Dec. 19, 1879, gave him and Mrs. Grant a notable reception with about seven hundred prominent guests. He was one of the pall-bearers at Grant's funeral in 1885.

Mr. Drexel was always a generous giver. He was a large contributor to the University of Pennsylvania, to hospitals, to churches of all denominations, and to asylums. With Mr. Childs and others he built an Episcopal church at Elberon, Long Branch, where he usually went in the summer.

His largest and best gift, for which he will be remembered, is that of about three million dollars to found and endow Drexel Institute, erected in his lifetime. He wished to fit young men and women to earn their living; and after making a careful examination of Cooper Institute, New York, and Pratt Institute, Brooklyn, and sending abroad to learn the best methods and plan of buildings for such industrial education, he began his own admirable Drexel Institute of Art, Science, and Industry in West Philadelphia. He erected the handsome building of light buff brick with terra-cotta trimmings, at the corner of Thirty-second and Chestnut Streets, at a cost of $550,000, and then gave an endowment of $1,000,000. At various times he gave to the library, museum, etc., over $600,000.

The Institute was dedicated on the afternoon of Dec. 17, 1891, Chauncey M. Depew making the dedication address, and was opened to students Jan. 4, 1892. James MacAlister, LL.D., superintendent of the public schools of Philadelphia, a man of fine scholarship, great energy, and enthusiastic love for the work of education, was chosen as the president.

From the first the school has been filled with eager students in the various departments. The art department gives instruction in painting, modelling, architecture, design and decoration, wood-carving, etc.; the department of science and technology, courses in mathematics, chemistry, physics, machine construction, and electrical engineering; the department of mechanic arts, shopwork in wood and iron with essential English branches; the business department, commercial law, stenography, and typewriting, etc.; the department of domestic science and arts gives courses in cooking, dressmaking, and millinery. There are also courses in physical training, in music, library work, and evening classes open five nights in the week from October to April.

The Institute was attended by more than 2,700 students in 1893-1894; and 35,000 persons attended the free public lectures in art, science, technology, etc., and free concerts, chiefly organ recitals, weekly, during the winter months.

The Institute has been fortunate in its gifts from friends. Mr. George W. Childs gave to it his rare and valuable collection of manuscripts and autographs, fine engravings, ivories, books on art, etc.; Mrs. John R. Fell, a daughter of Mr. Drexel, a collection of ancient jewellery and rare old clocks; Mrs. James W. Paul, another daughter of Mr. Drexel, $10,000 as a memorial of her mother, to be used in the purchase of articles for the museum; while other members of the family have given bronzes, metal-work, and unique and useful gifts.

Mr. Drexel lived to see his Institute doing its noble work. So interested was he that he stopped daily as he went to the bank to see the young people at their duties. He was greatly interested in the evening classes. "This part of the work," says Dr. MacAlister, "he watched with great eagerness, and he was specially desirous that young people who were compelled to work through the day should have opportunities in the evening equal to those who took the regular daily work of the Institution."

Mr. Drexel died suddenly, June 30, 1893, about two years after the building of the Institute, from apoplexy, at Carlsbad, Germany. He had gone to Europe for his health, as was his custom yearly, and seemed about as well as usual until the stroke came. Two weeks before he had had a mild attack of pleurisy, but would not permit his family to be told of it, thinking that he would fully recover.

Mr. Drexel left behind him the memory of a modest, unassuming man; so able a financier that he was asked to accept the position of Secretary of the Treasury of the United States, but declined; so generous a giver, that he built his monument before his death in his elegant and helpful Institute, an honor to his native city, Philadelphia, and an honor to his family.

PHILIP D. ARMOUR
AND HIS INSTITUTE

Philip D. Armour was born in Stockbridge, Madison County, N.Y., and spent his early life on a farm. In 1852, when he was twenty years of age, he went to California, and finally settled in Chicago, where he has become very wealthy by dealing in packed meat, which is sent to almost every corner of the earth.

"He pays six or seven millions of dollars yearly in wages," writes Arthur Warren in an interesting article in *McClure's Magazine*, February, 1894, "owns four thousand railway cars, which are used in transporting his goods, and has seven or eight hundred horses to haul his wagons. Fifty or sixty thousand persons receive direct support from the wages paid in his meatpacking business alone, if we estimate families on the census basis. He is a larger owner of grain-elevators than any other individual in either hemisphere; he is the proprietor of a glue factory, which turns out a product of seven millions of tons a year; and he is actively interested in an important railway enterprise."

He manages his business with great system, and knows from his heads of departments, some of whom he pays a salary of $25,000 yearly, what takes place from day to day in his various works. He is a quiet, self-centred man, a good listener, has excellent judgment, and possesses untiring energy.

"All my life," he says, "I have been up with the sun. The habit is as easy at sixty-one as it was at sixteen; perhaps easier, because I am hardened to it. I have my breakfast at half-past five or six; I walk down town to my office, and am there by seven, and I know what is going on in the world without having to wait for others to come and tell me. At noon I have a simple luncheon of bread and milk, and after that, usually, a short nap, which freshens me again for the afternoon's work. I am in bed again at nine o'clock every night."

Mr. Armour thinks there are as great and as many opportunities for men to succeed in life as there ever have been. He said to Mr. Warren: "There was never a better time than the present, and the future will bring even greater opportunities than the past. Wealth, capital, can do nothing without brains to direct it. It will be as true in the future as it is in the present that brains make capital—capital does not make brains. The world does not stand still. Changes come quicker now than they ever did, and they will come quicker and quicker. New ideas, new inventions, new methods of manufacture, of transportation, new ways to do almost everything, will be found as the world grows older; and the men who anticipate them, and who are ready for them,

171

will find advantages as great as any their fathers or grandfathers have had."

Mr. Frank G. Carpenter, the well-known journalist, relates this incident of Mr. Armour:—

"He is a good judge of men, and he usually puts the right man in the right place. I am told that he never discharges a man if he can help it. If the man is not efficient he gives instructions to have him put in some other department, but to keep him if possible. There are certain things, however, which he will not tolerate; and among these are laziness, intemperance, and getting into debt. As to the last, he says he believes in good wages, and that he pays the best. He tells his men that if they are not able to live on the wages he pays them he does not want them to work for him. Not long ago he met a policeman in his office.

"'What are you doing here, sir?' he asked.

"'I am here to serve a paper,' was the reply.

"'What kind of a paper?' asked Mr. Armour.

"'I want to garnishee one of your men's wages for debt,' said the policeman.

"'Indeed,' replied Mr. Armour; 'and who is the man?' He thereupon asked the policeman into his private office, and ordered the debtor to come in. He then asked the clerk how long he had been in debt. The man replied that for twenty years he had been behind, and that he could not catch up.

"'But you get a good salary,' said Mr. Armour, 'don't you?'

"'Yes,' said the clerk; 'but I can't get out of debt. My life is such that somehow or other I can't get out.'

"'But you must get out,' said Mr. Armour, 'or you must leave here. How much do you owe?'

"The clerk then gave the amount. It was less than $1,000. Mr. Armour took his check-book, and wrote out an order for the amount. 'There,' he said, as he handed the clerk the check, 'there is enough to pay all your debts. Now I want you to keep out of debt, and if I hear of your getting into debt again you will have to leave.'

"The man took the check. He did pay his debts, and remodelled his life on a cash basis. About a year after the above incident happened he came to Mr. Armour, and told him that he had had a place offered him at a higher salary, and that he was going to leave. He thanked Mr. Armour, and told him that his last year had been the happiest of his life, and that getting out of debt had made a new man of him."

When Mr. Armour was asked by Mr. Carpenter to what he attributed his great success, he replied:—

"I think that thrift and economy have had much to do with it. I owe much to my mother's training, and to a good line of Scotch ancestors, who have always been thrifty and economical."

Mr. Armour has not been content to spend his life in amassing

172

wealth only. After the late Joseph Armour bequeathed a fund to establish Armour Mission, Philip D. Armour doubled the fund, or more than doubled it; and now the Mission has nearly two thousand children in its Sunday-school, with free kindergarten and free dispensary. Mr. Armour goes to the Mission every Sunday afternoon, and finds great happiness among the children.

To yield a revenue yearly for the Mission, Mr. Armour built "Armour Flats," a great building adjoining the Mission, with a large grass-plot in the centre, where in two hundred and thirteen flats, having each from six to seven rooms, families can find clean and attractive homes, with a rental of from seventeen to thirty-five dollars a month.

"There is an endowed work," says Mr. Armour, "that cannot be altered by death, or by misunderstandings among trustees, or by bickerings of any kind. Besides, a man can do something to carry out his ideas while he lives, but he can't do so after he is in the grave. Build pleasant homes for people of small incomes, and they will leave their ugly surroundings, and lead brighter lives."

Mr. Armour, aside from many private charities, has given over a million and a half dollars to the Armour Institute of Technology. The five-story fire-proof building of red brick trimmed with brown stone was finished Dec. 6, 1892, on the corner of Thirty-third Street and Armour Avenue; and the keys were put in the hands of the able and eloquent preacher, Dr. Frank W. Gunsaulus, "to formulate," says the Chicago *Tribune*, Oct. 15, 1893, "more exactly than Mr. Armour had done the lines on which this work was to go forward. Dr. Gunsaulus had long ago reached the conclusion that the best way to prepare men for a home in heaven is to make it decently comfortable for them here."

Dr. Gunsaulus put his heart and energy into this noble work. The academic department prepares students to enter any college in the country; the technical department gives courses in mechanical engineering, electricity, and electrical engineering, mining engineering, and metallurgy. The department of domestic arts offers instruction in cooking, dressmaking, millinery, etc.; the department of commerce fits persons for a business life, wisely combining with its course in shorthand and typewriting such a knowledge of the English language, history, and some modern languages, as will make the students do intelligent work for authors, lawyers, and educated people in general.

Special attention has been given to the gymnasium, that health may be fully attended to. Mr. Armour has spared neither pains nor expense to provide the best machinery, especially for electrical work. "In a few years," he says, "we shall be doing everything by electricity. Before long our steam-engines will be as old-fashioned as the windmills are now."

Dr. Gunsaulus has taken great pleasure in gathering books,

prints, etc., for the library, which already has a choice collection of works on the early history of printing.

The Institute was opened in September, 1893, with six hundred pupils, and has been most useful and successful from the first.

LEONARD CASE
AND THE SCHOOL OF APPLIED SCIENCE

Technological schools are springing up so rapidly all over our country that it would be impossible to name them all. The Stevens Institute of Technology at Hoboken, N.J., was organized in 1871, with a gift of $650,000; the Towne Scientific School, Philadelphia, 1872, $1,000,000; the Miller School, Batesville, Va., 1878, $1,000,000; the Rose Polytechnic, Terre Haute, Ind., 1883, over $500,000; the Case School of Applied Science of Cleveland, Ohio, 1881, over $2,000,000.

Leonard Case, the giver of the Case School and the Case Library, born June 27, 1820, was a quiet, scholarly man, who gave wisely the wealth amassed by his father. The family on the paternal side came from Holland; on the maternal side from Germany. Mr. James D. Cleveland, in a recent sketch of the founder of Case School, gives an interesting account of the ancestors of Mr. Case.

The great-grandfather of Leonard Case, Leonard Eckstein, when a youth, had a quarrel with the Catholic clergy in Nuremberg, near which city he was born, and was in consequence thrown into prison, where he nearly starved. One day his sister brought him a cake which contained a slender silk cord baked in it. This cord was let down from his cell window to a friend, who fastened it to a rope which, when drawn up, enabled the young man to slide down a wall eighty feet above the ground.

After his escape, the youth of nineteen came to America, and landed in Philadelphia without a cent of money. Later he married and moved to Western Pennsylvania; and his daughter Magdalene married Meshach Case, the grandfather of Leonard Case.

Meshach was an invalid from asthma. In 1799 he and his wife came on horseback to explore Ohio, and perhaps make a home. They bought two hundred acres of the wilderness in the township of Warren, built a log cabin, and cleared an acre of timber around it. The following year others came to settle, and all celebrated the Fourth of July with instruments made on the grounds. Their drum was a piece of hollow pepperidge-tree with a fawn's skin stretched over it, and a fife was made from an elder stem.

The eldest son, Leonard, who was a hard worker from a child, at seven cutting wood for the fires, at ten thrashing grain, at fourteen ploughing and harvesting, took cold when heated, and became ill for two years and a cripple for the rest of his life, using crutches as he walked. Early in life, when it was the fashion to use intoxicating liquors, Leonard made a pledge never to use them, and was a total abstainer as long as he lived, thus setting a noble example to the growing community.

Determined to have an education, he invented some instruments for drafting, bottomed all the chairs in the neighborhood, made sieves for the farmers, and thus earned a little money for books. As his handwriting was good, he was made clerk of the little court at Warren, and later of the Supreme Court for Trumbull County, where he had an opportunity to study, and copy the records of the Connecticut Land Company.

A friend advised him to study law, and furnished him with books, which advice he followed. Later, in 1816, he moved to Cleveland, and was made cashier of a bank just organized. He was a man of public spirit, suggested the planting of trees which have made Cleveland known as the Forest City, was sent to the Legislature, and finally became president of a bank, as well as land agent of the Connecticut Land Company. He was universally respected and esteemed.

The hard-working invalid had become rich through increase in value of the large amount of land which he had purchased. He died Dec. 7, 1864, seven years after his wife's death, and two years after the death of his very promising son William, of consumption. The latter was deeply interested in natural history, and in 1859 had begun to erect a building for the Young Men's Library Association and the Kirtland Society of Natural History. This project his surviving brother, Leonard, carried out.

After the death of father, mother, and brother, Leonard Case was left to inherit the property. He had graduated at Yale College in 1842, and was admitted to the bar in 1844. He, however, devoted himself to literary pursuits, and travelled extensively over this country and abroad.

Ill health in later years increased his natural reticence and dislike of publicity. He gave generously where he became interested. To the Library Association he first gave $20,000. In 1876 he gave Case Building and grounds, then valued at $225,000, to the Library Association. It is now worth over half a million dollars, and furnishes a good income for its library of over 40,000 volumes. Under the excellent management of Mr. Charles Orr, the librarian, the building has been remodelled, and the library much enlarged. The membership fee is one dollar annually.

The same year, 1876, Mr. Case determined to carry out his plan of a School of Applied Science. He corresponded with various eminent men; and on Feb. 24, 1877, after gifts to his father's relatives, he conveyed his property to trustees for a school where should be taught mathematics, physics, mechanical and civil engineering, chemistry, mining and metallurgy, natural history, modern languages, etc., to fit young men for practical work in life.

"How well this foresight was inspired," says Mr. Cleveland, "is shown in the great demand by the city and country at large for the men who have received training at the Case School. Hundreds are called for by iron, steel, and chemical works, here and elsewhere, to act in laboratories or in direction of important engineering, in mines, railroads, construction of docks, waterworks, electrical projects, and architecture. Nearly forty new professions have been opened to the youth of Cleveland, which were unavailable before this school was founded."

Cady Staley, Ph.D. LL.D., is the president of Case School, which has an able corps of professors. There are nearly 250 students in the institution.

Leonard Case died Jan. 6, 1880; but his school and his library perpetuate his name, and make his memory honored.

177

ASA PACKER
AND LEHIGH UNIVERSITY

In the midst of twenty acres stands Lehigh University, at South Bethlehem, Penn., founded by Asa Packer,—a great school of technology, with courses in civil, mechanical, mining, and electrical engineering, chemistry, and architecture. The school of general literature of the University has a classical course, a Latin-scientific course, and a course in science and letters.

To this institution Judge Packer gave three and one-quarter millions during his life; and by will, eventually, the University will become one of the richest in the country.

He did not give to Lehigh University alone. "St. Luke's Hospital, so well known throughout eastern Pennsylvania for its noble and practical charity," says Mr. Davis Brodhead in the *Magazine of American History*, June, 1885, "is also sustained by the endowments of Asa Packer. Indeed, when we consider the scope of his generosity, of which Washington and Lee University of Virginia, Muhlenburg College at Allentown, Penn., Jefferson Medical College of Philadelphia, and many churches throughout his native State, of different denominations, can bear witness, we can the better appreciate how truly catholic were his gifts. His benefactions did not pause upon State lines, nor recognize sectional divisions.

"In speaking of his generosity, Senator T. F. Bayard once said, 'The confines of a continent were too narrow for his sense of human brotherhood, which recognized its ties everywhere upon this footstool of the Almighty, and decreed that all were to be united to share in the fruits of his life-long labor.'"

Asa Packer was born in Groton, Conn., Dec. 29, 1805. As his father had been unsuccessful in business he could not educate his boy, who found employment in a tannery in North Stonington. His employer soon died, and the youth was obliged to go to work on a farm.

He was ambitious, and determined to seek his fortune farther west; so with real courage walked from Connecticut to Susquehanna County, Penn., and in the new county took up the trade of carpenter and joiner.

For ten years he worked hard at his trade. He purchased a few acres in the native forest, cleared off the trees, and built a log house, to which he took his bride. When children were born into the home she made all the clothing, and in every way helped the poor, industrious carpenter to make a living.

In 1833, when he was twenty-eight years old, Mr. Packer moved

178

his family to Mauch Chunk in the Lehigh Valley, hoping that he could earn a little more money by his trade.

When he had leisure, his busy mind was thinking how the vast supplies of coal and iron in the Lehigh Valley could be transported East. In the fall of 1833 the carpenter chartered a canal boat, and doing most of the manual labor himself, he started with a load of coal to Philadelphia through the Lehigh Canal.

Making a little money out of this venture, he secured another boat, and in 1835 took his brother into partnership, and they together commenced dealing in general merchandise. This firm was the first to carry anthracite coal through to New York, it having been carried previously to Philadelphia, and from there re-shipped to New York.

With Asa Packer's energy, honesty, and broad thinking, the business grew to good-sized proportions. Then he realized that they must have steam for quicker transportation. He urged the Lehigh Coal and Navigation Company to build a railroad along the banks of their canal; but they refused, thinking that coal and lumber could only pay water freights. In September, 1847, a charter was granted to the Delaware, Lehigh, Schuylkill, and Susquehanna Railroad Company; but the people were indifferent, and the time of the charter was within seventeen days of expiring, when Asa Packer became one of the board of managers, and by his efforts graded one mile of the road, thus saving the charter. Two years later the name of the company was changed to the Lehigh Valley Railroad Company, and Mr. Packer had a controlling portion of the stock.

So much faith had he in the project that no one else, apparently, had faith in, that he offered to build the road from Mauch Chunk to Easton, a distance of forty-six miles, and take his pay in the stocks and bonds of the company.

The offer was accepted; and the road was finished in 1855, four years after it was begun, but not without many discouragements and great financial strain. Mr. Packer was made president of the railroad company, which position he held as long as he lived.

Already wealth and honors had come to the energetic carpenter. In 1842 and 1843 he was elected to the State Legislature, and became one of the two associate judges for the new county of Carbon.

In 1852, and again in 1854, he was elected to Congress as a Democrat, and made a useful record for himself. So universally respected was he in Pennsylvania for his Christian life, as well as for his successful business career, that he was prominently mentioned as a presidential candidate, Pennsylvania voting solidly for him through fourteen ballots; and when his name was withdrawn the delegates voted for Horatio Seymour.

In 1869, Judge Packer was nominated for governor; but the State was strongly Republican, having given General Grant the previous year

25,000 majority. Judge Packer was defeated by only 4,500 votes, showing his popularity in his own State.

Two years before this, in the autumn of 1867, his great gift, Lehigh University, had been opened to pupils. It has now considerably over four hundred students, from thirty-five various States and countries. It was named by Judge Packer, who would not allow his own name to be used. After his death the largest of the buildings was called Packer Hall, but by the wording of the charter the name of the University can never be changed. The Packer Memorial Church, a handsome structure, is the gift of Mrs. Packer Cummings, the daughter of the founder. To the east of Packer Hall is the University Library with 97,000 volumes, the building costing $100,000, erected by Judge Packer in memory of his daughter Mrs. Lucy Packer Linderman. At his death he endowed the library with a fund of $500,000.

Judge Packer died May 17, 1879, and is buried in the little cemetery at Mauch Chunk in the picturesque Lehigh Valley. He lived simply, giving away during the last few years of his life over $4,000,000.

Said the president of the University, Rev. Dr. John M. Leavitt, in a memorial sermon delivered in University Chapel, June 15, 1879, "Not only his magnificent bequests are our treasures; we have something more precious,—his *character* is the noblest legacy of Asa Packer to the Lehigh University....

"He was both gentle and inflexible, persuasive and commanding, in his sensibilities refined and delicate as a woman, and in his intellect and resolve clear and strong as a successful military leader.... Genial kindness flowed out from him as beams from the sun. Never at any period of his life is it possible to conceive in him a churlish or niggardly spirit.... During nearly fifty years he was connected with our church, usually as an officer, and for much of the long period was a constant and exemplary communicant.... Like the silent light giving bloom to the world, his faith had a vitalizing power. He grasped the truth of Christianity and the position of the church, and showed his creed by his life."

180

CORNELIUS VANDERBILT
AND VANDERBILT UNIVERSITY

Cornelius Vanderbilt, born May 27, 1794, descended from a Dutch farmer, Jan Aertsen Van der Bilt, who settled in Brooklyn, N.Y., about 1650, began his career in assisting his father to convey his produce to market in a sail-boat. The boy did not care for education, but was active in pursuit of business. At sixteen he purchased for one hundred dollars a boat, in which he ferried passengers and goods between New York City and Staten Island, where his father lived. He saved carefully until he had paid for it. At eighteen he was the owner of two boats, and captain of a third.

At nineteen he married a cousin, Sophia Johnson, who by her saving and her energy helped him to accumulate his fortune. At twenty-three he was worth $9,000, and was the captain of a steamboat at a salary of $1,000 a year. The boat made trips between New York City and New Brunswick, N.J., where his wife managed a small hotel.

In 1829, when he was thirty-five, he began to build steamboats, and operated them on the Hudson River, on Long Island Sound, and on the route to Boston. When he was forty his property was estimated at $500,000. When the gold-seekers rushed to California, in 1848-1849, Mr. Vanderbilt established a line by way of Lake Nicaragua, and made large profits. He also established a line between New York and Havre.

During the Civil War Mr. Vanderbilt gave the Vanderbilt, his finest steamship, costing $800,000, to the government, and sent her to the James River to assist when the Merrimac attacked the national vessels at Hampton Roads. Congress voted him a gold medal for his timely gift.

In 1863 he began to invest in railroads, purchasing a large part of the stock of the New York and Harlem Railroad. His property was at this time estimated at $40,000,000. He soon gained controlling interest in other roads. His chief maxim was, "Do your business well, and don't tell anybody what you are going to do until you have done it."

In February, 1873, Bishop McTyeire of Nashville, Tenn., was visiting with the family of Mr. Vanderbilt in New York City. The first wife was dead, and Mr. Vanderbilt had married a second time. Both men had married cousins in the city of Mobile, who were very intimate in their girlhood, and this brought the bishop and Mr. Vanderbilt into friendly relations. One evening when they were conversing about the effects of the Civil War upon the Southern States, Commodore

Vanderbilt, as he was usually called, expressed a desire to do something for the South, and asked the bishop what he would suggest.

The Methodist Church at the South had organized Central University at Nashville, but found it impossible to raise the funds needed to carry on the work. The bishop stated the great need for such an institution, and Mr. Vanderbilt at once gave $500,000. In his letter to the Board of Trust, Mr. Vanderbilt said, "If it shall through its influence contribute even in the smallest degree to strengthening the ties which should exist between all geographical sections of our common country, I shall feel that it has accomplished one of the objects that has led me to take an interest in it."

Later, in his last illness, he gave enough to make his gift a million. The name of the institution was changed to Vanderbilt University. Mr. Vanderbilt died in New York, Jan. 4, 1877, leaving the larger part of his millions to his son, William Henry Vanderbilt. He gave $50,000 to the Rev. Charles F. Deems to purchase the Church of the Strangers.

Founder's Day at Vanderbilt University is celebrated yearly on the late Commodore's birthday, May 27, the day being ushered in by the playing of music and the ringing of the University bell.

Bishop McTyeire, who, Mr. Vanderbilt insisted, should accept the presidency of the University, used to say, "My wife was a silent but golden link in the chain of Providence that led to Vanderbilt University."

When an attractive site of seventy-five acres of land was chosen for the buildings, an agent who was recommending an out-of-the-way place protested, and said, "Bishop, the boys will be looking out of the windows there."

"We want them to look out," said the practical bishop, "and to know what is going on outside."

The secretary of the faculty tells a characteristic incident of this noble man. "He once cordially thanked me for conducting through the University building a company of plain country people, among whom was a woman with a baby in her arms. 'Who knows what may come of that visit?' said he. 'It may bring that baby here as a student. He may yet be one of our illustrious men. Who knows? Who knows? Such people are not to be neglected. Great men come of them.'"

Vanderbilt University now has over seven hundred students, and is sending out many capable scholars into fields of usefulness.

Mr. William H. Vanderbilt, the son of Cornelius, gave over $450,000 to the University. His first gift of $100,000 was for the gymnasium, Science Hall, and Wesley Hall, the Home of the Biblical Department. Another $100,000 was for the engineering department. At his death, Dec. 8, 1885, he left the University by will $200,000.

Mr. Vanderbilt's estate was estimated at $200,000,000, double the amount left by his father. It is said that he left $10,000,000 to each of his eight children, the larger part of his fortune going to two of his sons, Cornelius and William K. Vanderbilt.

He gave for the removing of the obelisk from Egypt to Central Park, $103,000; to the College of Physicians and Surgeons of New York City, $500,000. His daughter Emily, wife of William D. Sloan, gave a Maternity Home in connection with the college, costing $250,000. Mr. Vanderbilt's four sons, Cornelius, William, Frederick, and George, have erected a building for clinical instruction as a memorial of their father.

Mr. Vanderbilt gave $100,000 each to the Home and Foreign Missions of the Primitive Episcopal Church, to the New York Missions of that church, to St. Luke's Hospital, the Metropolitan Museum of Art, the United Brethren Church at New Dorp, Staten Island, and to the Young Men's Christian Association. He gave $50,000 each to the Theological Seminary of the Episcopal Church, the New York Bible Society, the Home for Incurables, Seamen's Society, New York Home for Intemperate Men, and the American Museum of Natural History.

Cornelius Vanderbilt, the grandson of Commodore Vanderbilt, has given $10,000 for the library, and $20,000 for the Hall of Mechanical Engineering of Vanderbilt University. He has also given a building to Yale College in memory of his son, a large building at the corner of Madison Avenue and Forty-fifth Street to his railroad employees for reading, gymnasium hall, bathrooms, etc., $100,000 for the Protestant Cathedral, and much to other good works.

Another son of William H., George W. Vanderbilt, who is making at his home in Asheville, N.C., a collection as complete as possible of all trees and plants, established the Thirteenth Street Branch of The Free Circulating Library in New York City, in July, 1888, and has supported a normal training-school.

A daughter of William H., Mrs. Elliott F. Shepard, has given to the Young Women's Christian Association in New York the Margaret Louisa Home, 14 and 16 East Sixteenth Street, a handsome and well-appointed structure where working-women can find a temporary home and comfort. The limit of time for each guest is four weeks. The house contains fifty-eight single and twenty-one double rooms. It has proved a great blessing to those who are strangers in a great city, and need inexpensive and respectable surroundings.

It is stated in the press that Mrs. Frederick Vanderbilt uses a generous portion of her income in preparing worthy young women for some useful position in life,—as nurses, or in sewing or art, each individual having $500 expended for such training.

BARON MAURICE DE HIRSCH

"The death of Baron Hirsch," says the New York *Tribune*, April 22, 1896, "is a loss to the whole human race. To one of the most ancient and illustrious branches of that race it will seem a catastrophe. No man of this century has done so much for the Jews as he.... In his twelfth century castle of Eichorn in Moravia he conceived vast schemes of beneficence. On his more than princely estate of St. Johann in Hungary he elaborated the details. In his London and Paris mansions he put them into execution. He rose early and worked late, and kept busy a staff of secretaries and agents in all parts of the world. He not only relieved the immediate distress of the people, he founded schools to train them to useful work. He transported them by thousands from lands of bondage to lands of freedom, and planted them there in happy colonies. In countless other directions he gave his wealth freely for the benefit of mankind without regard to race or creed."

Baron Hirsch died at Presburg, Hungary, April 20, 1896, of apoplexy. He was the son of a Bavarian merchant, and was born in 1833. At eighteen he became a clerk in the banking-firm of Bischoffsheim & Goldschmidt, and married the daughter of the former. He was the successful promoter of the great railway system from Budapest to Varna on the Black Sea. He made vast sums out of Turkish railway bonds, and is said to have been as rich as the Rothschilds.

He gave away in his lifetime an enormous amount, stated in the press to have been $15,000,000 yearly, for the five years before his death.

The New York *Tribune* says he gave much more than $20,000,000 for the help of the Jews. He gave to institutions in Egypt, Turkey, and Asia Minor, which bear his name. He offered the Russian Government $10,000,000 for public education if it would make no discrimination as to race or religion; but it declined the offer, and banished the Jews.

To the Hirsch fund in this country for the help of the Jews the baron sent more than $2,500,000. The managers of the fund spent no money in bringing the Jews to this country, but when here, opened schools for the children to prepare them to enter the public schools, evening schools for adults, training-schools to teach them carpentry, plumbing, and the like; provided public baths for them; bought farm-lands for them in New Jersey and Connecticut, and assisted them to buy small farms; provided factories for young men and women, as at Woodbine, N.J., where 5,100 acres have been purchased for the Hirsch Colony, and a brickyard and kindling-wood factory established. The baron is said to have received 400 begging letters daily, some of them from crowned heads, to whom he loaned large amounts. The favorite home of the baron was in Paris, where he lost his only and idolized son Lucien, in 1888, at the age of twenty. Much of the fortune that was to be the son's the father devoted to charity, especially to the alleviation of the condition of the European Jews, in whom the son was deeply interested. Many millions were left to Lucienne, the extremely pretty natural daughter of his son Lucien.

ISAAC RICH
AND BOSTON UNIVERSITY

Isaac Rich left to Boston University, chartered in 1869, more than a million and a half dollars. He was born in Wellfleet, Mass., in 1801, of humble parentage. At the age of fourteen he was assisting his father in a fish-stall in Boston, and afterwards kept an oyster-stall in Faneuil Hall. He became a very successful fish-merchant, and gave his wealth for noble purposes.

Unfortunately, immediately after his death, Jan. 13, 1872, the great fire of 1872 consumed the best investments of the estate, and the panic of 1873 and other great losses followed; so that for rebuilding the stores and banks in which the estate had been largely invested money had to be borrowed, and at the close of ten years the estate actually transferred to the University was a little less than $700,000.

This sum would have been much larger had not the statutes of New York State made it illegal to convey to a corporation outside the State, like Boston University, the real estate owned by Mr. Rich in Brooklyn, which reverted to the legal heirs. It is claimed that Mr. Rich was "the first Bostonian who ever donated so large a sum to the cause of collegiate education."

The Hon. Jacob Sleeper, one of the three original incorporators of the University, gave to it over a quarter of a million dollars. The College of Liberal Arts is named in his honor.

Boston University owes much of its wide reputation to its president, the Rev. Dr. William F. Warren, a successful author as well as able executive. From the first he has favored co-education and equal opportunities for men and women. Dr. Warren said in 1890, "In my opinion the co-education of the sexes in high and grammar schools, as also in colleges and universities, is absolutely essential to the best results in the education of youth.

"I believe it to be best for boys, best for girls, best for teachers, best for tax-payers, best for the community, best for morals and manners and religion."

More than sixty years ago, in 1833, at its beginning, Oberlin College gave the first example of co-education in this country. In 1880 a little more than half the colleges in the United States, 51.3 per cent, had adopted the policy; in 1890 the proportion had increased to 65.5 per cent. Probably a majority of persons will agree with Dr. James MacAlister of Philadelphia, that "co-education is becoming universal throughout this country."

Concerning Boston University, the report prepared for the

admirable education series edited by Professor Herbert B. Adams of Johns Hopkins University, says, "This University was the first to afford the young women of Massachusetts the advantages of the higher education. Its College of Liberal Arts antedated Wellesley and Smith and the Harvard Annex. Its doors, furthermore, were not reluctantly opened in consequence of the pressure of an outside public opinion too great to be resisted. On the contrary, it was in advance of public sentiment on this line, and directed it. Its school of theology was the earliest anywhere to present to women all the privileges provided for men. In fact, this University was the first in history to present to women students unrestricted opportunities to fit themselves for each of the learned professions. It was the first ever organized from foundation to capstone without discrimination on the ground of sex. Its publications bearing upon the joint education of the sexes have been sought in all countries where the question of opening the older universities to women has been under discussion."

Boston University, 1896, has at present 1,270 students,—women 377, men 893,—and requires high grade of scholarship. It is stated that "the first four years' course of graded medical instruction ever offered in this country was instituted by this school in the spring of 1878."

DANIEL B. FAYERWEATHER
AND OTHERS

Mr. Fayerweather was born in Stepney, Conn., in 1821; he was apprenticed to a farmer, learned the shoemaker's trade in Bridgeport, and worked at the trade until he became ill. Then he bought a tin-peddler's outfit, and went to Virginia. When he could not sell for cash he took hides in payment.

Afterwards he returned to his trade at Bridgeport, where he remained till 1854, when he was thirty-three years old. He then removed to New York City, and entered the employ of Hoyt Brothers, dealers in leather. Years later, on the withdrawal of Mr. Hoyt, the firm name became Fayerweather & Ladew. Mr. Fayerweather was a retiring, economical man, honest and respected. At his death in 1890, he gave to the Presbyterian Hospital, St. Luke's Hospital, and Manhattan Eye and Ear Infirmary, $25,000 each; to the Woman's Hospital and Mount Sinai Hospital, $10,000 each; to Yale College, Columbia College, Cornell University, $200,000 each; to Bowdoin College, Amherst, Williams, Dartmouth, Wesleyan, Hamilton, Maryville, Yale Scientific School, University of Virginia, Rochester, Lincoln, and Hampton Universities, $100,000 each; to Union Theological Seminary, Lafayette, Marietta, Adelbert, Wabash, and Park Colleges, $50,000 each. The residue of the estate, over $3,000,000, was divided among various colleges and hospitals.

GEORGE I. SENEY,

Who died April 7, 1893, in New York City, gave away, between 1879 and 1884, to Seney Hospital in Brooklyn, $500,000, and a like amount each to the Wesleyan University, and to the Methodist Orphan Asylum, Brooklyn. To Emory College and Wesleyan Female College, Macon, Ga., he gave $250,000; to the Long Island Historical Society, $100,000; to the Brooklyn Library, $60,000; to Drew Theological Seminary, Madison, N.J., a large amount; to the Industrial School for Homeless Children, Brooklyn, $25,000, and a like amount to the Eye and Ear Infirmary of that city. He also gave twenty valuable paintings to the Metropolitan Museum of Art in New York.

The givers to colleges have been too numerous to mention. The College of New Jersey, at Princeton, has received not less than one and a half million or two million dollars from the John C. Greene estate.

188

Johns Hopkins left seven millions to found a university and hospital in Baltimore.

The Hon. Washington C. De Pauw left at his death forty per cent of his estate, estimated at from two to five million dollars, to De Pauw University, Greencastle, Ind. Though some of the real estate decreased in value, the university has received already $300,000, and will probably receive not less than $600,000, or possibly much more, in the future.

Mr. Jonas G. Clark gave to found Clark University, Worcester, Mass., about a million dollars to be devoted to post-graduates, or a school for specialists. Mr. Clark spent about eight years in Europe studying the highest institutions of learning. Matthew Vassar gave a million dollars to Vassar College for women at Poughkeepsie, N.Y. Ezra B. Cornell gave a million to Cornell University at Ithaca, N.Y. Mr. Henry W. Sage has also been a most munificent giver to the same institution. Dr. Joseph W. Taylor of Burlington, N.J., a physician and merchant, and member of the Society of Friends, founded Bryn Mawr College for Women, at Bryn Mawr, Penn. His gift consisted of property and academic buildings worth half a million, and one million dollars in invested funds as endowment.

Mr. Paul Tulane gave over a million to Tulane University, New Orleans. George Peabody gave away nine millions in charities,—three millions to educational institutions, three millions to education at the South to both whites and negroes, and three millions to build tenement houses for the poor of London, England.

HORACE KELLEY,

Of Cleveland, Ohio, left a half-million dollars for the foundation of an art gallery and school. His family were among the pioneer settlers, and their purchases of land in what became the heart of the city made their children wealthy. He was born in Cleveland, July 8, 1819, and died in the same city, Dec. 5, 1890.

He married Miss Fanny Miles, of Elyria, Ohio, and spent much of his life in foreign travel and in California, where they had a home at Pasadena. His fortune was the result of saving as well as the increase in real-estate values.

Mr. John Huntington made a somewhat larger gift for the same purpose. Mr. H. B. Hurlbut gave his elegant home, his collection of pictures, etc., valued at half a million, and Mr. J. H. Wade and others have contributed land, which make nearly two million dollars for the Cleveland Art Gallery and School. Mr. W. J. Gordon, of Cleveland, Ohio, gave land for Gordon's Park, bordering on Lake Erie, valued at a million dollars. It was beautifully laid out by him with drives, lakes, and flower-beds, and was his home for many years.

MR. HART A. MASSEY,

Formerly a resident of Cleveland, but in later years a manufacturer at Toronto, Canada, at his death, in the spring of 1896, left a million dollars in charities. To Victoria College, Toronto, $200,000, all but $50,000 as an endowment fund. This $50,000 is to be used for building a home for the women students. To each of two other colleges, $100,000, and to each of two more, $50,000, one of the latter being the new American University at Washington, D.C. To the Salvation Army, Toronto, $5,000. To the Fred Victor Mission, to provide missionary nurses to go from house to house in Toronto, and care for the sick and the needy, $10,000. Many thousands were given to churches and various homes, and $10,000 to ministers worn out in service. To Mr. D. L. Moody's schools at Northfield, Mass., $10,000. Many have given to this noble institution established by the great evangelist, and it needs and deserves large endowments. The Frederick Marquand Memorial Hall, brick with gray stone trimmings, was built as a dormitory for one hundred girls, in 1884, at a cost of $67,000. Recitation Hall, of colored granite, was built in 1885, at a cost of $40,000, and, as well as some other buildings, was paid for out of the proceeds of the Moody and Sankey hymn-books. Weston Hall, costing $25,000, is the gift of Mr. David Weston of Boston. Talcott Library, a beautiful structure costing $20,000, with a capacity for forty thousand volumes, is the gift of Mr. James Talcott of New York, who, among many other benefactions, has erected Talcott Hall at Oberlin College, a large and handsome boarding-hall for the young women.

CATHARINE LORILLARD WOLFE

In the Metropolitan Museum of Art in New York City, one sees an interesting picture of this noted giver, painted by Alexander Cabanel, commander of the Legion of Honor, and professor in the École des Beaux Arts of Paris.

Miss Wolfe, who was born in New York, March 8, 1828, and died in New York, April 4, 1887, at the age of fifty-nine, was descended from an old Lutheran family, her great-grandfather, John David Wolfe, coming to this country from Saxony in 1729. Two of his four children, David and Christopher, served with credit in the War of the Revolution. After the war, David and a younger brother were partners in the hardware business, and their sons succeeded them.

John David Wolfe, the son of David, born July 24, 1792, retired from business in the prime of his life, and devoted himself to benevolent work. He was a vestryman of Trinity Parish, and later senior warden of Grace Church, New York. He gave to schools and churches all over the country, to St. Johnland on Long Island, to the Sheltering Arms in New York, the High School at Denver, Col., the Diocesan School at Topeka, Kan., etc. He was a helper in the New York Historical Society, and one of the founders of the American Museum of Natural History in New York. He was its first president when he died, May 17, 1872, in his eightieth year, leaving only one child, Catharine, to inherit his large property.

A portion of Miss Wolfe's seven millions came from her mother, Dorothea Lorillard, and the rest from her father. She was an educated woman, who had read much and travelled extensively, and, like her father, used her money in doing good while she lived. Her private benefactions were constant, and she went much among the poor and suffering.

She built in East Broadway a Newsboy's Lodging House for not less than $50,000; the Italian Mission Church in Mulberry Street, $50,000, with tenement house in the same street, $20,000; the house for the clergy of the diocese of New York, 29 Lafayette Place, $170,000; St. Luke's Hospital, $30,000; Home for Incurables at Fordham, $30,000; Union College, Schenectady, N.Y., $100,000; Schools in the Western States, $50,000; Home and Foreign Missions, $100,000; American Church in Rome, $40,000; American School of Classical Studies at Athens, $20,000; Virginia Seminary, $25,000; Grace House, containing reading and lecture rooms for the poor, and Grace Church, $200,000 or more. She paid the expense of the exploring expedition to Babylonia under the leadership of the distinguished Oriental scholar,

Dr. William Hayes Ward, editor of the *Independent*. A friend tells of her sending him to New York, from her boat on the Nile, a check for $25,000 to be distributed in charities. She educated young girls; she helped those who are unable to make their way in the world.

Having given all her life, she gave away over a million at her death in money and objects of art. To the Metropolitan Museum of Art she gave the Catharine Lorillard Wolfe collection, with pictures by Rosa Bonheur, Meissonnier, Gérôme, Verboeckhoven, Hans Makart, Sir Frederick Leighton, Couture, Bouguéreau, and many others. She added an endowment of $200,000 for the preservation and increase of the collection.

One of the most interesting to me of all the pictures in the Wolfe collection is the sheep in a storm, No. 118, "Lost," souvenir of Auvergne, by Auguste Frederic Albrecht Schenck, a member of the Legion of Honor, born in the Duchy of Holstein, 1828. Those who love animals can scarcely stand before it without tears.

Others besides Miss Wolfe have made notable gifts to the Museum of Art. Mr. Cornelius Vanderbilt gave, in 1887, Rosa Bonheur's world-renowned "Horse Fair," for which he paid $53,500. It was purchased at the auction sale of Mr. A. T. Stewart's collection, March 25, 1887.

Meissonnier's "Friedland, 1807" was purchased at the Stewart sale by Mr. Henry Hilton for $66,000, and presented to the museum. Mr. Stephen Whitney Phoenix, who gave so generously to Columbia College, was also, like Mr. George I. Seney, a great giver to the museum.

MISS MARY ELIZABETH GARRETT

Of Baltimore gave to the Medical School of Johns Hopkins University over $400,000, that women might have equal medical opportunities with men.

President Daniel C. Gilman, in an article on Johns Hopkins University, says, "Much attention had been directed to the importance of medical education for women; and efforts had been made by committees of ladies in Baltimore and other cities to secure for this purpose an adequate endowment, to be connected with the foundations of Johns Hopkins. As a result of this movement, the trustees accepted a gift from the committee of ladies, a sum which, with its accrued interest, amounted to $119,000, toward the endowment of a medical school to which 'women should be admitted upon the same terms which may be prescribed for men.'

"This gift was made in October, 1891; but as it was inadequate for the purposes proposed, Miss Mary E. Garrett, in addition to her previous subscriptions, offered to the trustees the sum of $306,977, which, with other available resources, made up the amount of $500,000, which had been agreed upon as the minimum endowment of the Johns Hopkins Medical School. These contributions enabled the trustees to proceed to the organization of a school of medicine which was opened to candidates for the degree of doctor of medicine in October, 1893."

Several women have aided Johns Hopkins, as indeed they have most institutions of learning in America. Mrs. Caroline Donovan gave to the university $100,000 for the foundation of a chair of English literature. In 1887 Mrs. Adam T. Bruce of New York gave the sum of $10,000 to found the Bruce fellowship in memory of her son, the late Adam T. Bruce, who had been a fellow and an instructor at the university. Mrs. William E. Woodyear gave the sum of $10,000 to found five scholarships as a memorial of her deceased husband. Mr. and Mrs. Lawrence Turnbull endowed the Percy Turnbull memorial lectureship of poetry with an income of $1,000 per annum.

MRS. ANNA OTTENDORFER

"Whenever our people gratefully point out their benefactors, whenever the Germans in America speak of those who are objects of their veneration and their pride, the name of Anna Ottendorfer will assuredly be among the first. For all time to come her memory and her work will be blessed." Thus spoke the Hon. Carl Schurz at the bier of Mrs. Ottendorfer in the spring of 1884.

Anna Behr was born in Würzburg, Bavaria, in a simple home, Feb. 13, 1815. In 1837, when twenty-two years old, she came to America, remained a year with her brother in Niagara County, N.Y., and then married Jacob Uhl, a printer.

In 1844 Mr. Uhl started a job-office in Frankfort Street, New York, and bought a small weekly paper called the *New-Yorker Staats-Zeitung*. His young wife helped him constantly, and finally the weekly paper became a daily.

Her husband died in 1852, leaving her with six children and a daily paper on her hands. She was equal to the task. She declined to sell the paper, and managed it well for seven years. Then she married Mr. Oswald Ottendorfer, who was on the staff of the paper.

Both worked indefatigably, and made the paper more successful than ever. She was always at her desk. "Her callers," says *Harper's Bazar*, May 3, 1884, "had been many. Her visitors represented all classes of society,—the opulent and the poor, the high and the lowly. There was advice for the one, assistance for the other; an open heart and an open purse for the deserving; a large charity wisely used."

In 1875 Mrs. Ottendorfer built the Isabella Home for Aged Women in Astoria, Long Island, giving to it $150,000. It was erected in memory of her deceased daughter, Isabella.

In 1881 she contributed about $40,000 to a memorial fund in support of several educational institutions, and the next year built and furnished the Woman's Pavilion of the German Hospital of New York City, giving $75,000. For the German Dispensary in Second Avenue she gave $100,000, also a library.

At her death she provided liberally for many institutions, and left $25,000 to be divided among the employees of the *Staats-Zeitung*. In 1879 the property of the paper was turned into a stock-company; and, at the suggestion of Mrs. Ottendorfer, the employees were provided for by a ten-per-cent dividend on their annual salary. Later this was raised to fifteen per cent, which greatly pleased the men.

The New York *Sun*, in regard to her care for her employees, especially in her will, says, "She had always the reputation of a very clever, business-like, and charitable lady. Her will shows, however, that she was much more than that—she must have been a wonderful woman." A year before her death the Empress Augusta of Germany sent her a medal in recognition of her many charities.

Mrs. Ottendorfer died April 1, 1884, and was buried in Greenwood. Her estate was estimated at $3,000,000, made by her own skill and energy. Having made it, she enjoyed giving it to others.

Her husband, Mr. Oswald Ottendorfer, has given most generously to his native place Zwittau,—an orphan asylum and home for the poor, a hospital, and a fine library with a beautiful monumental fountain before it, crowned by a statue representing mother-love; a woman carrying a child in her arms and leading another. His statue was erected in the city in 1886, and the town was illuminated in his honor at the dedication of the library.

DANIEL P. STONE AND VALERIA G. STONE

When Mr. Stone, who was a dry-goods merchant of Boston, died in Malden, Mass., in 1878, it was agreed between him and his wife, Mrs. Valeria G. Stone, that the property earned and saved by them should be given to charity.

While Mrs. Stone lived she gave generously; and at her death, Jan. 15, 1884, over eighty years old, she gave away more than $2,000,000. To Andover Theological Seminary, to the American Missionary Association for schools among the colored people, $150,000 each, and much to aid struggling students and churches, and to save mortgaged homes. To Wellesley College to build Stone Hall, $110,000; to Bowdoin College, Amherst, Dartmouth, Drury, Carleton, Chicago Seminary, Hamilton, Iowa, Oberlin, Hampton Institute, Woman's Board for Armenia College, Turkey, Olivet College, Ripon, Illinois, Marietta, Beloit, Robert College, Constantinople, Berea, Doane, Colorado, Washburne, Howard University, each from five to seventy-five thousand dollars. She gave also to hospitals, city mission work, rescue homes, and Christian associations. For evangelical work in France she gave $15,000.

SAMUEL WILLISTON

The giver of over one million and a half dollars was born at Easthampton, Mass., July 17, 1795.

He was the son of the Rev. Payson Williston, first pastor of the First Church in Easthampton in 1789, and the grandson of the Rev. Noah Williston of West Haven, Conn., on his father's side, and of the Rev. Nathan Birdseye of Stratford, Conn., on his mother's.

As the salary of the father probably never exceeded $350 yearly, the family were brought up in the strictest economy. At ten years of age the boy Samuel worked on a farm, earning for the next six years about seven dollars a month, and saving all that was possible. In the winters he attended the district school, and studied Latin with his father, as he hoped to fit himself for the ministry.

He began his preparation at Phillips Academy, Andover, carrying thither his worldly possessions in a bag under his arm. "We were both of us about as poor in money as we could be," said his roommate years afterward, the Rev. Enoch Sanford, D.D., "but our capital in hope and fervor was boundless." Samuel's eyes soon failed him, and he was obliged to give up the project of ever becoming a minister. He entered the store of Arthur Tappan, in New York, as clerk; but ill health compelled him to return to the farm with its out-door life.

When he was twenty-seven he married Emily Graves of Williamsburg, Mass. She brought to the marriage partnership a noble heart, and every willingness to help. The story is told that she cut off a button from the coat of a visitor, with his consent, learned how it was covered, and soon furnished work for her neighbors as well as herself.

After some years Mr. Williston began in a small way to manufacture buttons, and the business grew under his capable management till a thousand families found employment. He formed a partnership with Joel and Josiah Hayden at Haydenville, for the manufacture of machine-made buttons in 1835, then first introduced into this country from England. Four years later the business was transferred to Easthampton.

Mr. Williston did not wait till he was very rich before he began to give. In 1837 he helped largely towards the erection of the First Church in Easthampton. In 1841 he established Williston Seminary, which became a most excellent fitting-school for college. During his lifetime he gave to this school about $270,000, and left it at his death an endowment of $600,000.

He was also deeply interested in Amherst College, establishing the Williston professorship of rhetoric and oratory, the Graves, now

Williston, professorship of Greek, and some others. "He began giving to Amherst College," writes Professor Joseph H. Sawyer, "when the institution was in the depths of poverty and well-nigh given over as a failure. He saved the college to mankind, and by example and personal solicitation stimulated others to give." He built and equipped Williston Hall, and assisted in the erection of other buildings.

He aided Mary Lyon, in establishing Mount Holyoke Seminary, gave to Iowa College, the Protestant College in Beirut, Syria, and to churches, libraries, and various other institutions.

He was active in all business enterprises, as well as works of benevolence. He was president of the Williston Cotton Mills, the First National Bank, Gas Company, and Nashawannuck (suspender) Company, all at Easthampton. He was the first president of the Hampshire and Hampden Railway, president of the First National Bank of Northampton, also of the Greenville Manufacturing Company (cotton cloths), member of both branches of the Legislature until he declined a re-election, one of the trustees of Amherst College, of the Westborough, Mass., Reform School, on the board of an asylum for idiots in Boston, a corporate member of the American Board, a trustee of Mount Holyoke Seminary, etc.

Mr. Williston overcame the obstacles of poor eyesight, ill health, and poverty, and became a blessing to tens of thousands. His wife was equally a giver with him. The Rev. William Seymour Tyler, D.D., of Amherst College, said at the semi-centennial celebration of Williston Seminary, June 14-17, 1891, "I knew its founders. I say 'founders,' for Mrs. Williston had scarcely less to do than Mr. Williston in planning and founding the building and endowing the seminary, as in all the successful measures and achievements of his remarkable and useful life; and the few enterprises in which he did not succeed were those in which he did not follow her advice. I knew the founders from the time when, at the beginning of their prosperity, their home and their factory were both in a modest wing of Father Williston's parsonage, until they had created Williston Seminary, made Easthampton, following out their great and good work, and entered into their rest."

Five children were born to Mr. and Mrs. Williston, but all died in childhood. They adopted five children, two boys and three girls, reared them, and educated them for honored positions in life.

Mr. Williston died at Easthampton, July 17, 1874; and his wife, two years younger than he, died April 12, 1885. Both are buried in the cemetery at Easthampton, to which burying-ground Mr. Williston gave, at his death, $10,000. He lived simply, and saved that he might give it in charities.

JOHN F. SLATER AND DANIEL HAND, AND THEIR GIFTS TO THE COLORED PEOPLE

One of the best charities our country has ever had bestowed upon it is the million-dollar gift of Mr. Slater, and the million and a half gift of Mr. Hand, for the education of the colored people in the Southern States. Other millions of dollars are yet needed to train these millions of the colored race to self-help and good citizenship.

Mr. John Fox Slater was born in Slatersville, R.I., March 4, 1815. He was the son of John Slater, who helped his brother Samuel to found the first cotton manufacturing industry in the United States.

Samuel Slater came from England; and setting up some machinery from memory, after arriving in this country, as nobody was permitted to carry plans out of England, he started the first cotton-mill in December, 1790. A few years later his brother John came from England, and together they started a mill at Slatersville, R.I.

They built mills also at Oxford, now Webster, Mass., and in time became men of wealth. Mr. Samuel Slater opened a Sunday-school for his workmen, one of the first institutions of that kind in this country.

His son John early developed rare business qualities, and at the age of seventeen was placed in charge of one of his father's mills at Jewett City, near Norwich, Conn. He had received a good academical education, had excellent judgment, would not speculate, and was noted for integrity and honor. He became not only the head of his own extensive business, but prominent in many outside enterprises.

His manners were refined, he was self-poised and somewhat reserved, and very unostentatious, thereby showing his true manhood. He read on many subjects,—finance, politics, and religion, and was a good conversationalist.

As he grew richer he felt the responsibility of his wealth. He gave generously to the country during the Civil War; he contributed largely to the establishment of the Norwich Free Academy and to the Congregational Church in Norwich with which he was connected, and to other worthy objects.

He determined to do good with his money while he lived. After the war, having given largely for the relief of the freedmen, he decided to give to a board of trustees $1,000,000, for the purpose of "uplifting the lately emancipated population of the Southern States and their posterity by conferring on them the blessings of Christian education."

When asked the precise meaning of the phrase "Christian education," he replied, "that in the sense which he intended, the common school teaching of Massachusetts and Connecticut was

199

Christian education. That it is leavened with a predominant and salutary Christian influence."

He said in his letter to the trustees, "It has pleased God to grant me prosperity in my business, and to put it into my power to apply to charitable uses a sum of money so considerable as to require the counsel of wise men for the administration of it." In committing the money to their hands he "humbly hoped that the administration of it might be so guided by divine wisdom as to be, in its turn, an encouragement to philanthropic enterprise on the part of others, and an enduring means of good to our beloved country and to our fellow-men."

Mr. Slater's gift awakened widespread interest and appreciation. The Congress of the United States voted him thanks, and caused a gold medal to be struck in his honor.

Mr. Slater lived to see his work well begun, intrusted to such men as ex-President Hayes at the head of the trust, Phillips Brooks, Governor Colquitt of Georgia, his son William A. Slater, and others. He died May 7, 1884, at Norwich, at the age of sixty-nine.

The general agent of the trust for several years was the late Dr. A. G. Haygood of Georgia, who resigned when he was made a bishop in the Methodist Church. Since 1891 Dr. J. L. M. Curry of Washington, D.C., chairman of the Educational Committee, and author of "The Southern States of the American Union" and other works, has been the able agent of the Slater as well as Peabody Funds. Dr. Curry, member of both National and Confederate Congresses, and minister to Spain for three years, has been devoted to education all his life, and gives untiring industry and deep interest to his work.

The Slater Fund is used in normal schools to fit students for teaching and for industrial education, and much of it is paid in salaries to teachers.

Dr. Curry, in his Report for 1892-1893, gives a list of the schools aided in that year, all of which he visited during the year. To Bishop College, Marshall, Tex., with 248 colored students, $1,000 was given for normal work and manual training; to Central Tennessee College, Nashville, with 493 students, $2,000, to pay the teachers in the mechanical shop, carpentry, sewing, cooking, etc.; to Clark University, Atlanta, Ga., 415 students, $2,500, mostly to the mechanical department, etc.; to Spelman Female Institute, Atlanta, with 744 pupils, $5,000; the institute has nine buildings, with property valued at $200,000.

To Claflin University, Orangeburg, S.C., with 635 students, both men and women, $3,096, chiefly to the industrial department,—iron-working, harness-making, masonry, painting, etc.; to Hampton Normal Institute, Hampton, Va., the noble institution to which General S. C. Armstrong gave his life, $5,000, for training girls in housework, to the

200

machine-shop, for teachers in natural history, mathematics, etc. There are nearly 800 pupils in the school.

To the Leonard Medical School, Shaw University, Raleigh, N.C., $1,000. The medical faculty are all white men. To the university itself, with 462 pupils, $2,500; to the Meharry Medical College, Nashville, 117 men and four women, $1,500; to the State Normal School, Montgomery, Ala., with 900 students, $2,500; to the Normal and Industrial Institute, Tuskegee, Ala., with 400 men and 320 women, $2,100, given largely to the departments of agriculture, leather and tin, brick-making, saw-mill work, plastering, dressmaking, etc. "This institution is an achievement of Mr. Booker T. Washington, a graduate of Hampton Normal Institute," says the Report of the Commissioner of Education, 1891-1892. "Opened in 1881 with one teacher and thirty pupils, it attained such success that in 1892 there were 44 officers and teachers and over 600 students. It also owns property estimated at $150,000, upon which there is no encumbrance. General S. C. Armstrong said of it, 'I think it is the noblest and grandest work of any colored man in the land.'"

To Straight University, New Orleans, La., with 600 pupils, the Slater Fund gave $2,000. The late Thomas Lafon, a colored man, left at death $5,800 to this excellent institution; to Talladega College, Talladega, Ala., with 519 students, $2,500; to Tougaloo University, Tougaloo, Miss., with 392 students, $3,000. This institute, under the charge of the American Missionary Association, began twenty-five years ago with one small building surrounded by negro cabins. Now there are ten buildings in the midst of five hundred acres. Most of these institutions for colored people have small libraries, which would be greatly helped by the gift of good books.

In nine years, from 1883 to 1892, nearly $400,000 was given from the Slater Fund to push forward the education of the colored people. Most of them were poor and left in ignorance through slavery; but they have made rapid progress, and have shown themselves worthy of aid. The *American Missionary*, June, 1883, tells of a law-student at Shaw University who helped to support his widowed mother, taught a school of 80 scholars four miles in the country, walking both ways, studying law and reciting at night nearly a mile away from his home. When admitted to the bar, he sustained the best examination in a class of 30, all the others white.

The *Howard Quarterly*, January, 1893, cites the case of a young woman who prepared for college at Howard University. She led the entire entrance class at the Chicago University, and received a very substantial reward in a scholarship that will pay all expenses of the four years' course.

Mr. La Port, the superintendent of construction of the George R. Smith College, Sedalia, Mo., was born a slave; he ran away at twelve, worked fourteen years to obtain money enough to secure his freedom, is now worth $75,000, and supports his aged mother and the widow of the man from whom he purchased his freedom.

The highest honor at Boston University in 1892 was awarded to a colored man, Thomas Nelson Baker, born a slave in Virginia in 1860. The class orator at Harvard College in 1890 was a colored man, Clement Garnett Morgan.

DANIEL HAND

Was born in Madison, Conn., July 16, 1801. He was descended from good Puritan ancestors, who came to this country in 1635 from Maidstone, Kent, England. His grandfather on his father's side served in the War of the Revolution, and his ancestors on his mother's side both in the old French War and the Revolutionary War.

Daniel, one of seven boys, lived on a farm till he was about sixteen years of age, when he went to Augusta, Ga., in 1818, with an uncle, Daniel Meigs, a merchant of that place and of Savannah. Young Hand proved most useful in his uncle's business; in time succeeded him, and became one of the leading merchants of the South. Some fifteen years before the war Mr. Hand took into business partnership in Augusta Mr. George W. Williams, a native of Georgia, who later established a business in Charleston, S.C., Mr. Hand furnishing the larger part of the capital. The business in Augusta was given in charge to a nephew, and Mr. Hand temporarily removed to New York City.

When the Civil War became imminent, Mr. Hand went South, was arrested as a "Lincoln spy" in New Orleans; but no basis being found for the charge, was released on parole that he would report to the Confederate authority at Richmond. On his way thither, passing the night in Augusta, he would have been mobbed by a lawless crowd who gathered about his hotel, had not a few of the leading men of Atlanta hurried him off to jail in a carriage with the mayor and a few friends as a guard.

Reporting at Richmond, Mr. Hand was allowed to go where he chose, if within the limits of the Confederacy, and chose Asheville, N.C., for his home until the war ended, spending his time in reading, of which he was very fond, and then came North.

The Confederate Courts at Charleston tried to confiscate his property, but this was prevented largely through the influence of Mr. Williams. Some years later, when the latter became involved, and creditors were pressing for payment, Mr. Hand, the largest creditor, refused to secure his claim, saying, "If Mr. Williams lives, he will pay his debts. I am not at all concerned about it." The money was paid by Mr. Williams at his own convenience after several years.

Mr. Hand had married early in life his cousin, Elizabeth Ward, daughter of Dr. Levi Ward of Rochester, N.Y., who died early, as well as their young children. Mr. Hand remained a widower for more than fifty years.

Bereft of wife and children, fond of the Southern people, yet heartily opposed to slavery, and realizing the helplessness and ignorance of the slaves, Mr. Hand decided to give to the American Missionary Association $1,000,894.25, the income to be used "for the purpose of educating needy and indigent colored people of African descent, residing, or who may hereafter reside, in the recent slave States of the United States of America.... I would limit," he said, "the sum of $100 as the largest sum to be expended for any one person in any one year from this fund." The fund, transferred Oct. 22, 1888, was to be known as the "Daniel Hand Educational Fund for Colored People."

Upon Mr. Hand's death, at Guilford, Conn., Dec. 17, 1891, in the family of one of his nieces, it was found that he had made the American Missionary Association his residuary legatee. About $500,000 passed into the possession of the Association, to be used for the same purpose as the million dollars; and about $200,000, it is believed, will eventually go to the organization after life-use by others.

The American Missionary Association is a noble society, organized in 1846 and chartered in 1862, for helping the poor and neglected races at our own doors, by establishing churches and schools in the South among both negroes and whites, in the West among the Indians, and in the Pacific States among the Chinese.

The Rev. Dr. A. D. Mayo says, in his book on the Southern women in the recent educational movement in the South, "Perhaps the most notable success in the secondary, normal, and higher training of colored youth has been achieved by the American Missionary Association.... At present its labors in the South are largely directed to training superior colored youth of both sexes for the work of teaching in the new public schools. It now supports six institutions called colleges and universities, in which not only the ordinary English branches are taught, but opportunity is offered for the few who desire a moderate college course." Fisk University of Nashville, which has sent out over 12,000 students, is one of the most interesting.

The American Missionary Association assists 74 schools for colored people with 12,000 pupils, 198 churches for the same with over 10,000 members and a much larger number in the Sunday-schools; 14 churches among the Indians with over 900 members; 20 schools among the Chinese at the West with over 1,000 pupils and over 300 Christian Chinese.

Mr. Hand's noble gift aids about fifty schools in the various Southern States from its income of over $50,000 yearly.

Mr. Hand was a man of fine personal presence, of extensive reading, and wide observation. He gave, says his relative, Mr. George A. Wilcox, "for the well-being of many, both within and without the family connection, who have come within the province of deserved assistance; befriending those who try to help themselves, whether successfully or not, but unalterably stern in his disfavor when idleness or dissipation lead to want." He gave the academy bearing his name to his native town of Madison, Conn. He joined the First Presbyterian Church in Augusta, Ga., when he was twenty-eight years of age, and was for thirty years its efficient Sunday-school superintendent. He organized a teachers' meeting, held every Saturday evening, which proved of great benefit.

He always loved the Scriptures. He said one day to a friend, as he laid his hand on his well-worn Bible, "I always read from that book every morning, and have done so from my boyhood, except in a comparatively few cases of unusual interruption or special hindrance."

He was often heard to say, "I have now a very short time for this world, but I take no concern about that; no matter where or when I die, I hope I am ready to go when called."

The temperance work needs another Daniel Hand to furnish a million dollars for its labors among the colored men of the South, where, says the thirtieth annual report of the National Temperance Society, "the saloon is everywhere working their ruin. It destroys their manhood, despoils their homes, impoverishes their families, defrauds their wives and children, and debauches the whole community."

The National Temperance Society, whose efficient and lamented Secretary, John N. Stearns, died April 21, 1895, was organized in 1865. It has printed and scattered over 900,000,000 pages of total-abstinence literature. With its board of thirty managers representing nearly all denominations and temperance organizations, ever on the alert to assist in making and enforcing helpful laws and to lessen the power of the liquor traffic, it is doing its work all over the nation. Says one who has long been identified with this organization, "I believe there is no Missionary Society, either Home or Foreign, that is doing more for the cause of Christ than this society, especially in saving the boys and girls; and yet, so far as I know, it receives less donations than any other society, and very rarely a legacy." Mr. William E. Dodge, the well-known merchant of New York, left the Society, by will, $5,000. Mr. W. B. Spooner of Boston, and Mr. James H. Kellogg of Rochester, N.Y., each left $5,000.

It is a hopeful sign of the times when laws are passed in thirty-nine States and all the Territories requiring the teaching of the nature and effects of alcoholic drinks upon the human system. It is encouraging when a million members of Christian Endeavor societies pledge themselves "to seek the overthrow of this evil at all times in every lawful way." Our country has given grandly for education; it will in the future give more generously to reforms which help to do away with poverty and crime.

GEORGE T. ANGELL

George T. Angell, the president and founder of "The American Humane Education Society," and president and one of the founders of "The Massachusetts Society for the Prevention of Cruelty to Animals," deserves, with the late lamented Henry Bergh of New York, the thanks of the nation for their noble work in teaching kindness to dumb creatures, and preventing cruelty. No charity can lie nearer to my own heart than the societies for the prevention of cruelty to animals.

Mr. Angell, now seventy-three years of age,—he was born at Southbridge, Mass., June 5, 1823,—the son of a minister, a graduate of Dartmouth College, a successful lawyer, gave up his practice of seventeen years, in 1868, to devote himself and his means, without pay, to humane work all over the world. He has enlisted the highest and the lowest in behalf of dumb animals. He has spoken before schools and conventions, before legislatures and churches, before kings and in prisons, in behalf of those who must patiently submit to wrong, and have no voice to plead for themselves.

Mr. Angell helped to establish the first "American Band of Mercy;" and now there are nearly 25,000 bands, with a membership of between one and two million persons, all pledged "to try to be kind to all living creatures, and try to protect them from cruel usage."

He has helped to scatter more than two million copies, in nearly all European and some Asiatic languages, of Anna Sewell's charming autobiography of an English horse, "Black Beauty," telling both of kind and cruel masters. Ten thousand copies have recently been printed for circulation in the schools of Italy.

A thousand cruel fashions, such as that of docking horses, or killing for mere sport, will be done away when men and women have given these subjects more careful thought.

> "Evil is wrought by want of thought
> As well as want of heart,"

wrote Thomas Hood in "The Lady's Dream."

"Our Dumb Animals," published in Boston, of which Mr. Angell is the editor, and which should be in every home and school in the land, has a circulation of about 50,000 to 60,000 a month, and is sent to the editors of 20,000 American publications. Over one hundred and seventeen million pages of humane literature are printed in a single year by the American Humane Education Society and the Massachusetts S. P. C. A.; the latter society has convicted about 5,000 persons in the last few years of overloading horses, beating dogs or inciting them to fight, starving animals, or other forms of cruelty.

In most large cities drinking fountains have been provided for man and beast; transportation and slaughter of animals have been rendered more humane; children have been taught kindness to the weakest and smallest of God's creatures; to feel with Cowper,—

> "I would not enter on my list of friends
> (Though graced with polished manners and fine sense,
> Yet wanting sensibility) the man
> Who needlessly sets foot upon a worm."

Some persons are following the example of Baroness Burdett-Coutts in London, who has provided a home for lost dogs, where they are kept till their owners call for them, or are given away to those who know that to have a pet in the home is a sure way to make people more tender and more noble in character. Such a place is found on Lake Street, Brighton, Mass., in the Ellen M. Gifford Sheltering Home for Animals, where each year several hundred dogs and cats are received, and homes found for them. There is a large playground for the dogs, and greater space for the cats. It is stated in the Report that the Boston police "have always generously and humanely aided the work of the Shelter." The objects of the "Sheltering Home" are:—

"First, to aid and succor the waifs and strays of the city.

"Second, to alleviate the sufferings of sick, abused, and homeless animals.

"Third, to find good homes for all those who come to the Shelter, as far as possible.

"Fourth, to spread the gospel of humanity towards dumb creatures by practical example."

It would be difficult to find in history a truly great person, like Wellington, Abraham Lincoln, Dr. Samuel Johnson, or Sir Walter Scott, who has not been a lover of dogs or birds or cats. Frederick the Great when dying asked an attendant to cover one of his dogs which seemed to be shivering with the cold.

"Our Dumb Animals" for May, 1896, gives the names of more than a hundred persons who have left legacies in the last few years to the Massachusetts Society for the Prevention of Cruelty to Animals. Every State and city needs more of these generous givers. A letter lies before me from Mr. E. C. Parmelee, the general agent of the society in Cleveland, Ohio, which says, "I regret to say that we have no dog shelter.... We should very much like to have one, and a hospital for broken-down and neglected horses.... We have very much hoped that we should have a bequest at no very distant day sufficiently large to build such a block as we need, with dormitories for children who are picked up in the night, and with an apartment for keeping our horse-ambulance, with a pair of horses and driver always at command, to remove such horses as are disabled, and fall in the streets from various causes."

Every society needs more agents to watch carefully the dumb creatures who carry heavy loads, or are neglected or ill treated; and the gospel of kindness to animals needs to be carried to every part of the earth.

WILLIAM W. CORCORAN
AND HIS ART GALLERY

William Wilson Corcoran was born Dec. 27, 1798, at Georgetown, D.C. He was the son of Thomas Corcoran, who settled in Georgetown when a youth, and became one of its leading citizens. He was mayor, postmaster, and one of the founders of the Columbian College, of which institution he was an active trustee while he lived. He was also one of the principal founders of two Episcopal churches in Georgetown, St. John's and Christ's Church, and was always a vestryman in one or the other.

His son William, after a good preparatory education, spent a year at the Georgetown College, and a year at the school of the Rev. Addison Belt, a graduate of Princeton. His father desired that he should complete his college course; but William was eager to enter upon a business life, and when he was seventeen went into the dry-goods store of his brothers, James and Thomas Corcoran. Two years later they established him in business under the firm name of W. W. Corcoran & Co. The firm prospered so well that the wholesale auction and commission business was begun in 1819.

For four years the firm made money; but in the spring of 1823, they, with many other merchants in Georgetown and Baltimore, failed, and were obliged to settle with their creditors for fifty cents on the dollar.

Young Corcoran, then twenty-five years of age, devoted himself to caring for the property of his father, who was growing old. The father died Jan. 27, 1830. Five years later, in 1835, Mr. Corcoran married Louise A. Morris, who lived but five years after their marriage, dying Nov. 21, 1840, leaving a son and daughter. The son died soon after the death of his mother; the daughter grew to womanhood, and became a great joy to her father. She married the Hon. George Eustis, a member of Congress from Louisiana, and died in early life at Cannes, France, 1867, leaving three small children.

Mr. Corcoran long before this had become a very successful banker. Two years after his marriage, in 1837, he moved his family to Washington, and began the brokerage business in a small store, ten by sixteen feet, on Pennsylvania Avenue near Fifteenth Street. After three years he took into partnership Mr. George W. Riggs, the son of a wealthy man from Maryland, under the firm name of Corcoran & Riggs.

In 1845 they purchased the old United States Bank building,

corner of Fifteenth Street and New York Avenue; and two years later Mr. Corcoran settled with his creditors of 1823, paying principal and interest, about $46,000. During the Mexican war the firm made extensive loans to the government, which conservative bankers regarded as a hazardous investment. Mr. Riggs retired from the firm July 1, 1848; and his younger brother, Elisha, was made a junior partner.

"In August, 1848, having about twelve millions of the six-percent loan of 1848 on hand, and the demand for it falling off in this country, and the stock being one per cent below the price at which Corcoran & Riggs took it, Mr. Corcoran determined to try the European markets; and, after one day's reflection, embarked for London, where, on arrival, he was told by Mr. Bates, of the house of Baring Bros. & Co., and Mr. George Peabody, that no sale could be made of the stock, and no money could be raised by hypothecation thereof, and they regretted that he had not written to them to inquire before coming over. He replied that he was perfectly satisfied that such would be their views, and therefore came, confident that he could convince them of the expediency of taking an interest in the securities; and that the very fact that London bankers had taken them would make it successful.

"Ten days after his first interview with them, Mr. Thomas Baring returned from the Continent, and with him he was more successful. A sale of five millions at about cost (one hundred and one here) was made to six of the most eminent and wealthy houses in London, viz., Baring Bros. & Co., George Peabody, Overend, Gurney & Co., Dennison & Co., Samuel Jones Lloyd, and James Morrison.

"This was the first sale of American securities made in Europe since 1837; and on his return to New York he was greeted by every one with marked expressions of satisfaction, his success being a great relief to the money market by securing that amount of exchange in favor of the United States. On his success being announced, the stock gradually advanced until it reached one hundred and nineteen and one-half, thus securing by his prompt and successful action a handsome profit which would otherwise have resulted in a serious loss."

On April 1, 1854, Mr. Corcoran withdrew from the banking-firm, and devoted himself to the management of his property and to his benevolent projects.

In 1859 he began, at the northeast corner of Pennsylvania Avenue and Seventeenth Street, a building for the encouragement of the Fine Arts. The structure was used during the Civil War for military purposes. In 1869 Mr. Corcoran deeded this property to trustees. "I shall ask you to receive," he wrote the trustees, "as a nucleus, my own gallery of art, which has been collected at no inconsiderable pains; and I have assurances from friends in other cities, whose tastes and liberality have taken this direction, that they will contribute fine works of art from their respective collections.... I venture to hope that with your kind co-operation and judicious management we shall have provided, at no distant day, not only a pure and refined pleasure for residents and visitors of the national metropolis, but have accomplished something useful in the development of American genius."

In 1869 Mr. Corcoran also deeded to trustees the Louise Home, erected in memory of his wife and daughter, as a home for refined and educated gentlewomen who had "become reduced by misfortune."

The deed specified that "there shall be no discrimination or distinction on account of religious creed or sectarian opinions, in respect to the trustees, directresses, officers, or inmates of the said establishment; but all proper facilities that may be possible in the judgment of the trustees shall be allowed and furnished to the inmates for the worship of Almighty God, according to each one's conscientious belief."

The building and grounds of the Louise Home in 1869 were estimated at $200,000, and are now worth probably over $500,000. The endowment consisted of an invested fund of $325,000.

Mr. Corcoran gave generously as long as he lived, having decided early in life that "at least one-half of his moneyed accumulations should be held for the welfare of men."

In Oak Hill Cemetery he erected a beautiful monument to the memory of John Howard Payne, author of "Home, Sweet Home." It is a shaft of Carrara marble, surmounted by a bust one and one-half times the size of the average man.

In his old age he purchased the Patapsco Institute at Ellicott's Mills, and gave the title-deeds to the two grand-nieces of John Randolph of Roanoke, who were in reduced circumstances, that they might open a school.

He gave to Columbian University, it is stated, houses and lands and money, amounting to a quarter of a million dollars. The University of Virginia, the Ascension Church, and other colleges and churches, were enriched through his generosity.

Mr. Corcoran died in Washington, Feb. 24, 1888, at the age of ninety years. He had given away over five million dollars.

"The treasures of the Corcoran Art Gallery," said its president in laying the corner-stone of a new building two years ago, "represent a money cost of $346,938 (exclusive of donations), a cost value which, of course, is greatly below the real value which these treasures represent to-day. The total value of the gallery, in its treasures, its endowments, and its buildings, is estimated to-day at $1,926,938. The total number of visitors who have inspected the paintings and sculpture exhibited in the gallery from the date of its opening down to the beginning of this month [May, 1896] was 1,696,489."

JOHN D. ROCKEFELLER
AND CHICAGO UNIVERSITY

From our windows we look out upon a forest of beautiful beech-trees, great oaks, and maples. There are well-kept drives, cool ravines with tasteful walks, a pretty lake and boat-house, and great stretches of lawn, in the four hundred or more acres, such as one sees in England. The gravelled roadways are appropriately named. "Blithedale" leads into a charming valley, through which a brook winds in and out, under a dozen bridges. The "Maze" leads through clusters of beeches and other undergrowth, and opens upon a magnificent view of blue Lake Erie at the right and the busy city at the left. In the distance, on a hilltop, stands a large white frame house, with red roof. Vines clamber over the broad double porches, red trumpet-creepers twine and blossom about some of the big oaks, beds of roses send out their fragrance, and the place looks most attractive and restful.

It is "Forest Hill," at Cleveland, Ohio, the summer home of Mr. John D. Rockefeller, probably the greatest giver in America. Our largest giver heretofore, so far as known, was George Peabody, who gave at his death $9,000,000. Mr. Rockefeller has given about $7,500,000 to one institution, besides several hundred thousand dollars each year for the past twenty-five years to various charities.

Mr. Rockefeller comes from very honorable ancestry. The Rockefellers were an old French family in Normandy, who moved to Holland, and came to America about 1650, settling in New Jersey. Nearly a century ago, in 1803, Mr. Rockefeller's grandfather, Godfrey, married Lucy, one of the Averys of Groton, Conn., a family distinguished in the Revolutionary War, and which has since furnished to our country many able men and women.

The picturesque home of the Averys, built in 1656, in the town of New London (now Groton), by Captain James Avery, was occupied by his descendants until it was destroyed by fire in 1894. A monument has been erected upon the site, with a bronze tablet containing a *fac-simile* of the old home.

The youngest son of Captain James Avery was Samuel, whose fine face looks out from the pages of the interesting Avery Genealogy, which Homer D. L. Sweet, of Syracuse, spent thirty years in writing. Samuel, an able and public-spirited man, married, in 1686, in Swanzey, Mass., Susannah Palmes, a direct descendant, through thirty-four generations, of Egbert, the first king of England. The name has always been retained in the family, Lucy Avery Rockefeller naming her

212

youngest son Egbert. Her eldest son, William Avery, married Eliza Davison; and of their six children, John Davison Rockefeller is the second child and eldest son.

He was born in Richford, Tioga County, N.Y., July 8, 1839. His father, William Avery, was a physician and business man as well. With great energy he cleared the forest, built a sawmill, loaned his money, and, like his noted son, knew how to overcome obstacles.

The mother, Eliza Davison, was a woman of rare common sense and executive ability. Self-poised in manner, charitable, persevering in whatever she attempted, she gave careful attention to the needs of her family, but did not forget that she had Christian duties outside her home. The devotion of Mr. Rockefeller to his mother as long as she lived was marked, and worthy of example.

The Rockefeller home in Richford was one of mutual work and helpfulness. The eldest child, Lucy, now dead, was less than two years older than John; the third child, William, about two years younger; Mary, Franklin and Frances, twins, each about two years younger than the others; the last named died early. All were taught the value of labor and of economy.

The eldest son, John, early took responsibility upon himself. Willing and glad to work, he cared for the garden, milked the cows, and acquired the valuable habit of never wasting his time. When about nine years old he raised and sold turkeys, and instead of spending the money, probably his first earnings, saved it, and loaned it at seven per cent. It would be interesting to know if the lad ever dreamed then of being perhaps the richest man in America?

In 1853 the Rockefeller family moved to Cleveland, Ohio; and John, then fourteen years of age, entered the high school. He was a studious boy, especially fond of mathematics and of music, and learned to play on the piano; he was retiring in manner, and exemplary in conduct. When between fourteen and fifteen years of age, he joined the Erie Street Baptist Church of Cleveland, Ohio, now known as the Euclid Avenue Baptist Church, where he has been from that time an earnest and most helpful worker in it. The boy of fifteen did not confine his work in the church to prayer-meetings and Sunday-school. There was a church debt, and it had to be paid. He began to solicit money, standing in the church-door as the people went out, ready to receive what each was willing to contribute. He gave also of his own as much as was possible; thus learning early in life, not only to be generous, but to incite others to generosity.

When about eighteen or nineteen, he was made one of the Board of Trustees of the church, which position he held till his absence from the city in the past few years prevented his serving. He has been the superintendent of the Sunday-school of the Euclid Avenue Baptist Church for about thirty years. When he had held the office for twenty-five years the Sunday-school celebrated the event by a reception for their leader. After addresses and music, each one of the five hundred or more persons present shook hands with Mr. Rockefeller, and laid a flower on the table beside him. From the first he has won the love of the children from his sympathy, kindness, and his interest in their welfare. No picnic even would be satisfactory to them without his presence.

After two years passed in the Cleveland High School, the school-year ending June, 1855, young Rockefeller took a summer course in the Commercial College, and at sixteen was ready to see what obstacles the business world presented to a boy. He found plenty of them. It was the old story of every place seeming to be full; but he would not allow himself to be discouraged by continued refusals. He visited manufacturing establishments, stores, and shops, again and again, determined to find a position.

He succeeded on the twenty-sixth day of September, 1855, and became assistant bookkeeper in the forwarding and commission house of Hewitt & Tuttle. He did not know what pay he was to receive; but he knew he had taken the first step towards success,—he had obtained work. At the end of the year, for the three months, October, November, and December, he received fifty dollars,—not quite four dollars a week.

The next year he was paid twenty-five dollars a month, or three hundred dollars a year, and at the end of fifteen months, took the vacant position with the same firm, at five hundred dollars, as cashier and bookkeeper, of a man who had been receiving a salary of two thousand dollars.

Desirous of earning more, young Rockefeller after a time asked for eight hundred dollars as wages; and, the firm declining to give over seven hundred dollars a year, the enterprising youth, not yet nineteen, decided to start in business for himself. He had industry and energy; he was saving of both time and money; he had faith in his ability to succeed, and the courage to try. He had managed to save about a thousand dollars; and his father loaned him another thousand, on which he paid ten per cent interest, receiving the principal as a gift when he became twenty-one years of age. This certainly was a modest beginning for one of the founders of the Standard Oil Company.

Having formed a partnership with Morris B. Clark, in 1858, in produce commission and forwarding, the firm name became Clark & Rockefeller. The closest attention was given to business. Mr. Rockefeller lived within his means, and worked early and late, finding little or no time for recreation or amusements, but always time for his accustomed work in the church. There was always some person in sickness or sorrow to be visited, some child to be brought into the Sunday-school, or some stranger to be invited to the prayer-meetings.

The firm succeeded in business, and was continued with various partners for seven years, until the spring of 1865. During this time some parts of the country, especially Pennsylvania and Ohio, had become enthusiastic over the finding of large quantities of oil through drilling wells. *The Petroleum Age* for December, 1881, gives a most interesting account of the first oil-well in this country, drilled at Titusville, on Oil Creek, a branch of the Alleghany River, in August, 1859.

Petroleum had long been known, both in Europe and America, under various names. The Indians used it as a medicine, mixed it with paint to anoint themselves for war, or set fire at night to the oil that floated upon the surface of their creeks, making the illumination a part of their religious ceremonies. In Ohio, in 1819, when, in boring for salt, springs of petroleum were found, Professor Hildreth of Marietta wrote that the oil was used in lamps in workshops, and believed it would be "a valuable article for lighting the street-lamps in the future cities of Ohio." But forty years went by before the first oil-well was drilled, when men became almost as excited as in the rush to California for gold in 1849.

Several refineries were started in Cleveland to prepare the crude oil for illuminating purposes. Mr. Rockefeller, the young commission merchant, like his father a keen observer of men and things, as early as 1860, the year after the first well was drilled, helped to establish an oil-refining business under the firm name of Andrews, Clark, & Co.

The business increased so rapidly that Mr. Rockefeller sold his interest in the commission house in 1865, and with Mr. Samuel Andrews bought out their associates in the refining business, and established the firm of Rockefeller & Andrews, the latter having charge of the practical details.

Mr. Rockefeller was then less than twenty-six years old; but an exceptional opportunity had presented itself, and a young man of exceptional ability was ready for the opportunity. A good and cheap illuminator was a world-wide necessity; and it required brain, and system, and rare business ability to produce the best product, and send it to all nations.

The brother of Mr. Rockefeller, William, entered into the partnership; and a new firm was established, under the name of William Rockefeller & Co. The necessity of a business house in New York for the sale of their products soon became apparent, and all parties were united in the firm of Rockefeller & Co.

In 1867 Mr. Henry M. Flagler, well known in connection with his improvements in St. Augustine, Fla., was taken into the company, which became Rockefeller, Andrews, & Flagler. Three years later, in 1870, the Standard Oil Company of Ohio was established with a capital of $1,000,000, Mr. Rockefeller being made president. He was also made president of the National Refiners' Association.

He was now thirty-one years old, far-seeing, self-centred, quiet and calm in manner, but untiring in work, and comprehensive in his grasp of business. The determination which had won a position for him in youth, even though it brought him but four dollars a week, the confidence in his ability, integrity, and sound judgment, which made the banks willing to lend him money, or men willing to invest their capital in his enterprise, made him a power in the business world thus early in life.

Amid all his business and his church work, he had found time to form another partnership, the wisest and best of all. In the same high school with him for two years was a young girl near his own age, Laura C. Spelman, a bright scholar, refined and sensible.

Her father was a merchant, a Representative in the Legislature of Ohio, an earnest helper in the church, in temperance, and in all that lifts the world upward. He was the friend of the slave; and the Spelman home was one of the restful stations on that "underground railroad" to which so many colored men and women owe their freedom. He was an active member for years of Plymouth Congregational Church in Cleveland, and later of Dr. Buddington's church in Brooklyn, and of the Broadway Tabernacle, New York, under Dr. Wm. M. Taylor. He died in New York City, Oct. 10, 1881.

Mrs. Spelman, the mother, was also a devoted Christian. She now lives, at the age of eighty-six, with her daughter, grateful, as she says, for life's beautiful sunset. She is loved by everybody, and her sweet face and voice would be sadly missed. She retains all her faculties, and has as deep an interest as ever in all religious, philanthropic, and political affairs.

The Spelman ancestors are English. Sir Henry Spelman, knighted by King James I., died in 1641, and lies buried in Westminster Abbey. Henry S., the third son of Sir Henry, and first of the name in America, came to Jamestown, Va., in 1609, and was killed by the Indians. Richard Spelman, born in Danbury, England, in 1665, came to Middletown, Conn., in 1700, and died in 1750. Laura's grandfather, Samuel, was the fourth in line from Richard. He was one of the pioneers in Ohio, moving thither from Granville, Mass. Her father, Harvey B. Spelman, was born in a log cabin in Rootstown, Ohio. Her mother's family came also from Massachusetts, from the town of Blanford; and her father and mother met and were married in Ohio.

Laura Spelman was a member of the first graduating class of the Cleveland High School, and has always retained the deepest interest in her classmates. After graduating, and spending some time in a boarding-school at the East, she taught very successfully for five years in the Cleveland public schools, being assistant in one of the large grammar schools.

At the age of twenty-five Mr. Rockefeller married Miss Spelman,

Sept. 8, 1864. Disliking display or extravagance, fond of books, a wise adviser in her home, a leader for many years of the infant department in the Sunday-school, like her father a worker for temperance and in all philanthropic movements, Mrs. Rockefeller has been an example to the rich, and a friend and helper to the poor. Comparatively few men and women can be intrusted with millions, and make the best use of the money. With Mr. Rockefeller's married life thus happily and wisely begun, business activities went on as before, perchance with less wear of body and mind. It was, of course, impossible to organize and carry forward a great business without anxiety and care.

In Cleave's "Biographical Cyclopædia of Cuyahoga County," it is stated that, in 1872, two years after the organization of the Standard Oil Company, "nearly the entire refining interest of Cleveland, and other interests in New York and the oil-regions, were combined in this company [the Standard Oil], the capital stock of which was raised to two and a half millions, and its business reached in one year over twenty-five million dollars,—the largest company of the kind in the world. The New York establishment was enlarged in its refining departments; large tracts of land were purchased, and fine warehouses erected for the storage of petroleum; a considerable number of iron cars were procured, and the business of transporting oil entered upon; interests were purchased in oil-pipes in the producing regions.

"Works were erected for the manufacture of barrels, paints, and glue, and everything used in the manufacture or shipment of oil. The works had a capacity of distilling twenty-nine thousand barrels of crude oil per day, and from thirty-five hundred to four thousand men were employed in the various departments. The cooperage factory, the largest in the world, turned out nine thousand barrels a day, which consumed over two hundred thousand staves and headings, the product of from fifteen to twenty acres of selected oak."

Ten years after this time, in 1882, the Standard Oil Trust was formed, with a capital of $70,000,000, afterwards increased to $95,000,000, which in a few years became possessed of large oil-producing interests, and of the stock of the companies controlling the greater part of the refining of petroleum in this country.

Ten years later, in 1892, the Supreme Court of Ohio having declared the Trust to be illegal, it was dissolved, and the business is now conducted by separate companies. In each of these Mr. Rockefeller is a shareholder.

Mr. Rockefeller has proved himself a remarkable organizer. His associates have been able men; and his vast business has been so systematized, and the leaders of departments held responsible, that it is managed with comparative ease.

The Standard Oil Companies own hundreds of thousands of acres of oil-lands, and wells, refineries, and many thousand miles of pipe-lines throughout the United States. They have business houses in the principal cities of the Old World as well as the New, and carry their oil in their own great oil-steamships abroad as easily as in their pipe-lines to the American seaboard. They control the greater part of the petroleum business of this country, and export much of the oil used abroad. They employ from forty to fifty thousand men in this great industry, many of whom have remained with the companies for twenty or thirty years. It is said that strikes are unknown among them.

When it is stated, as in the last United States Census reports, that the production of crude petroleum in this country is about thirty-five million barrels a year, the capital invested in the production $114,000,000, and the value of the exports of petroleum in various forms amounts to nearly $50,000,000 a year, the vastness of the business is apparent.

With such power in their hands, instead of selling their product at high rates, they have kept oil at such low prices that the poorest all over the world have been enabled to buy and use it.

Mr. Rockefeller has not confined his business interests to the Standard Oil Company. He owns iron-mines and land in various States; he owns a dozen or more immense vessels on the lakes, besides being largely interested in other steamship lines on both the ocean and the great lakes; he has investments in several railroads, and is connected with many other industrial enterprises.

With all these different lines of business, and being necessarily a very busy man, he never seems hurried or worried. His manner is always kindly and considerate. He is a good talker, an equally good listener, and gathers knowledge from every source. Meeting the best educators of the country, coming in contact with leading business and professional men as well, and having travelled abroad and in his own country, Mr. Rockefeller has become a man of wide and varied intelligence. In physique he is of medium height, light hair turning gray, blue eyes, and pleasant face.

He is a lover of trees, never allowing one to be cut down on his grounds unless necessity demands it, fond of flowers, knows the birds by their song or plumage, and never tires of the beauties of nature.

He is as courteous to a servant as to a millionnaire, is social and genial, and enjoys the pleasantry of bright conversation. He has great power of concentration, is very systematic in business and also in his every-day life, allotting certain hours to work, and other hours to exercise, the bicycle being one of his chief out-door pleasures. He is fond of animals, and owns several valuable horses. A great Saint Bernard dog, white and yellow, called "Laddie," was for years the pet of the household and the admiration of friends. When recently killed accidentally by an electric wire, the dog was carefully buried, and the grave covered with myrtle. A pretty stone, a foot and a half high, cut in

218

imitation of the trunk of an oak-tree, at whose base fern-leaves cluster, marks the spot, with the words "Our dog Laddie; died, 1895," carved upon a tiny slab.

It may be comparatively easy to do great deeds, but the little deeds of thoughtfulness and love for the dumb creatures who have loved us show the real beauty and refinement of character.

Mr. Rockefeller belongs to few social organizations, his church work and his home-life sufficing. He is a member of the New England Society, the Union League Club of New York, and of the Empire State Sons of the Revolution, as his ancestors, both on his father's and mother's side, were in the Revolutionary War.

His home is a very happy one. Into it have been born five children,—Bessie, Alice, who died early, Alta, Edith, and John D. Rockefeller, Jr.

Bessie is married to Charles A. Strong, Associate Professor of Psychology in Chicago University, a graduate of both the University of Rochester and Harvard, and has been a student at the Universities of Berlin and Paris. He is a son of the Rev. Dr. Augustus H. Strong, President of Rochester Theological Seminary.

Edith is married to Harold F. McCormick of Chicago, a graduate of Princeton, and son of the late Cyrus H. McCormick, whose invention of the reaper has been a great blessing to the world. Mr. McCormick gave generously of his millions after he had acquired wealth.

John D. Rockefeller, Jr., is at Brown University, and will probably be associated with his father in business, for which he has shown much aptitude.

The children have all been reared with the good sense and Christian teaching that are the foundations of the best homes. They have dressed simply, lived without display, been active in hospital, Sunday-school, and other good works, and found their pleasures in music, in which all the family are especially skilled, and in reading. They enjoy out-door life, skating in winter, and rowing, walking, and riding in the summer; but there is no lavish use of money for their pleasures.

The daughters know how to sew, and have made many garments for poor children. They have been taught the useful things of home-life, and often cook delicacies for the sick. They have found out in their youth that the highest living is not for self. A recent gift from Miss Alta Rockefeller is $1,200 annually to sustain an Italian day-nursery in the eastern part of Cleveland. This summer, 1896, about fifty little people, two years old and upwards, enjoyed a picnic in the grounds of their benefactor. Mrs. Rockefeller's mother and sister, Miss Lucy M. Spelman, a cultivated and philanthropic woman, are the other members of the Rockefeller family.

Besides Mr. Rockefeller's summer home in Cleveland, he has

another with about one thousand acres of land at Pocantico Hills, near Tarrytown on the Hudson. The place is picturesque and historic, made doubly interesting through the legends of Washington Irving. From the summit of Kaakoote Mountain the views are of rare beauty. Sleepy Hollow and the grave of Irving are not far distant. The winter home in New York City is a large brick house, with brown-stone front, near Fifth Avenue, furnished richly but not showily, containing some choice paintings and a fine library.

Mr. Rockefeller will be long remembered as a remarkable financier and the founder of a great organization, but he will be remembered longest and honored most as a remarkable giver. We have many rich men in America, but not all are great givers; not all have learned that it is really more blessed to give than to receive; not all remember that we go through life but once, with its opportunities to brighten the lives about us, and to help to bear the burdens of others.

Mr. Rockefeller began to give very early in life, and for the last forty years has steadily increased his giving as his wealth has increased. Always reticent about his gifts, it is impossible to learn how much he has given or for what purposes. Of necessity some gifts become public, such as his latest to Vassar College of $100,000, a like amount to Rochester University and Theological Seminary, and the same, it is believed, to Spelman Seminary, at Atlanta, Ga., named as a memorial to his father-in-law.

This is a school for colored women and girls, with preparatory, normal, musical, and industrial departments. The institute opened with eleven pupils in 1881, and now has 744, with nine buildings on fourteen acres of land. Dr. J. L. M. Curry said in his report for 1893, "In process of erection is the finest school building for normal purposes in the South, planned and constructed expressly with reference to the work of training teachers, which will cost over $50,000." In the industrial department, dress-cutting, sewing, cooking, and laundry work are taught. There is also a training-school for nurses.

In a list of gifts for 1892, in the New York Tribune, Mr. Rockefeller's name appears in connection with Des Moines College, Ia., $25,000; Bucknell College, $10,000; Shurtleff College $10,000; the Memorial Baptist Church in New York, erected through the efforts of Dr. Edward Judson in memory of his father, Dr. Adoniram Judson, $40,000; besides large amounts to Chicago University. It is probable that, aside from Chicago University, these were only a small proportion of his gifts during that year.

An article in the press states that the recent anonymous gift of $25,000 to help purchase the land for the site of Barnard College of Columbia University was from Mr. Rockefeller. He has also pledged $100,000 towards a million dollars, which are to be used for the construction of model tenement houses for the poor in New York City.

He has given largely to the Cleveland Young Men's Christian Association, and to Young Men's and Women's Christian Associations both in this country and abroad. He has built churches, given yearly large sums to foreign and home missions, charity organization societies, Indian associations, hospital work, fresh-air funds, libraries, kindergartens, Societies for the Prevention of Cruelty to Animals, for the education of the colored people at the South, and to the Woman's Christian Temperance Unions and to the National Temperance Society. He is a total abstainer, and no wine is ever upon his table. He does not use tobacco in any form.

Mr. Rockefeller's private charities have been almost numberless. He has aided young men and women through college, sometimes by gift and sometimes by loan. He has provided the means for persons who were ill to go abroad or elsewhere for rest. He does not forget, when his apples are gathered at Pocantico Hills, to send hundreds of barrels to the various charitable institutions in and near New York, or, when one of his workingmen dies, to continue the support to his family while it is needed. Some of us become too busy to think of the little ways of doing good. It is said by those who know him best, that he gives more time to his benevolences and to their consideration than to his business affairs. He employs secretaries, whose time is given to the investigation of requests for aid, and attending to such cases as are favorably decided upon.

Mr. Rockefeller's usual plan of giving is to pledge a certain sum on condition that others give, thus making them share in the blessings of benevolence. At one time he gave conditionally about $300,000, and it resulted in $1,700,000 being secured for some twenty or thirty institutions of learning in all parts of the country. It is said by a friend, that on his pledge-book are hundreds of charities to which he gives regularly many thousand dollars each month.

His greatest gift has been that of $7,425,000 to the University of Chicago. The first University of Chicago existed from 1858 to 1886, a period of twenty-eight years, and was discontinued from lack of funds. When the American Baptist Education Society, formed at Washington, D.C., in May, 1888, held its first anniversary in Tremont Temple, Boston, it was resolved "to take immediate steps toward the founding of a well-equipped college in the city of Chicago." Mr. Rockefeller had already become interested in founding such an institution, and made a subscription of $600,000 toward an endowment fund, conditioned on the pledging by others of $400,000 before June 1, 1890. The Rev. T. W. Goodspeed, and the Rev. E. T. Gates, Secretary of the Education Society, succeeded in raising this amount, and in addition a block and a half of ground as a site for the institution, valued at $125,000, given by Mr. Marshall Field of Chicago. Two and a half blocks were purchased for $282,500, making in all twenty-four acres, lying between the two great south parks of Chicago, Washington and Jackson, and fronting on the Midway Plaisance, a park connecting the other two. These parks contain a thousand acres.

The university was incorporated in 1890, and Professor William Rainey Harper of Yale University was elected President. The choice was an eminently wise one, a man of progressive ideas being needed for the great university. He had graduated at Muskingum College in 1870, taken his degree of Ph.D. at Yale in 1875, been Professor of Hebrew and the cognate languages at the Baptist Union Theological Seminary for seven years, Professor of the Semitic Languages at Yale for five years, and Woolsey Professor of Biblical Literature at Yale for two years, besides filling other positions of influence.

In September, 1890, Mr. Rockefeller made a second subscription of $1,000,000; and, in accordance with the terms of this gift, the Theological Seminary was removed from Morgan Park to the University site, as the Divinity School of the University, and dormitories erected, and an academy of the University established at Morgan Park.

The University began the erection of its first buildings Nov. 26, 1891. Mr. Henry Ives Cobb was chosen as the architect, and the English Gothic style is to be maintained throughout. The buildings are of blue Bedford stone, with red tiled roofs. The recitation buildings, laboratories, chapel, museum, gymnasium, and library are the central features; while the dormitories are arranged in quadrangles on the four corners.

Mr. Rockefeller's third gift was made in February, 1892, "one thousand five per cent bonds of the par value of one million dollars," for the further endowment of instruction. In December of the same year he gave an equal amount for endowment, "one thousand thousand-dollar five per cent bonds." In June, 1893 he gave $150,000; the next year, December, 1894, in cash, $675,000. On Jan. 1, 1896, another million, promising two millions more on condition that the University should also raise two millions. Half of this sum was obtained at once through the gift of Miss Helen Culver. In her letter to the trustees of the University, she says, "The whole gift shall be devoted to the increase and spread of knowledge within the field of biological science.... Among the motives prompting this gift is the desire to carry out the ideas, and to honor the memory, of Mr. Charles J. Hull, who was for a considerable time a member of the Board of Trustees of the old University of Chicago."

Miss Culver is a cousin of the late Mr. Hull, who left her his millions for philanthropic purposes. Their home for many years was the mansion since known as Hull House.

The University of Chicago has been fortunate in other gifts. Mr. S. A. Kent of Chicago gave the Kent Chemical Laboratory, costing

222

$235,000, opened Jan. 1, 1894. The Ryerson Physical Laboratory, costing $225,000, opened July 2, 1894, was the gift of Mr. Martin A. Ryerson, as a memorial to his father. Mrs. Caroline Haskell gave $100,000 for the Haskell Oriental Museum, as a memorial of her husband, Mr. Frederick Haskell. There will be rooms for Egyptian, Babylonian, Greek, Hebrew, and other collections. Mr. George C. Walker, $130,000 for the Walker Museum for geological and anthropological specimens; Mr. Charles T. Yerkes, nearly a half million for the Yerkes Observatory and forty-inch telescope; Mrs. N. S. Foster, Mrs. Henrietta Snell, Mrs. Mary Beecher, and Mrs. Elizabeth G. Kelley have each given $50,000, or more, for dormitories. It is expected that half a million will be realized from the estate of William B. Ogden for "The Ogden (graduate) School of Science." The first payment has amounted to half that sum. Considerably over $10,000,000 have been given to the University. The total endowment is over $6,000,000.

The University opened its doors to students on Oct. 1, 1892, in Cobb Lecture Hall, given by Mr. Silas B. Cobb of Chicago, and costing $150,000. The number of students during the first year exceeded nine hundred. The professors have been chosen with great care, and number among them some very distinguished men, from both the Old World and the New. The University of Chicago is co-educational, which is matter for congratulation. Its courses are open on equal terms to men and women, with the same teachers, the same studies, and the same diplomas. "Three of the deans are women," says Grace Gilruth Rigby in *Peterson's Magazine* for February, 1896, "and half a dozen women are members of its faculty. They instruct men as well as women, and in this particular it differs from most co-educational schools."

The University has some unique features. Instead of the usual college year beginning in September, the year is divided into four quarters, beginning respectively on the first day of July, October, January, and April, and continuing twelve weeks each, with a recess of one week between the close of each quarter and the beginning of the next. Degrees are conferred the last week of every quarter. The summer quarter, which was at first an experiment, has proved so successful that it is now an established feature.

The instructor takes his vacation in any quarter, or may take two vacations of six weeks each. The student may absent himself for a term or more, and take up the work where he left off, or he may attend all the quarters, and thus shorten his college course. Much attention is given to University Extension work, and proper preparatory work is obtained through the affiliation of academies with the University. Instruction is also given by the University through correspondence with those who wish to pursue preparatory or college studies.

"Chicago is, as far as I am aware," writes the late Hjalmar Hjorth Boyesen in the *Cosmopolitan* for April, 1893, "the first institution which, by the appointment of a permanent salaried university extension faculty, has formally charged itself with a responsibility for the outside public. This is a great step, and one of tremendous consequence."

A non-resident student is expected to matriculate at the University, and usually spends the first year in residence. Non-resident work is accepted for only one-third of the work required for a degree.

The University has eighty regular fellowships and scholarships, besides several special fellowships.

The institution, according to Robert Herrick, in *Scribner's Magazine* for October, 1895, seems to have the spirit of its founder. "Two college settlements in the hard districts of Chicago," he writes, "are supported and manned by the students.... The classes and clubs of the settlements show that the college students feel the impossibility of an academic life that lives solely to itself. On the philanthropic committee, and as teachers in the settlement classes, men and women, instructors and students, work side by side. The interest in sociological studies, which is commoner at Chicago than elsewhere, stimulates this modern activity in college life."

The University of Chicago has been successful from the first. In 1895 it numbered 1,265 students, of whom 493 were in the graduate schools, most of them having already received their bachelor's degree at other colleges. In 1896 there are over 1,900 students. The possibilities of the university are almost unlimited.

Dr. Albert Shaw writes in the *Review of Reviews* for February, 1893, "No rich man's recognition of his opportunity to serve society in his own lifetime has ever produced results so mature and so extensive in so very short a time as Mr. John D. Rockefeller's recent gifts to the Chicago University."

The *New York Sun* for July 4, 1896, gives Mr. Rockefeller the following well-deserved praise: "Mr. John D. Rockefeller has paid his first visit to the University of Chicago, which was built up and endowed by his magnificent gifts. The millions he has bestowed on that institution make him one of the very greatest of private contributors to the foundation of a school of learning in the whole history of the world. He has given the money, moreover, in his lifetime, and thus differs from nearly all others of the most notable founders and endowers of colleges.

"By so giving, too, he has distinguished himself from the great mass of all those who have made large benefactions for public uses. He has taken the millions from his rapidly accumulating fortune; and he has made the gifts quietly, modestly, and without the least seeking for popular applause, or to win the conspicuous manifestations of honor their munificence could easily have obtained for him. The reason for this remarkable peculiarity of Mr. Rockefeller as a public benefactor is that, being a deeply religious man, he has made his gifts as an obligation of religious duty, as it seems to him."

Mr. Rockefeller's latest gift, of $600,000, was made to the people of Cleveland, Ohio, when that city celebrated her one hundredth birthday, July 22, 1896. The gift was two hundred and seventy-six acres of land of great natural beauty, to complete the park system of the city. For this land Mr. Rockefeller paid $600,000. The land is already worth a million dollars, and will be worth many times that amount in the years to come.

When announcing Mr. Rockefeller's munificent gift to the city, Mr. J. G. W. Cowles, president of the Chamber of Commerce, said of the giver: "His modesty is equal to his liberality, and he is not here to share with us this celebration. The streams of his benevolence flow largely in hidden channels, unseen and unknown to men; but when he founds a university in Chicago, or gives a beautiful park to Cleveland, with native forests and shady groves, rocky ravines, sloping hillsides and level valleys, cascades and running brook and still pools of water, all close by our homes, open and easy of access to all our people, such deeds cannot be hid—they belong to the public and to history, as the gift itself is for the people and for posterity."

The Centennial gift has caused great rejoicing and gratitude, and will be a blessing forever to the whole people, but especially to those whose daily work keeps them away from the fresh air and the sunshine.

A day or two after the gift had been received, a large number of Cleveland's prominent citizens visited the giver at his home at Forest Hill, to express to him the thanks of the city. After the address of gratitude, Mr. Rockefeller responded with much feeling.

"This is our Centennial year," he said. "The city of Cleveland has grown to great proportions, and has prospered far beyond anything any of us had anticipated. What will be said by those who will come after us when a hundred years hence this city celebrates its second Centennial anniversary, and reference is made to you, gentlemen, and to me? Will it be said that this or that man has accumulated great treasures? No; all that will be forgotten. The question will be, What did we do with our treasures? Did we, or did we not, use them to help our fellow-man? This will be forever remembered."

After referring to his early school-life in the city, and efforts to find employment, he told how, needing a little money to engage in business, and in the "innocence of his youth and inexperience" supposing almost any of his business friends would indorse his note for the amount needed, he visited one after another; and, said Mr. Rockefeller, "each one of them had the most excellent reasons for refusing!"

Finally he determined to try the bankers, and called upon a man whom the city delights to honor, Mr. T. P. Handy. The banker received the young man kindly, invited him to be seated, asked a few questions, and then loaned him $2,000, "a large amount for me to have all at one time," said Mr. Rockefeller.

Mr. Rockefeller is still in middle life, with, it is hoped, many years before him in which to carry out his great projects of benevolence. He is as modest and gentle in manner, as unostentatious and as kind in heart, as when he had no millions to give away. He is never harsh, seems to have complete self-control, and has not forgotten to be grateful to the men who befriended and trusted him in his early business life.

His success may be attributed in part to industry, energy, economy, and good sense. He loved his work, and had the courage to battle with difficulties. He had steadiness of character, the ability to command the confidence of business men from the beginning, and gave close and careful attention to the matters intrusted to him.

Mr. Rockefeller will be remembered, not so much because he accumulated millions, but because he gave away millions, thereby doing great good, and setting a noble example.

226